KT-393-721

Praise for *Are You Dave Gorman?*

When Danny Wallace bet Dave Gorman he couldn't find 54 other people called Dave Gorman, neither of them could have imagined this daft quest would become a theatre show, a TV series and a book. However this trivial pursuit takes comedy and journalism to an altogether different level. Their madcap odyssey covered 25,000 miles, carrying them to Italy, Israel and the Channel Islands. They lost their shoes in Norway. They were caught in a tornado in New York. They appeared on page three of The Sun, and became front-page news in Denmark, without even going there. They met a carpet fitter, a semi-retired lighthouse keeper and the assistant manager of East Fife football club, all called Dave Gorman, and an American actor who played a character called Dave Gorman in a film. The end result of this spectacularly pointless adventure is a warm, funny, life-enhancing book about absolutely nothing.

Guardian

A magnificent tale of obsession and adventure.

Independent

… heightens an elegantly simple concept to the peak of absurdity, as a drunken boast leads to obsession, betrayal, exhilarating victories, devastating setbacks and maxed-out credit cards. In a way, we are all Dave Gorman… an international sensation… a magnificent docu-comedy… a true story that's as simple and accessible as it is maddeningly addictive.

Time Out New York

This is a much better book about why boys are how they are than *Men are from Mars Women are from Venus*.

Jenny Colgan

Are You Dave Gorman? is the oddly touching story of how comic Dave Gorman went in search of all the world's other Dave Gormans … It's the very frivolousness and absurdity of *Are You Dave Gorman?* that makes it so boyishly likeable.

Amazon.co.uk

You would think, much like the poor chaps at school with the surnames Bates, Pratt and Smallcock, Mr Gorman would positively shun publicity, or at the very least, come up with a more public-appeasing moniker. But no, the impressively mutton chopped comic had to go and make a bet with his best mate Danny Wallace, that he could find someone else with his daft name. This was played out, week-by-week in Gorman's gently pleasing, but genuinely funny BBC2 series, but its retelling on pages of flattened twig takes nothing away from the writer's friendly style or indeed the humour inherent in the appealingly daft situation. This is one trivial piece of nonsense that comes with 'recommended' stamped all over it.

FHM magazine

Nick Hornby may have explored the idea of men bringing security to their lives through obsessive devotion to music or football, but this raises the stakes to the nth degree... It's the sheer madness of the quest that proves the compelling hook, complemented by the author's lightness of touch and quickness of pace. And, of course, it is funny too. Above all, though, this is a cracking adventure and one which anyone can enjoy, even if you've never met a Dave Gorman.

Chortle.co.uk

You'll like this so much you may want to change your name to Dave Gorman.

Big Issue

What starts out as a drunken bet grows into an existential odyssey and a life-affirming, heart-warming chapter in the history of English eccentricity.

Independent on Sunday

Gorman is becoming the Bill Bryson of stand-up.

Sunday Times

Dave Gorman's
GOOGLE WHACK!
Adventure

Acknowledgements

I'd like to thank: Jake Lingwood (sorry it's not a novel), all the reps at Ebury (G.T.Y.M.A.S!), Stina Smemo, Hannah Telfer, Claire Kingston, (not *the*) Ken Barlow and Dave Breen. Rob Aslett and all at Avalon, especially Alex Godden and Dan Lloyd. Simon Streeting for intercontinental help and wisdom, Matt Welton for advice, guidance, encouragement and constancy, Geoff Lloyd and Chris Maher for being wrong over a curry but so, so right about so many other things in life and Simon Singh for lending me some of his precision.

For taking a leap of faith, my thanks go to Susan Provan, Fiona Pride, Rebecca Austin and all at the Melbourne International Comedy Festival. For making me so welcome: everyone at the Sydney Opera House Studio Theatre and the George Square Theatre, Edinburgh. Julie James and Dan Cutforth, Eillen Sellam, and the Butterworth clan, likewise. Thanks to Lib Williams, Katrina Mathers, Jon Primrose and Rupert 'Two Pints' Potts too.

But most importantly, for agreeing to meet and help a stranger, my gratitude and undying admiration goes out to all the googlewhacks I met along the way.

I didn't invent googlewhacking. Gary Stock did. If you find a googlewhack, why not visit googlewhack.com and leave it in the Whack Stack.

Dave Gorman's
GOOGLE WHACK!
Adventure

Dave Gorman

EBURY PRESS

First published in Great Britain in 2004

10 9 8 7 6 5 4 3 2 1

Google is a trademark of Google Technology Inc. Google is not affilated in any way with Dave Gorman's Googlewhack Adventure.

Text © Dave Gorman 2004

Dave Gorman has asserted his right to be identified as the author of this work under the Copyright, Designs and Patents Act 1988.

All rights reserved. No part of this publication may be reproduced, stored in a retrieval system, or transmitted in any form or by any means, electronic, mechanical, photocopying, recording or otherwise without the prior permission of the copyright owners.

First published by Ebury Press
Random House, 20 Vauxhall Bridge Road, London SW1V 2SA

Random House Australia (Pty) Limited
20 Alfred Street, Milsons Point, Sydney, New South Wales 2061, Australia

Random House New Zealand Limited
18 Poland Road, Glenfield, Auckland 10, New Zealand

Random House South Africa (Pty) Limited
Endulini, 5A Jubilee Road, Parktown 2193, South Africa

The Random House Group Limited Reg. No. 954009

www.randomhouse.co.uk

A CIP catalogue record for this book is available from the British Library.

Cover Design by Dave Breen
Text design and typesetting by Textype
Cover photo © Laura Knox
All photography © Dave Gorman unless otherwise stated
Woman and Dog photo © womenanddogsuk.co.uk
The First and Second Laws of Thermodynamics © Flanders and Swann.
Lyric used by kind permission of Laura and Steph Flanders.

ISBN 0091891965

Printed and bound in Great Britain by Clays of St Ives PLC

Papers used by Ebury Press are natural, recyclable products made from wood grown in sustainable forests.

Australian history is almost always picturesque, indeed it is so curious and strange, that it is itself the chiefest novelty the country has to offer. It does not read like history, but like the most beautiful lies. And all of a fresh sort, not mouldy old stale ones. It is full of surprises, and adventures, and incongruities, and incredibilities, but they are all true, they all happened.

Mark Twain, Following the Equator *(1897)*

I am asleep. Now I'm not asleep. But I'm not yet awake. I'm in the twilight zone somewhere in between; no longer dreaming, not yet conscious. The synapses of my brain are just beginning to fire up, sensations drip, drip, dripping into my central nervous system, each drip bringing me closer to reality.

I pull the covers to me for warmth. Drip. Not yet prepared to open my eyes, not yet ready for the world. Drip. My head aches, my body aches, if I can stay in the land of nod I can delay these unpleasant sensations. I try to rewind the dream to delay the inevitable but the video of my mind has broken and the dream is not only over but gone. Something to do with lemons, but maybe not. No. Forgotten. Lost without trace. Drip. My hands start to wander, a scratch here, another there. Drip. Nothing untoward going on – it's just that certain things need to be checked, counted, rearranged. Drip, drip, drip. Yep, one of those, two of these. OK. Best to just shift everything to the left like so. Drip. Hang on. Drip. Why have I had to push my hand under my trousers? If I'm asleep I should be in bed and if I'm in bed I should be naked. Drip. What's the last thing I remember? Drip. New Year's Eve. Drip, drip, drip, drip, drip. Oh hell. Drip. So where am I? Think. Drip. Think. Drip. Nothing. Blank. Oh well, I need to work this out. I need more information. I have no option, I'm going to have to open my eyes and let reality in. Drip. Here goes.

Eyes open.

Drip, drip, drip. But the drips become a flood; information overload. I'm looking directly at a young Chinese boy. His face is only inches from mine. I don't live with any young Chinese boys which means that something is very, very wrong and someone, perhaps me, is going to have a lot of explaining to do.

He pulls his head back a little but he doesn't avert his gaze. He's crouching down, on his haunches, staring at me, studying me with an expression of curious fascination as if I'm some kind of exotic creepy-crawly. I try to say 'hello' but my mouth is dry and all that emerges is a dead croak. This seems to frighten the boy and he jumps backwards. Then I see that he isn't jumping of his own accord, rather he is being yanked back by the concerned hand of his mother.

My frame of reference is no longer filled by his inquisitive, silent gaze and I am able to take in the scenery. I'm definitely not at home. Not unless builders have knocked through and built a lifesize working model of a newsagents in my living room. Overnight. Some of my friends like a practical joke every now and then, but this, I think, is beyond even them.

My eyes are still adjusting to the light and it takes a few seconds for the scene to find its focus. I'm in an airport. Heathrow to be precise. I close my eyes and shake my head as if shaking a kaleidoscope, rearranging the sands to form a different image. But when I open my eyes again the picture hasn't changed. It isn't an illusion. I'm in Heathrow Airport. It's New Year's Day.

I'm very confused. Scared, even. I look back to the Chinese boy forlornly hoping that he will be able to explain the situation to me. Instead, he stares back at me, emotionless, curious, still. I think he's scared of me so I offer him a weak smile. He smiles back and tugs at his mother's sleeve, eager to point out that the croaky man is smiling. She turns to see me but doesn't smile. Instead she shoots me a glance so fierce that I wince with pain when it hits me. She bundles up her young charge and scuttles away. I'm alarmed at the urgency with which she escapes whatever threat I supposedly pose.

Suddenly I realise that my hand is still inside my trousers.

I look around. Hundreds of people are milling around. I'm on the cold hard floor. Fully clothed. Sweating. There are no covers pulled up around me, just a coat. It's January the 1st and my first conscious action of the New Year has been to touch myself and smile at a young Chinese boy. No wonder his mum had shown such concern. 'Happy New Year, Dave', I think, 'Happy New Year'.

I need to pull myself together so, perhaps it's ironic that the first thing I do is take my hand out of my trousers. The second thing I do is run my hands through my coat pockets and discover with a mixture of relief and alarm, what possessions I have about my person. Wallet, mobile phone; relief. Passport; shit. That's not good. And then … oh no, that familiar shape, the shiny paper envelope, the stiff cardboard. Surely not? No! Please? An airline ticket. Scared to learn the truth, I lift the flap of the envelope, and peek inside.

Oh.

My.

Life.

Washington DC! A ticket to Washington DC!

But it is much more than that. It is a ticket to insanity, to obsession, to the start of an adventure; a googlewhack adventure.

PART ONE

HOW I CAME TO WAKE UP IN HEATHROW
AIRPORT ON NEW YEAR'S DAY WITH A TICKET TO
WASHINGTON DC IN MY POCKET

one

Francophile Namesakes

Francophile   noun: one who admires France and the French.

Namesakes   noun: plural of namesake. A person or thing with the same name as another.

A lot of people find turning 30 a bit traumatic. It's a wake-up call. They take stock of their lives, realise how little they've achieved and decide it's time to take life a little more seriously. Perhaps the hope is that if they take life a bit more seriously, life might take them a bit more seriously in return.

In particular this seems to afflict a lot of people in what is laughingly referred to as the entertainment 'industry'. At the age of 30 it seems that all singers want to be actors, all actors want to play Hamlet and all comedians want to write novels. This is, of course, an act of vanity and should be abhorred.

Now, as it goes, nothing could have been further from my mind as I hit 30. I'd been making a living of sorts, treading the boards in the name of comedy since I was 19 and on my thirtieth birthday life conspired to take me to the millionaire's ski resort of Aspen, Colorado where, having already performed a show of my own, I was then taken to a theatre where I watched one of my childhood heroes, Steve Martin, perform live. He did a routine about his singing testicles. There was a strange dignity to the performance and it brought the house down.

The lesson was clear; turning 30 didn't mean I had to grow up. On 2 March 2001 there was not one single part of me that wanted to be taken seriously. As far as I was concerned, life was good, I was having fun and I could see no reason to change my course.

A year later, however, it hit me like a train. I woke up on my 31st birthday and was gripped by a sudden desire to be taken seriously. It was time to stop acting the fool and behave like a grown-up. (This may or may not be connected but among my presents was a novel called *Shopgirl.* Written by Steve Martin; childhood hero, testicular vocalist, comedian, movie star ... and novelist.)

I'd often idly talked about writing a novel, but I'd never done anything about it. All of a sudden that just wasn't good enough! Me, not yet a novelist?! At 31?! Oh, how I'd let myself down! Oh, how I'd let the world of literature down. It was time to do something about it. It was time for David James Gorman to be taken seriously.

I sat down at my computer and looked at a blank screen. *Here goes*, I thought, *here comes the Booker Prize, let's see what the world thinks about me when I've finished this.* I stared at the blank screen, locked my fingers together, stretched my arms, palms out and cracked my knuckles because that's how I'd seen writers do it in the movies. Then I put the kettle on. I wanted a cup of tea but coffee seemed more like a writer's drink. Maybe I should start smoking? I could think about that later. Eight cups of coffee into the day and there were still no words on the screen. This whole *writing-a-novel* malarkey was looking a lot harder than it seemed. That night, as I stayed awake, shaking the caffeine through my system, I came up with a plan: at ten o'clock the next morning I would ring my agent, Rob.

'Hello, Rob.'

'Dave.'

'I've been thinking ... I want to write a novel. What do you reckon?'

'Don't be ridiculous, Dave. You're very busy. I've got a lot of work lined up for you, things are on a roll, if it ain't broke, don't fix it.'

'Well, OK, Rob, if that's what you think. I'll give up on the whole crazy idea. It was a pipedream anyway.'

That was how I imagined the conversation would go, that was my plan. After all, I *was* very busy. My diary was full and so were the theatres. It wouldn't last forever but the sun was shining and surely any agent worth his salt would want to make hay. If I was *told* not to write a novel, that was better than just *failing* to write a novel, wasn't it? That way I could get drunk in a few bars and complain to strangers about how I *wanted* to write a novel but that circumstances just wouldn't let me. I could be a frustrated novelist! Oh yes, I could make drunk strangers in bars take me seriously, and to be honest, wouldn't that be enough? Admittedly this plan contained only a tiny fraction of the kudos of winning the Booker Prize but it involved absolutely none of the work.

I picked up the phone.

'Hello, Rob.'

'Dave.'

'I've been thinking ... I want to write a novel. What do you think?'

'Good.'

'What?'

'I'll make a few calls.'

'What?'

'Set up a meeting.'

'But what about the theatres?'

'They can wait.'

'But ...'

'I'll call you back.'

'...'

*

'I think you're just the right kind of person to write a novel,' said Jake.

The three of us were in Rob's office and it seemed that *everyone* was taking me seriously.

Jake was in publishing, an editor working for Random House, the world's largest publisher. He was young and very enthusiastic and he demanded the same kind of enthusiasm in others.

'Fiction is hard work. It's just you, your imagination and your computer,' he said, 'You have to take it seriously.'

'That's exactly what I want. I *want* to take it seriously,' I said, before offering a completely unnecessary, 'I'm 31.'

Crikey; Rob and Jake were both giving my literary ambitions real considered thought. This plumped up my ego and made me take the idea seriously too. I was trying to convince Jake to give me the deal, and in doing so I was starting to convince myself. Maybe, if I *had* to write a novel it would be easier. If I had a publishing deal, most importantly, if I had a deadline to meet, I was sure I'd be able to do it. Because everyone else was taking the idea seriously, I was being seduced by it all over again.

'Are you really serious, Dave?'

'I am, Jake, I really am.'

And I was. But I needed to convince Jake somehow. I had to demonstrate how serious I was. I had an idea.

'I'll tell you how serious I am, Jake. I'm actually thinking—' pause for effect '—of growing a beard.'

Jake stared at me. I stared back at him but only because I didn't dare look at Rob. I knew what he was thinking: *please don't screw up this meeting with your stupid beard talk.* I could feel his eyes burning into the side of my face. There was an awkward silence but I continued to meet Jake's stare and refused to blink. Rob coughed but Jake and I kept on staring.

'Really?' Jake seemed impressed but unsure.

'Really,' I said with a solemn nod.

Jake sucked some air through his teeth, clearly weighing up

my beardly potential. Rob coughed again.

'OK, er ...' Rob seemed embarrassed, 'the beard is ... a bold offer, Dave, but I think the meeting would be best served if we concerned ourselves with the real business in hand.'

'Rob. This *is* the business in hand,' I said, Jake still fixed in my stare.

'OK... but...'

'Gentlemen,' Jake interrupted, breaking out of my gaze, 'I think we have a deal.'

Jake offered his hand and I shook it. There was a pause while we all sat and contemplated what had just occurred. As far as I could work out, the world's largest publisher had just offered me a publishing deal on the condition that I grew a beard. Rob, as my agent, was the first to speak.

'I'm glad we have that sorted out, but there are, of course, some details still to negotiate.'

'Of course,' said Jake.

'Of course,' I said. 'Just so you know; you might not think it to look at me with my brown hair, but the beard will be ginger.'

There was a long pause.

'I was thinking more in terms of contract details. For the book,' said Rob, who clearly couldn't see the important message contained within the subject of my beard.

'Right,' I said, trying to invest the word with great understanding.

'Right,' said Jake, with abundant common sense.

'Right,' said Rob with finality.

'Right,' I said because I wanted to see if we'd go round again. We didn't.

Instead there was another pause, during which I realised there was something important we hadn't yet discussed.

'Oh, by the way ... I have an idea ... for a story, for a novel, if anyone would like to hear it?'

Rob looked at his watch. Jake looked slightly bemused. He was probably wondering what witchcraft we'd worked in order for him to agree a publishing deal solely on the status of my facial hair. I suspect it was the first literary deal of its kind.

'Of course,' he said, remembering his job, 'I'd love to hear it. In fact, I *need* to hear it.'

'Why don't you two get a coffee and discuss it?' said Rob, who had other business to attend to. He represented a few people, and some of them, being female, couldn't rely on facial hair tactics to secure employment.

In the comfy leather armchairs of the café next door I explained my idea to Jake while we shared a pot of tea.

'OK. It's about a man who, in his mind's eye, can see a new primary colour,' I said. 'It torments him because it's impossible to describe it to anyone. If there was nothing red in the world but it existed in your imagination you couldn't begin to describe it to me, could you? It's the colour of tomatoes, buses, postboxes, blood and so on, but if you couldn't refer to an example of red you couldn't describe it.'

'And how do we know that we both see the same red in the first place?' asked Jake.

'Exactly, we don't. That's why it's impossible to describe. That's why this man is going mad. Eventually he figures if he can see it, it must exist somewhere. So he decides to search for it ...'

'Travel,' said Jake scribbling some notes down, 'good.'

'... so he swims the deepest oceans and penetrates the densest rain-forests in search of obscure flora and fauna hoping to discover a speck of this mysterious hue.'

'Nice.'

'Oh ... and his name,' I said, leaning forward, thinking on my feet, 'is Hugh! Hugh Brown! So when he eventually finds the colour in a ... in a ... in a ... butterfly, he's really frustrated because he can't ...'

'... name it after himself?' guessed Jake.

'Exactly!' I squealed, 'You can't call a colour "brown" because the name's been taken and you can't call it "hugh" because that's like calling it ... "colour".'

'But he's found it?'

'Yeah. So he isolates it as a chemical compound and then all hell breaks loose.'

I sat back in my chair, proud of myself. Jake looked at me with big eyes, clearly expecting me to tell him more about the hell that was going to break loose.

'So … for example,' I started, 'some people are so freaked by the sight of this new colour, they descend into madness. Hugh Brown will have that on his conscience for the rest of his life. TVs, computer monitors, all electronic media need to be completely redesigned in order to display the new colour *and* the world's cereal manufacturers are fighting to own the colour just so that *their* boxes stand out on the shelves.'

I was sure that was enough. I sat back. Jake said nothing.

'Well?' I said, 'Do you like it?'

'How long will it take you to grow a beard?'

*

Later that day Rob and Jake set about the process of negotiating the contract details while I started my side of the bargain and gave up shaving. I expect they finished before me, but in any case, four weeks later, the deal was on. We met again, this time in Jake's office, I signed a contract, and we popped open a bottle of ceremonial champagne to mark the occasion.

To demonstrate just how committed people were I even got given a big cheque. I find it impossible to explain this sort of thing; it makes far more sense to pay someone after they've done some work than before and yet here I was being given an advance. I wasn't sure if this demonstrated that I was with a stupid publisher or a brilliant agent (or both) but I did know that I now had no choice; I would have to write a novel and there would no longer be any room for excuses. And because everyone else had taken the idea so seriously, I was convinced too.

'I'll need the first couple of chapters by the end of the year,' said Jake.

'No problem.' I said, scratching at my neck. I was brimming with confidence.

*

You've probably gathered by now that the book you're reading isn't the book I was supposed to write. This isn't a novel. This isn't a work of fiction; this is a true story. This is the story of what happened to me while I was supposed to be writing a novel. What can I say? We don't always get what we want in life, it's as simple as that. My parents always wanted a girl.

I started off with good intentions. I stared at the blank screen for at least 40 minutes before putting the kettle on, but making coffee was only the simplest form of displacement activity in which I indulged. It wasn't long before my CD collection was alphabetised, my wardrobe colour co-ordinated and my fridge defrosted, but the worst distraction of all was the computer.

Jake had said it would be just me, my imagination and my computer. He was wrong. My computer is connected to the internet and the internet contains everything in the whole wide world ever. I don't know about you, but I sometimes find everything in the whole wide world ever to be a bit distracting. Surely it's the curse of the modern world that so many people now work at a computer while the computer also provides the biggest distraction from work ever devised by man.

Even when I sat down at my desk with the best of intentions I would find myself thinking: I'll crack on with Chapter 1 of the novel … just as soon as I've checked my emails. Well, that's a day wiped out right there. After three weeks I had written one page. It read as follows:

```
Hugh's Hue.
A novel
by Dave Gorman
```

Having written one whole page I reckoned I'd earned myself a proper break, so I thought I'd have a cup of coffee and quickly check my emails. For the seventh time that day. Amongst the mail from strangers offering me pornography, human growth hormones, generic viagra, cheap inkjet cartridges, get-rich-quick schemes, get-rich-even-quicker schemes and get-rich-really-quick-no-honestly-we-mean-it schemes, there was one particular email that caught my attention and pricked my curiosity.

The subject of the email was 'Googlewhack', which meant nothing to me but seemed a curious enough word. The sender was a stranger but his email address revealed that he was called Steven. I guessed that Steven was Australian. I didn't know this for sure because obviously he didn't start the email by saying *Hello, I'm Australian,* but he might as well have:

G'day Davo

You see what I mean? There was a certain antipodean flavour there. It went on:

Did you know that you're a googlewhack?

Stevo

Hmmm? I'd never heard the term 'googlewhack' before and I didn't know who Stevo was. But it seemed to me there was a distinct possibility he was sending me some kind of Australian insult. After all, there was only one part of my anatomy I could imagine the folk down under calling a 'google' and Stevo seemed to be accusing me of whacking mine.

Well, I don't know if you've ever tried writing a novel when you suspect a stranger on the other side of the world is sending you a random insult but let me tell you it just isn't possible. My mind just couldn't focus on anything else. Until I knew what a *googlewhack* was, there was simply no way I could concentrate elsewhere. So I hit the 'reply' button and fired off an email to Stevo:

Stevo,

What the hell is a googlewhack?

Dave

That seemed to be more than enough work for one day. Besides, I'm sure I'd read somewhere that it was unwise to write on an empty stomach, and I was certain it was foolhardy to write on an empty head. Right now, I had to fill my belly and my mind. I told myself that I would begin work, proper, the next morning and like a fool I believed me. Right now there was a restaurant to visit, friends to meet, food to eat, drink to drink and some thoughts to think.

*

I'd arranged to meet three mates, Geoff, Chris and Chris, in a little restaurant tucked away on a Soho side street, a simple little place that serves simple food. They serve cheap plonk too but they don't mind if you bring your own wine so we brought a couple of bottles of even cheaper, plonkier plonk.

The conversation meandered, as good conversation so often does, but it returned time and again to the possible meaning of 'googlewhack'. No-one at the table was at all sure, but most had a theory. Most of the theories agreed that it was probably some kind of Australian slang but no-one had a convincing explanation as to what it could mean.

'Maybe he's calling you a nutter? A headcase? Whacko?' offered one of the Chrises.

'Or maybe he means you're ugly?' suggested the other Chris. 'Maybe looking at you is like being whacked in the goggles?'

'That would make me a gogglewhack,' I said, 'and according to Stevo I'm a *google*whack.'

'I reckon you were probably right first time. He's calling you a wanker,' said our waiter, who had joined the conversation and clearly wasn't overly concerned with tips.

'You're clearly not overly concerned with tips, are you?' I said, smiling.

'All right!' he said, full of mock offence. 'No need to be such a googlewhack about it!'

It seemed that everyone who heard the phrase wanted to know what it meant. No-one was able to shrug it off and move the conversation on, so perhaps it's not surprising that when I got up the next morning and turned my computer on, ready to get to work (honest, guv) the first thing I did was check my emails in the hope that Stevo had provided the answer. I wasn't disappointed.

Essentially, it seemed 'googlewhacking' was a kind of internet word game that you played using the search engine www.google.com. Anyone who's used the site before (and in recent years it has become the search engine of choice for most internet users) will have a head start here. I'll try to explain as best I can.

The internet contains lots and lots and lots and lots and lots and lots and lots of information. All human life is there: there are great truths, there are whopping lies and there is plenty of sex and videotape. In essence, anyone can put anything on to the world wide web. And for the large part it isn't organised.

This disorganisation makes it impossible to have a Dewey Decimal System taking you to the subject you're looking for. Instead, people use search engines. Google's job is to look through the internet on your behalf. It tries to read whatever it can find and while it doesn't find absolutely everything it currently indexes more than three billion pages. And it actually reads them. It takes in their content. So, let's say you want to know about balloons. You type in the word balloon and then ask Google to go to work. In a split second Google will show you every single one of the three billion pages that contain the word balloon. Be warned: it will involve some bizarre pornography. But, say you typed in the word animal instead? Well, then Google will come back showing you a list of every page that contains the word animal. Be warned: it will involve some very bizarre pornography. But maybe you want to know about balloon animals? In which case you type in both the words and this time Google comes racing back with every page on the web that contains both the word balloon and the word animal. This will involve some very, very bizarre pornography. This is in part because it has searched for both the words rather than the phrase. It will come back with pages that include the phrase 'balloon animal', as well as pages that include the phrase 'animal balloon' and, for that matter, it will also come back with all the pages that include sentences such as 'I inserted the balloon into the animal ...', in fact every page that contains the two words whether they share a sentence or not.

Try it with any two words of your choice and you will probably find that Google points you at quite a lot of different sites. I just tried it with custard and fandango and, at the time of writing, Google can find over 500 pages that use both those words.

However, on very rare occasions, instead of showing you 548 possible web pages, Google can only find one. It looks through three billion pages and only finds one that delivers. A site that, in its own way, is special and unique.

This is a googlewhack and there are people out there who like to find them for fun.

Aspiring googlewhackers should be aware that there are also a few supplementary rules, as follows.

1. You don't put the two words in inverted commas. That's a useful way of improving your search results should you be using Google as a search tool. But in googlewhacking terms, it's cheating.

2. The words you use must be 'real words' that can be found in www.dictionary.com, the googlewhacker's dictionary of choice; no other resource counts.
3. The page that Google finds cannot be a word list of any kind. Not a page from a dictionary or a thesaurus, nor any other kind of word list, just a regular web page, with regular content.

Stevo, my Australian correspondent, had been amusing himself by trying to find a googlewhack and he'd succeeded, with the words Francophile Namesakes.

There was only one page in the whole world wide web that contained both those two words and it was part of my website: www.davegorman.com. So, as far as Stevo was concerned I *was* a googlewhack! He'd had a look around my site, found my email address and decided to let me know. So now I knew.

So, that put my mind at rest. It wasn't a random insult, it was just a strange email from down under, letting me know that my website contained a little bit of uniqueness; a one in three billion bit of uniqueness. Now that I knew it wasn't an insult to my sanity or face it didn't bother me. Now that my curiosity was satisfied and I knew what a googlewhack was, surely I'd be able to crack on with Chapter 1 of my literary masterpiece?

Only life isn't that simple, is it? Because now a whole new curiosity had been pricked. Because now I knew what a googlewhack was, *I wanted to know if I could find one*. I felt sure that I could, after all I had a pretty good vocabulary. Maybe it would be a good exercise to get my brain in gear. Yes, I'd find myself a googlewhack and *then* I would crack on with Chapter 1 of the novel.

I got online and another day of my life soon disappeared. My first attempts were very wide of the mark. No matter how obscure the words were, they always seemed to be shared by thousands of pages on the Web. (Why on earth were there 3000 hits for Hedgehog Bazooka? Could 1190 websites really contain Alfalfa and Beefsteak?) Slowly, my technique started improving. Karaoke Hubcap: 429; Quiche Gorgon: 75; Prosthetic Vassal: 41; Haphazard Frugivore: 15.

Best yet. I should hold on to one of those:

Haphazard Applejacks: 7. Come on!

Haphazard Cockboat: 3. Oof.

And then … then it happened: Haphazard Hatstands: 1 hit!

I stared at the screen. The space which would normally be filled up with hits two, three and four was instead a strange white emptiness, an emptiness that filled me with an inexplicable pride. I punched the air with my fist and a small, half-whispered 'yes' fell from my mouth. I'd finally done it.

I went to the kettle to make a celebratory cup of tea and prepared myself to begin work. I sat back down at the computer and looked at my lovely googlewhack again. But hold on, something was wrong. There was the page with my search results. In the familiar blue stripe across the page I read the words:

Searched the web for <u>Haphazard</u> Hatstands.
Results: 1-1 of 1. Search took 0.2 seconds

But yes, something was wrong: haphazard was underlined, but hatstands wasn't. I knew what this meant because Stevo had explained it in his email. The underlining shows you that there is a link to dictionary.com. If it's underlined it means that the word is found there and if it isn't, then it isn't. So that meant that hatstands couldn't be found in dictionary.com!

I started to fume at the injustice of it all.

I mean, obviously hatstands is a word; what kind of dictionary is it that doesn't include hatstands! Then I looked at the page again and realised it was worse than that. The one page out of three billion to contain both haphazard and hatstands was a wordlist. A page full of words beginning with H. This wasn't a googlewhack at all and for *two separate* reasons. It seemed my celebration was premature. I sipped at my tea but all of a sudden it tasted sour. *Hugh's Hue*, it seemed, would have to wait a little longer …

*

… another hour passed in which I must have tried hundreds of different pairs to no avail. Pork Turncoat? 381 hits. Useless. Porky Turncoat? 43. Getting better. Dork Turncoat? 78. Damn. Dork Turnspit?

BINGO! I had it. Dork Turnspit delivered one hit and one hit only. I hurriedly took in the details, not wanting to be fooled again. It passed all the tests. Oh yes, my Google had been well and truly whacked! A few hours ago I was a mere 'whackee; a chance discovery by a mysterious Aussie, but now I too was a proper googlewhacker.

At last my tea tasted sweet. I'd done it. I'd found one. But what exactly had I found? I took in the address of the website and found myself shocked once more. It was a site with an alarming address: www.WomenAndDogsUK.co.uk.

A site, as you'll have guessed by now, that was based in the UK and concerned with women … and dogs!

two

Dork Turnspit

Dork   noun: pejorative term to describe
                    someone with specialised interests.

Turnspit   1. noun: a rod on which an animal is
                    skewered for rotating while it cooks over a
                    fire.
                    2. noun: a breed of terrier-like dog that no
                    longer exists. In the early twentieth
                    century they were used to power butter
                    churns or other kitchen equipment.

My mouse hovered over the link. Did I really want to look at a
website about women and dogs? I was certainly curious; I
wanted to know the nature of the googlewhack I'd found. I
looked over my shoulder to make sure no-one else was in the
room – which is particularly cautious behaviour for a man who
lives alone – and then, throwing caution to the wind, my finger
pulsed on the mouse and the world of women and dogs
opened up before me.

I needn't have worried. What I found was, by turns
charming, intriguing, naïve, funny and, well, bizarre. The site,
it appeared, was run by a man called Marcus whose hobby was
to collect secondhand photographs of women and dogs. There
was nothing distasteful about the photos – absolutely nothing
there you wouldn't show your mum. In fact your mum might
well be in some of the photos because they were largely

domestic snaps of homely women sharing a frame with man's best friend. It might be a big jolly gran petting a dog in some anonymous 1970s high street, it might be a young girl swamped by both an armchair and a border collie or it might be a mysterious skirted figure walking a dog in the distance. So long as there was both a woman (or girl) and a dog (or puppy) in the photo then it counted.

Marcus didn't take his own photos: what he loved to do was *find* them and this seemed to be an important part of it to him – he wanted to have the actual photo, he didn't want to find images of women and dogs online because then he couldn't *own* them. As hobbies go, it seemed a strange one. At first glance it was just that I suppose: strange. But as I worked my way through the collection of photos I found it to be quite enchanting. Each photo was, in itself, incredibly ordinary and while the idea of collecting other people's mundane, domestic ephemera might appear odd, when viewed as a collection it seemed to take on some kind of meaning.

Or was it just bizarre? And funny? Marcus provided a line of commentary to accompany each snap. In one picture a woman crouches in her garden holding the dog steady for the camera. The caption read simply: *'Her red shoes suggest that she is lively!'* Surely it's sites like this that make the internet so endlessly fascinating.

More than the site itself, I found myself becoming strangely fascinated by Marcus. What kind of man was he? What drove him on? Why, of all things, did he collect photos of such a specific and yet abstract nature? Did he know that people found it funny? Did other people find it funny or was it just me? Not that I felt I was laughing *at* Marcus because I really did find something touching and beautiful about the site, about the normality it portrayed and celebrated. As I read Marcus's notes on the pictures in which he wondered not just about the correlation between shoe colour and personality but about who these women were and how they lived I found myself sharing his sense of wonder.

Marcus immensely although I could never quite work out how self-aware he was. He possessed great charm, intelligence and a wonderfully dry sense of humour. Whenever I saw his name loitering in my inbox I was sure to open his email first as I knew it would provide something of a chuckle. Here was a man with diverse interests and opinions on current affairs, politics, sport and art. I couldn't help but wonder what part of him had developed such an obsessive interest in secondhand photos of women and dogs? I knew I found Marcus funny, but I couldn't tell you if he knew his website was funny. Was it a serious hobby to him or a deliberately arcane collection intended to amuse? I didn't know the answer and I never plucked up the courage to ask him directly for fear of causing offence. After all, he seemed to take his website very seriously. But maybe that was part of the joke? I had come to value his friendship too much to risk losing it by delving too far in to precisely where the real Marcus began. Even though our friendship only existed in email correspondence it wasn't long before the odd nature of how we had virtually 'met' was virtually forgotten and I stopped thinking of him as a mere email buddy. He was a friend, plain and simple, and that was good enough for me.

Incidentally, during this time my progress as a novelist was still nil. You'll be glad to know however, that I painted the kitchen. Then some other work arrived to provide me with a more genuine distraction. I had a few engagements lined up in theatres. This pleased me greatly because it meant I was no longer *failing* to write the novel, I was just *doing something else*. It was a small tour and along the way it would take me to the Warwick Arts Centre for three nights. The Warwick Arts Centre is a peculiar name for the venue because it tends to give people the impression that it's in Warwick when actually it's in Coventry. Mind you, if I was based in Coventry I might not be quick to admit it either. Anyway, I was going to be staying in Coventry for three nights and seeing as it was only 20 miles from Birmingham (and 10 from Warwick) I thought I'd let

Marcus know I was nearby and suggest we meet up. I sent him an email to tell him I was going to be in town and gave him details of my hotel, my mobile phone number and so on. I thought it would be nice to put a face to the emails.

Marcus didn't call. I returned from Coventry and checked my email but there was no reply. Weird. He seemed to have disappeared. I was worried that I'd scared him away. Had I crossed some kind of line? Maybe internet buddies were meant to remain just that. Maybe he only wanted to exist within the confines of the world wide web where he could be whoever he wanted. Oh well. I shrugged my shoulders and carried on. I obviously didn't know him as well as I thought.

Back in London, I returned my attention to the novel. Or rather I tried. And failed. Instead life became a series of self-imposed distractions, my flat a temple dedicated to the God of displacement activity and I its high priest. My mantra: *'I'll crack on with Chapter 1 just as soon as I've ... vacuumed the carpets* or *cleaned out the attic* or *ironed my smalls* or *archived my photos* or *changed the sheets* or *mopped the floor* or ...well, or *displaced my activity.'*

The one thing I can say for displacement activity is that you sure do get a lot done. It's just that the one thing you don't do is the one thing you're supposed to do. In my case, the one thing I'd been paid to do. I didn't have the guts to own up. I didn't have the guts to admit defeat. I should have called Jake, said I was having trouble starting, asked for help, advice, guidance. I didn't. I remained convinced that when I actually got round to starting it would flow. Every day I failed to put any words down, I convinced myself that the words were there somewhere, building up inside me. One day, I reckoned, the dam would burst and a complete novel would flow out of me in a torrent.

I'll crack on with Chapter 1 just as soon as I've cleaned the oven.

I'll crack on with Chapter 1 just as soon as I've done these accounts.

I'll crack on with Chapter 1 just as soon as I've done this crossword.

*

I had a freshly brewed pot of tea on the go and the Sunday papers spread out on the floor around me. I was whiling away the afternoon by slowly working my way through the *Observer*'s cryptic crossword. With cryptic clues the solutions are often a little obtuse and, as there was no theme to this puzzle, the words were unrelated to each other; the only thing they had in common was that they happened to share a crossword grid.

As I put more of these words down I found a theory forming in my head. I hadn't thought about googlewhacking for weeks; my curiosity had been sated when I found my first 'whack but for some reason on this lazy Sunday it entered my consciousness once more. It occurred to me that two obtuse but unconnected words were the basic ingredients for a googlewhack. Perhaps a cryptic crossword might turn out to be a treasure trove of 'whacks? Word disassociation was clearly the order of the day. After all, if two words are connected in some way, the chances are they will inevitably share many a page on the internet. We all know that pizza and pineapple shouldn't go together but, like it or not, they are connected and if you search for the two words on Google you'll find hundreds of hits as a result. But word disassociation is a difficult game for the human brain to play; the moment you have one word lodged in your brain, all manner of connected words clamour for your attention. In a crossword, however, someone else has done the disassociating for you. Here before me was a collection of unconnected, obtuse words. Here was a checkerboard full of words that must surely be ripe for googlewhacking. My theory, *Gorman's First Theory of Googlewhacking*, was that a cryptic crossword would be a good googlewhack generator.

I'll crack on with Chapter 1, just as soon as I've finished this crossword and tested Gorman's First Theory of Googlewhacking.

A couple of hours later I found myself with a completed cryptic crossword. This was a rare achievement for me but I think I must have been especially motivated by the whack factor. There were 26 words within the crossword and I set about trying them out in various likely, or rather unlikely, pairs. My first few goes didn't yield a 'whack, but they did return low numbers: 7 hits, 4 hits, 2 hits, far closer to the elusive one than I had achieved with my first wild stabs in the dark all those weeks before.

But then, before my very eyes, a 'whack appeared. I'll admit that there was a little manipulation on my part: 3 down gave me varsity and 17 across gave bonnet. Varsity Bonnet wasn't a 'whack in itself, but with a little pluralisation from me … Varsities Bonnets: whack! My theory held water.

I looked for more: 7 down gave me nutter. I wasn't sure a slang term like that would be in dictionary.com but it had to be worth a go. I tried pairing it up with 23 across, rarebit. Hmmm, four hits, but at least both words were 'legal'. I tried pluralising again and … whack! Rarebit Nutters did the job: one hit!

I kept going, trying different combinations and pretty soon the crossword yielded its third and final 'whack: Termagant Holbein. I was wary of including the name of a German painter but Holbein *was* underlined so I knew it was in dictionary.com. I was more than happy to allow my doubts to pass and international googlewhacking rules to prevail.

Twenty-six solutions had given me three googlewhacks and it had only taken a few minutes to find them. My theory was correct: a cryptic crossword *was* an excellent googlewhack generator. I had discovered, nay, invented, a googlewhack engine. I was delighted! No doubt I was experiencing the same rush of excitement shared by all the great scientific pioneers. Alexander Graham Bell probably felt exactly like this when he invented the telephone. Except I was alone and I imagine Bell had someone to share his excitement with and if he didn't, he could always call someone ... and so could I.

I picked up my mobile phone and scrolled through the stored numbers wondering which of my friends would be most interested in this exciting revelation. When I saw *DannyW* highlighted my thumb moved to the green button. Of course, Dan would like this kind of thing.

I lowered my thumb but in the very instant that I hit the button my phone rang. Instead of dialling my mate, I found myself answering a call. I looked at the screen to see who it was but there was no name, just a number. 0121 something; Birmingham.

'Hello?' I said, tentatively.

'Hellow Dive, it's Marcus!'

I was astounded. I hadn't thought about Marcus in weeks and I hadn't thought about googlewhacking for even longer. It was as if I'd somehow summoned up the googlewhack genie.

'Oi just wanted yower advoice?'

It might have tallied with his phone number but the strength of Marcus's Brummie accent still took me by surprise. Now that I knew his voice, reading his emails would never be the same again.

'My advice?'

'Yuss.'

'Roit.'

'What?'

'Right,' I said, correcting myself.

I suffer from Wandering Accent Syndrome at times. My own origins lie in Stafford which, while in the West Midlands, refuses to cave into the familiar twang of the region. What it does have is a wishy-washy sort of non-accent. Southerners always think I'm from the North and Northerners always think I'm from the South. Midlanders never have a clue. It's such a blank canvas that, when it's confronted by a strong accent, it sometimes gives in and I end up adopting the accent of whoever I'm talking to. If I'm not careful it can sound like mockery, a fact that once saw me running faster than I've ever run before through the streets of Newcastle Upon Tyne. Or *Noocassel! 'Pon Teen! Mon!,* as I think I'd called it.

I won't continue to try and type Marcus's words in a Birmingham accent by the way as it always seems unfair to readers from Birmingham when that happens. I'm assuming that if you speak with a Birmingham accent you must read with one too, so you'll be reading 'Hellow Dive' with a Birmingham accent squared and no-one needs that in their life. I'm sorry, the rest of you will just have to use your imaginations.

'Look, I'm coming down to London in a couple of weeks' time, for the weekend, like. I thought you might want to meet up,' said Marcus.

Well, that was a bit rich! When I tried to arrange a meeting on his patch, he just disappeared!

'OK. We'll play your rules,' I said, a note of sarcasm entering my voice.

'What?'

'Nothing. Forget it. It'd be good to see you. Have you anything in mind?'

'Well, is there anywhere near you that would be good for photos?'

'Photos?'

'Of women and dogs,' he said, seemingly surprised that it wasn't my first thought. 'You know, for my collection.'

I had no idea where to buy secondhand photos of women and dogs and I didn't really fancy placing an advert. I thought about it for a moment.

'We could try Spitalfields market?'

'Do you think they'll have some?'

'Well, there's lots of secondhand *stuff,*' I said, hedging my bets. I looked around me. On the wall directly in front of me was a large dented metal sign reclaimed from some old office supplies company. It was now screwed to my wall and acting as a magnetic noticeboard. To my right, on the kitchen wall the word 'eat' was spelt out in two-foot tall 3D letters that had once been part of a car dealer's shopfront. The underside of my coffee table was illuminated by a lightbox, originally designed for viewing x-rays but long since removed from some hospital wall. This was all junk I'd bought from Spitalfields in order to decorate my home (and delay the start of Chapter 1) so there was no telling what could be found there.

'Look, I can't promise you there'll be any photos, but of all the places I know, it's the most likely.'

'Wicked!' said Marcus.

He took a long time on the word 'wicked', filling it with zest, taking the two syllables to their limit, stretching the word from Birmingham to London and back again. If it's possible to hear someone giving you a thumbs up, I think I heard it then.

*

There were no photos of Marcus on his website, which wasn't surprising as he was neither a woman nor a dog, but it did mean that when we met two weeks later I had no real idea what to expect.

We had arranged to meet outside Liverpool Street Station, at a small Starbucks coffee shed. So, what would a man who collects secondhand photos of women and dogs look like? What should I expect? Maybe he'd have greasy hair and bad teeth, wear a dark suit with brown shoes? Or would it be a tweed jacket with leather elbow patches? Surely the voice that delivered that 'wicked' must have emerged from a round rosy-cheeked face, a jolly butcher, a clean-shaven Santa. Potential Marcuses flicked through my head and every time someone approached the coffee counter I weighed up the possibility that this was my man.

'You must be Dave.'

I knew the voice immediately and shook the hand that was being offered. He'd appeared from nowhere, managing to get from the station door to me without being picked up by my radar. In his late thirties, Marcus had neatly trimmed hair that had greyed before its time. He was wearing a navy blue sweatshirt with the words 'Warwick Castle' written in mock gothic script and neatly pressed blue jeans that he wore like smart trousers that just happened to be made out of denim. He had a small canvas rucksack, which I assumed he'd used to carry the electronic cloaking device that had so effectively disabled my radar.

Within the walls of the market, Marcus was like a laser guided missile. He paid no heed to the organic vegetables, the health drinks, the handmade soaps, antique mirrors, imported exotica, circuit-board lampshades, leather jackets, retro track suits and ironic T-shirts and instead walked directly to a stall loaded up with military memorabilia, 1970s tennis rackets, a battered oboe, three shop dummies and a box full of Rubik's Cubes. Beneath the table, in a fruit box, covered in a tea towel was a collection of photos. I don't know how he knew they were there unless he could smell them, but he went straight to them without pause, crouched down and started riffling through the box.

I stood and watched, amazed at the speed with which his fingers worked. There must have been several thousand photos in the box and Marcus gave each one a cursory glance, taking in the essential facts in the blink of an eye. I watched as black and white images of strangers, most likely dead strangers, flashed by. I saw the same faces repeated over and over – this must have been one family's collection. I saw kids grow up and parents age and wondered what journey they'd been on to land here in a market, somebody else's memories for sale. Then the hypnotic, repetitive flicking of fingers and flickering eyes paused. Marcus pulled a photo out of the box and, with a tiny punch of the air exhaled a breathy 'Wicked!'

He passed the photo to me and I held on to it while he returned to the search. I looked at the photo, at the woman and her dog. I guessed from her clothes and demeanour that both she and the twentieth century were in their forties when the picture had been taken. The dog stared blankly back at me.

I hoped that photos of my nearest and dearest wouldn't end up for sale to strangers, but if they ever did, I hoped they would be bought by someone like Marcus. He cared for his photos, he gave them some kind of value at least. This woman and her dog would be better served as treasures in Marcus's collection than they would in this box beneath a table in a damp East London market. A second photo emerged moments later and then a third and, with each one, Marcus grew more excited. And the strange thing was, so did I. Somehow I'd become a part of this world. For a few brief moments the idea of collecting these snaps, these moments from other people's lives made complete sense to me. The search became sport and each photo Marcus thrust in my direction was a goal scored. A fourth photo was passed to me.

'Wicked!' That was me this time. Marcus didn't bat an eyelid.

The fourth photo turned out to be the last and I watched as Marcus handed over some small change in return for his quarry. He was clearly delighted and I was delighted for him. And, in some strange way, I realised I was delighted for myself too.

To celebrate I treated Marcus to Sunday lunch at my local, the Approach Tavern, a marvellous free house that serves great food. It has an art gallery upstairs that I've never been to but I find the food tastes better knowing it's there.

'I've had a great day, Dave,' said Marcus, supping from his pint of bitter.

'So have I, mate,' I said. Because I had.

'It's amazing, isn't it? That something this good can come from something so random? You're a googlewhack and I'm a googlewhack and here we both are!'

'Francophile Namesakes and Dork Turnspit.'

'They must be almost impossible to find, these googlewhacks.'

'Well, they're not *that* hard,' I said because, of course, I knew that a googlewhack engine was printed in the newspaper each day.

'They must be. I mean it's one in three billion'.

'Yeah. But there must be lots of them,' I said. 'Google indexes three billion pages, but there might be millions of 'whacks out there.'

'Do you think?'

'Tell you what, if you want, you can try and find one now. See for yourself.'

*

'Sugar?' I asked, pushing the plunger of the cafetiere down.

'No ta, Dave.'

We were back in my flat. Marcus was sat at my desk staring at Google, trying to think of two whackable words. I passed him his coffee.

'How're you doing?'

'I'm still thinking.'

I decided that a bit of showing off was in order. I left Marcus's mind to wander through the extremes of his vocabulary and sat myself down on the sofa. I picked up the *Observer* and turned to the crossword. Oh yes, I'd fill this baby in, let Gorman's First Theory of Googlewhacking take over and the resulting haul of whacks would be sure to impress.

I looked up and saw Marcus sitting at the computer, tip-tapping away at the keyboard. I felt a small pang of guilt. I knew that that chair should have been filled by a 31-year-old aspiring novelist with a ginger beard. I knew that all of this, this meeting, this day, this demonstration of googlewhacking, all of this was really just another way of putting off the novel.

I shook the guilt out of me and tried to refocus on the crossword, but somehow, knowing what was really going on in the back of my mind rather killed my enthusiasm. Maybe it was the lunchtime pint but try as I might I couldn't concentrate on any of the clues. It didn't matter if I did the crossword or not, it was all just play-acting. The only thing I was really doing was *not* writing. My mind started to wander instead and my eyes drifted around the page. And then I saw something remarkable. Something that made me leap out of my chair in celebration.

'WICKED!' I shouted, but it sounded odd.

My voice seemed to have an echo. The echo seemed to have a Birmingham accent. I turned to see that Marcus was also out of his chair and in a similar state of celebration. He stood with one arm aloft, like a cricketer acknowledging applause from the pavilion. We had both leapt to our feet in celebration at the same moment but for completely different reasons.

My celebrations were inspired by something on the page. Besides that week's crossword was the solution from a week before and beneath that were the names of the winners from a fortnight ago. And I was one of them! *D Gorman, London E2;* there it was in the middle of the list of five names. I was a winner!

Now you might well feel that winning the *Observer* cryptic crossword competition doesn't really merit a hands-in-the-air-shouting-out-wicked style celebration, but bear in mind that earlier that day I had been almost as excited by the discovery of a photo of a woman and her dog. I was clearly highly susceptible to celebration that day.

At the foot of the page it explained that the winners would receive the *New Penguin English Dictionary* worth £15.99 but that wasn't what excited me. In fact, I didn't even realise there was a prize to begin with. I was just genuinely delighted to *be* a winner. Winning felt good! Sixteen quid's worth of dictionary was neither here nor there, I'm not normally one of life's winners and sampling a taste of victory was ... well, it was wicked.

Excitedly I explained my excitement to Marcus while excitedly he explained his to me. The cause of *his* celebration was the discovery of his first googlewhack: Unconstructive Superegos. I looked at the Google page a bit closer, taking in the details. It obeyed all the rules, it was clearly a legal 'whack.

'Well done, Marcus, nice one,' I said patting him on the back.

'Well done yourself, Dave, that's very impressive, that is,' said Marcus nodding in the direction of the newspaper.

'Let's have a look at the site then,' I said and Marcus moved the mouse and clicked on the link in one swift move.

The website opened up, and what I saw made me feel uneasy. Gradually, I was consumed by an eerie feeling, as if I'd seen a ghost. I felt like I'd been to this website before, I suppose what I was experiencing was a sort of online déjà vu only it was stronger than that. I didn't just *feel* like I'd been there before, I *knew* I'd been there before. But that couldn't possibly be true, could it? Marcus was a googlewhack, which meant that he represented a one in three billion chance. If a one in three billion chance sits in your living room and takes another one in three billion chance, the result just should not be what you'd call familiar territory.

And yet I couldn't shake that sense of familiarity. www.LearningMethods.com didn't ring any immediate bells but I scoured the page looking for evidence, determined to confirm for myself that I wasn't imagining things.

And then I saw it.

At the bottom of the page I saw the copyright information with the name of the site's owner. Not only had I been to this site before but, I was stunned to discover, I *knew* the man responsible for creating it. I knew him well. His was a name I would never forget. Unconstructive Superegos led to www.LearningMethods.com and that led to … Dave Gorman.

three

Unconstructive Superegos

Unconstructive   adjective: unhelpful, serving to
                       dismantle or worsen. Negative.

Superegos   noun: plural of superego; that part of
                       the unconscious mind that acts as a
                       conscience for the ego.

As it goes I happened to know a lot of people called Dave Gorman. Perhaps I should explain.

A few years ago I was having a late-night drink with my then flatmate Danny and the conversation had turned to my namesakes. Danny, for reasons best known to himself, didn't believe me when I told him that the Assistant Manager of East Fife Football Club was also called Dave Gorman and so, a few hours later we were on a train to Scotland. It was *that* kind of late night drink. We tracked down the Assistant Manager of East Fife football club. He was indeed called Dave Gorman.

It turned out that Dave Gorman had a son called Dave Gorman and so we met him the next day. And then things started to get a little odd. Meeting Dave Gormans (or Dave Gormen, which I think is the correct plural) became something of an all-consuming quest and we ended up travelling all over Britain as well as visiting France, Germany, Italy, Norway, Ireland, Israel, New York and Jersey, only stopping when I had met 54 of my namesakes (one for every card of the deck, including the jokers) and Danny had a photograph of each encounter as proof.

There isn't space here to explain exactly how this all happened, indeed that would take a whole other book, but let's just say that a lot of tequila was involved along with salt, lemon and idiocy.

I look back on that time of my life with great fondness, but also with a big dose of embarrassment. It is clearly no way for a grown-up to behave. When the journey came to an end Danny and I were so scared of our ability to egg each other on that we decided our flatshare must come to an end too. We went our separate ways and gave each other a bottle of tequila to mark the occasion. I placed mine on my new flat's kitchen shelf where it would act as both a reminder of our stupid past while also serving as a warning for the future.

This was the past I wanted to put behind me. That was what I was like in my twenties; a reckless fool concerned only with frippery and nonsense. When drunk I would accept any challenge and I would always have to prove myself right at any cost. But I was 31 now; I wanted to be taken seriously. I wanted to grow up. I think it's fair to say that my embarrassment at this most ridiculous chapter in my life went a long way towards explaining my desire to change. In many ways it was the reason I now had a contract to write a novel. It was the reason there was a pot of publishing money in my bank account. It was the reason I now had a ginger beard bristling on the end of my chin.

Despite this, I had yet to write a word of the novel and I was now finding myself, quite by accident, looking at the website of a Dave Gorman. It seemed the harder I struggled to put my past behind me, the more likely I was to be confronted by it at the next turn.

The Dave Gorman in question was a man I'd come to regard as something of a friend. Canadian but living in St Alexandre, a tiny village in the South of France, when I'd first learned of his existence that was all I knew of him: his name, his nationality and his location. Danny and I had flown to France, hired a car and driven to St Alexandre in the belief that a North American would stand out in the South of France. This supposition had proved correct and with the help of friendly but confused villagers we had found his house. Unfortunately we had also discovered that Dave wasn't in. Worse still, on further investigation it turned out Dave was away visiting friends… in London. The next day I met him in Greenwich, approximately five miles from my own front door!

But we'd got on really well and had stayed in touch ever since. David and I (he prefers his name unabbreviated and it does make things easier) have had drinks together two or three times in London and even found our paths coinciding in New York for one particularly drunken evening. It hadn't been unusual for the two of us to exchange the odd email or phone call.

What was unusual was to find myself staring at his website because a relative stranger by the name of Marcus, a man who collected secondhand photographs of women and dogs, had tried randomly searching the web for the words unconstructive and superegos.

Especially when you consider that I only knew Marcus because I had once randomly searched for the words dork and turnspit and I had only done *that* because a mystery Australian called Stevo had randomly searched the internet for the words francophile and namesakes!

It seemed to me that it was a pretty remarkable series of coincidences that led me back to my namesake. I didn't know what the odds of something like this happening were but I did know it made me want to buy a lottery ticket. It also made me want to ring David.

'You're not going to believe what's just happened!' I said, once we'd dispensed with formalities.

'What?' he asked.

I told him the story. The whole thing, from start to finish.

'I don't believe it!'

'I told you you wouldn't.'

'You did, didn't you? That is amazing, eh!'

David and I chatted for a while. Marcus was still sitting at my desk and even though he seemed to have been struck dumb by his part in this most extreme series of coincidences, I didn't want to be impolite so I wrapped up the phone call and promised to call David another time.

When Marcus left later that day he had four new photos in his rucksack and a spring in his step. I had one hell of a story and a problem. I'd taken a glimpse at my past and it frightened me. But it tempted me too. I had to resist that temptation, I had to put that life of youthful folly behind me and be the 31-year-old I wanted to be. I had to start writing the novel. I sat at the computer, opened up a new Word document and stared into its clean white abyss. The day's events had only served to make the task seem even more distant. How was I supposed to sit down and write a novel when reality had proved itself to be stranger than anything my imagination could conjure? I was already more than struggling with the task in hand but when truth was so resolutely stranger than fiction what was the point in writing fiction? I needed to clear my head.

My fingers hovered over the keyboard. Write. Write anything. Just start.

Hugh Brown woke up one morning. He'd been dreaming again. Dreaming of the colour, that colour, that…

Dreadful. Delete, delete, delete.

Imagine a colour that only you can see. It isn't purple or red or any of the colours in the rainbow…

No, no, no. Far too camp. Start again.

Hugh strode into the DIY superstore like a man possessed. He barged his way through to the paints, running down the aisles pulling cans down, tearing up colour charts. Tins of Apricot Crush, First Dawn and Smooth Pistachio all came tumbling down, spilling their gooey contents over the floor. A crowd gathered (it was a Bank Holiday Monday after all) and somewhere a child cried.

'Why!' Hugh screamed at the top of his voice, 'Why isn't it here?'

How did those words get on my screen. Did I really type that? Nonsense. Dreadful, dreadful nonsense. Come on Gorman; *write*. And then my head collapsed. I gave in:

I'll crack on with Chapter 1 just as soon as I've checked my email.

*

To: Dave Gorman
From: David Gorman
Subject: Absolutely Googlewhacking Amazing!

Hi Dave,

Good to talk earlier. So you've been googlewhacked and I've been googlewhacked too, eh? Strange serendipity indeed!

Congratulations on the publishing contract! Writing can be hard work so if you ever need a break you know you're welcome to come and stay with us for a few days any time you like. You can finally see the inside of the house and there's a spare bedroom with

your name on it. (Well, our name, but you know what
I mean.)

It's very peaceful at this time of year so if you need
to clear your head, it'd be great to see you again,

Warmly,

David

I'd told David about the publishing deal but I guess I hadn't
been entirely honest about my lack of progress. Writing was
proving to be even harder work than he knew ... but my eyes
were inexorably drawn to the phrase: *'if you need to clear your
head ...'*

I did. I needed to clear my head more than anything else. But
could I afford a jolly to France? There was money in the bank
but it didn't really feel like *my* money. Until I'd actually done
some writing surely I was just keeping some of Jake's money
warm for a while. Then again, how much money was I talking
about? At the end of the day it all depended on how much a trip
to France was going to cost so at the start of the next day I
decided to look it up. I knew that Ryanair flew to Nîmes, David's
nearest airport, so I found my way to their website to see how
much the journey would cost with this no-frills, low-budget
carrier. I punched in all the details and waited for the page to
load. I couldn't believe my eyes and when I'd convinced myself
my eyes were right, I couldn't believe my luck.

The website told me I could fly from Stansted to Nîmes for
one penny. And, what's more, the return flight would cost one
penny too. Two pence! To fly to France! And back! On a plane
of all things! I didn't know how it was possible but I didn't care.
I was just frightened that if I looked away the offer would
disappear so I said yes immediately. Then I remembered that
the internet couldn't hear me so I hit the Yes button instead.
Then I rang David and told him I'd be coming along in a couple

of weeks' time. I nearly told him I'd be coming every week at that price.

'Two pence!?' he said disbelievingly. 'Are you sure the plane has wings?'

*

Maybe I'm old-fashioned, maybe I'm naïve, but I like to think that if I read something in a newspaper it must be true. So it's with deep regret that I'm forced to reveal to you, dear reader, that this is not always the case. I know for a fact that the *Observer* – that august journal of repute – told at least one cold and calculated lie in December 2002. The lie was as follows: *The first three correct solutions opened will receive the New Penguin English Dictionary (worth £15.99).*

As a winner I did not receive a copy of the dictionary. In its stead I received book tokens but, and this is the part that makes the lie so heinous, the book tokens were only worth £15.00. That's right! What is the world coming to when a newspaper short-changes its crossword winners to the tune of 99 pence? That's nearly a pound! Oh, I know it might not sound like a lot of money but to put it in context, bear in mind you can fly to France and back 49 and a half times for that kind of money!

As angry as I was about this outrageous situation, after serious consideration I decided to be big about it. I didn't even post my letter of complaint.

*

I didn't know very much about Nîmes but I could learn. The first thing I found out was this: if you have a strong Belfast accent, the word *Nîmes* is indistinguishable from the word *name*. I discovered this at Departure Gate 42 of Stansted Airport where a young man with a strong Belfast accent had been given the job of checking both our destination and our names.

'Nîmes?'

'Gorman.'

'Nîmes?'

'Dave … Gorman.'

'Are you going to Nîmes, sir?'

'Sorry? Am I going to name sir what?'

'What's your destination, sir?'

'Nîmes.'

'That's what I was trying to establish, sir.'

'Right, sorry, I thought you said "Name".'

'I see, sir. So you are going to Nîmes?'

'Yes.'

'Right. Now, name?'

'That's right.'

'Name?'

'Yes, that's right. I'm going to Nîmes.'

I was surprised to see that the flight was nowhere near full. There couldn't have been more than 60 passengers on the flight. It was nice to get three seats to myself but I crossed my fingers and hoped everyone else had paid more than me because I was rather hoping there'd be more than £12 worth of fuel in the tank.

There must have been because two hours later we were in Nîmes where a fellow passenger taught me my second fact about the city. Nîmes is, apparently, known as the *Rome of France*. I'm not sure why but presumably all roads lead there which would explain why my taxi driver wanted to show me quite so many of them.

Maybe it was the language barrier. I speak almost no French and he spoke almost no English, so maybe when I asked him to take me to the bus station he quite innocently thought I had said: 'Please take me on a guided tour of the city, kind sir. Please show me every sight you can. I will be delighted if you can take the time to explain it all to me in a language I clearly don't understand.' At least that would explain why what should have been a quick five-mile hop turned into something far more extensive. And expensive.

The bus journey took a further hour and a half but at least this journey had no incomprehensible commentary and I was happy just to drink in the view. Tiny little hamlets appeared and disappeared, and there were olive groves and vineyards and cypress trees tapering into impossible points, showing the rustic church spires how it should be done.

Each village we passed through seemed to outdo the last for its picture postcard quality. There were old ramshackle buildings; all weather-beaten stone, cracked plaster and battered wooden shutters that looked like they were only held together by the ivy that sprawled across them. But they didn't look neglected the way they might in an English setting, they just seemed right. The whole scene seemed to have been painted with the most muted of colours, it was like watching TV with the contrast turned down which gave the area something of a restful quality. I felt my head clearing already. I was doing the right thing.

Suddenly, as we cleared the brow of a beautiful little hill, a glorious little sunlit village loomed on the horizon. Memories came flooding back; this was St Alexandre. I got off the bus.

It was two and a half years since I'd been here but somehow I knew exactly where I was going. When we arrived it seemed as though nothing in the village had moved. I passed the same blue and grey, 1950s Renault parked in exactly the same spot. There were no people around, but weren't those two cats sitting in that same suntrap the last time I'd been here? Wasn't that skateboard lying upended in the middle of the road last time too?

As I arrived at the top of David's driveway I paused to breathe in the air. Fresh, crisp, clean air. You don't get that in East London. I remembered the last time I'd been here. I remembered the hollow feeling at discovering the empty house, the disappointment that flooded through me at the painful realisation that it had been a wasted journey. This time it was different. This time David was expecting me. This time I strode confidently.

There was a note pinned to the door. It was folded over so

that its contents were secret but on the outside I could see the name Dave Gorman. I paused. Which Dave Gorman was it meant for? What if his doctor had called by with the results of some embarrassing test for David and pinned them to the door? No. A doctor wouldn't ignore a perfectly good letterbox. And I was Dave to his David. So it must be for me. I unpinned it and had a look:

Dave,

We're really sorry but some urgent business has come up and we've had to leave at short notice. We are on our way to London. We are truly very sorry.

David and Eillen

I felt myself go weak. My bag dropped to the floor. How could this be? Not again! I felt tired suddenly, my legs started to give at the knees. I lowered myself down, sat on the bag and held my head in my hands. What would I do? Where would I go?

'Surprise!'

I turned and saw David and Eillen smiling broadly. They looked more than a little pleased with themselves.

'Gotcha!' said David with a wag of the finger.

'You git!' I yelled but any anger I felt was outweighed by the relief. I embraced them both.

'I am 'ugging two David Gormans!' said Eillen to laughter all round.

'It's a David Gorman sandwich!' I said and the laughter continued. Until we all realised that could be taken the wrong way. Someone coughed and the hug parted.

'I'll put the kettle on,' David said.

*

It was a crisp December evening but it was warm enough to sit outside so we sat by the pool while we ate dinner. David barbecued some fish, the wine (from a vineyard not three miles away) flowed freely and so did the conversation. I knew that David and Eillen were teachers in what is known (and indeed trademarked) as LearningMethods, a system that David had created and that aimed, I think, to teach people how to analyse and solve their own problems, be they problems with tension, pain, phobias, relationships, whatever.

They had both travelled the world teaching and so always had a fund of stories with which to entertain and of course my life is a non-stop rollercoaster of excitement so I was more than able to hold my own.

David told me how he had just finished teaching his LearningMethods work on an International Business Negotiation course at the University of Avignon and I returned fire by telling him about my recent failure to write a novel. David told me how he was aggressively developing the work and that a LearningMethods teacher was now employed at the Royal Academy of Music in Stockholm and I told him all about my failure to write a novel. And then David told me that he'd just finished writing a 30,000 word article on his work and so I told him all about my failure to write one word ... of a novel. I think it's fair to say my rollercoaster had stalled.

Eillen had to travel to Avignon the next morning so she retired early to bed while David and I continued talking late into the night.

'So, Dave, tell me more about these ... googlewhacks?'

I told him everything. Everything I've told you.

'So I'm number two in a chain?' said David.

'What do you mean?'

'Well, you didn't find *my* googlewhack, did you? You found Dork Turnspit and he found Unconstructive Superegos so I'm number two in a chain,' said David, drawing a little diagram on the back of an envelope.

'I see what you mean.'

'Every link in the chain takes you one step further from your own imagination,' said David. '*Your* imagination conjures up two words. Those two words lead you to someone and *their* imagination conjures up two new words ... it would be interesting to see how long a chain you could get, eh?'

'Yeah, I guess so,' I said, guessing so.

'How many do you think it would be possible to get?' asked David, pouring me another glass of wine.

'I have no idea.'

'I bet you couldn't get ten in a row.'

'Well, let's think about this,' I said, warming to the conversation. For my sins I used to study maths and, while I dropped out of university, there is a small part of me that will always be that maths student. You put a couple of glasses of wine inside me and then give me a hypothetical mathematical problem like this and that part of my brain fires up automatically. If I'm ever in a coma, don't play me my favourite music, don't bring in my favourite celebrity, just start every sentence with '*If an apple costs 7p and an orange costs 9p how many ...*'

'Apart from you, I've emailed four different 'whacks,' I said. 'I mailed the three I found using the *Observer* crossword and I emailed Marcus. He was the only one I got a reply from.'

'So?'

'So, let's say that's the hit rate: one in four.' I took the pen and the envelope from David. It was my turn to draw a diagram. 'So it's simple. If you want to create a chain, every time you meet a googlewhack, you just persuade them to find four 'whacks. One of them should reply so then you meet them and persuade them to find four and so on. It'd be easy. There you go: a statistically likely ten in a row. Problem solved.'

'OK ...' said David, stroking his chin, 'but what about ... if they each only found you ... two? That wouldn't be possible, right?'

'Well, it would be harder but it's far from impossible. It's an infinite task. It's basically the same as the infinite-number-of-monkeys-and-typewriters thing. If you just keep trying forever, however unlikely it seems, you will eventually get ten googlewhacks in a row.'

'Yeah, but you don't have *forever* do you?' David snorted derisively. 'You need to put some kind of deadline on it.'

I suddenly realised that, while I was talking hypothetically, David seemed to be talking about this as a reality. I was using the word 'you' in the general sense. The same way it's used in sentences like '*You*'ve got to have a hobby' or '*You*'ll always find me in the kitchen at parties.' David was using the word 'you' in the specific sense. The same way it's used in sentences like, 'Oi, *you*, get off my land' or '*You* make me feel like dancing' or 'I, David Gorman, challenge *you*, Dave Gorman, to meet ten googlewhacks in a row', say. One knows the sort of thing, doesn't one?

'Hang on,' I said. 'You actually think I might do this?'

'Yeah … why not?'

'Let me be really clear about this, David: I. Am. Not. Doing. This. What kind of man do you think I am?'

'I thought you liked this kind of thing!' he protested.

'What? Why?'

'Because the first time I met you, you travelled all the way from England to France and back again in order to meet me! Why did you do that, Dave? Do tell.'

'Because …' I was sheepish now, 'because … you're also … called … Dave Gorman.'

'Exactly! You *love* doing this sort of thing.'

I suppose I did have something of a reputation. And I could see why. But I obviously hadn't explained to David that I was trying to change.

'Look, all that stupidity is behind me now,' I said. 'You know I'm trying to write a novel. You can see I've got a beard. I'm a grown-up now, David. *I'm 31.*'

David simply scoffed. A mischievous grin played across his face.

'What's that for? Why are you grinning?'

'I'm older than you, Dave,' he said.

'So?'

'So … you think 31 is the age to grow up! I don't know where you got that idea from but take it from an older man, Dave, 31 is too young to be growing up,' he sipped from his wine. '32. That's when you should grow up.'

'What?'

'32,' he smirked, 'I think you should grow up when you're 32.'

'What do you mean?'

'I mean,' he paused. He spun the moment out, as if he was Hercule Poirot about to reveal the murderer, 'I mean: if you personally find no more googlewhacks, but every googlewhack you meet finds you two more, *I bet you can't get ten googlewhacks in a row before your 32nd birthday.*'

I was drunk. A friend, a fellow Dave Gorman no less, was issuing me with a challenge. Could I meet ten googlewhacks in a row? Was I tempted? A couple of years ago I'd have leaned across the table and shaken David's hand without a thought. But I'd moved on since then. Or had I? Here was my chance to prove myself. Here was my chance to be the man I wanted to be and not the man I'd become. If I could resist the challenge I could prove to David, to the world and to myself that I was no longer the idiot clown. I could be a grown-up.

'No, David,' I said firmly. I would have raised my voice but Eillen was asleep so instead I spoke with a resolute whisper. 'No. I'm not doing it. *This* is my plan: I'm going to have a nice couple of days here in France. Then I'm going to go back to England. I'm going to have a nice, quiet, family Christmas at my mum's and then, in the New Year, I'm going to crack on with my novel.'

There. I was proud of myself. I felt like an alcoholic refusing a drink for the first time, I'd spent the last few years of my life addicted to childish idiocy, but no more. I had given up. It was all behind me.

Hello, my name is Dave Gorman and I used to be an idiot.

As I went to bed I found I was at peace with the world and with myself and as a consequence I had the best night's sleep I'd had in months. I woke late the next day and followed the smell of freshly brewed coffee through to the kitchen.

'Good morning, David Gorman.'

'Good *afternoon*, Dave Gorman.'

We smiled.

'Hey, while you're away from home, if you want to use the phone and things, just go right ahead. You don't need to ask. Treat the place like your own home . . . you might as well; your name's on the mortgage.'

'Thanks. It's only a couple of days, I think I can manage.'

'Well, if you want to check your emails, there's a computer through there … feel free.'

'Now that I might do. Are you sure you don't mind?'

'Go for it.'

I wandered through to the study and within a couple of minutes was online, checking my mail, deleting the spam and replying where appropriate. I'd only been there a short while when David popped in with a fresh cup of coffee. A few minutes later he popped in with a nicely warmed pain au chocolat. A few minutes more and he appeared again. I wondered what fresh treat he had in store this time.

'While you're online, here's a couple of people I thought you might want to get in touch with,' he said, handing me a piece of paper.

He said it casually as if it was almost not worth mentioning but there was a glint in his eye. Something was up, but I couldn't work out what. I looked at the paper and saw two email addresses. The names were completely unfamiliar to me.

'Why would I want to get in touch with these people? Who are they?'

David beamed; it was the smile of a magician about to reveal his finest trick: 'They're the two googlewhacks I found! Remember? Every googlewhack you find can find you two more and you have to try and get a chain of ten in a row before you're 32?'

He looked at me in the same way that a cat looks at its owner when it's brought a dead bird into the house, seeking reward and approval. I gave David the look an owner gives to his cat in such circumstances; a withering look of reproach.

'No. David. Remember: I'm not doing that,' I was astounded. He seemed to have completely forgotten the conversation from last night. I tried to jog his memory.

'Beard?' I said, pointing at my face.

'grown-up?' I said, pointing at my face again.

'Novel?' I said, pointing at my face yet again. I know it didn't make sense but I was on a roll.

'But I thought you—'

'Oh, David. I'm not doing it,' I sighed, refusing to be worn down.

'Oh. I got up early this morning especially.'

Was he sulking? Was it a pretend sulk? He still had an air of mischief about him.

'I found my two. I thought you'd be interested,' he continued. 'I thought you'd want to … you know?'

'I know, David,' I fought for control of my temper. I won. I was calm and precise, 'Believe me; I didn't take the bait last night and I'm sober now so there's no chance. My mind is made up.'

'OK.'

He smiled and I smiled back. We looked each other in the eye to make sure we both knew we were still friends. David turned to leave. As he got to the door he turned, paused and then almost whispered, 'They were good googlewhacks too.'

He'd got me. He'd fished for my interest and finally I'd taken the bait.

'Really?' I asked. 'What were they…?'

'…What do you mean?' I asked asthmatically.

'I mean…' said David, pausing for one, two, three breaths, 'Dauphin Gormandise is a googlewhack! Dauphin Gormandise! That's got to be as close as you can get to Dave Gorman with only one hit.'

I laughed again. David laughed again.

'How long did that one take you?' I asked, amazed at the efforts he'd gone to.

'Oh … not *that* long,' he said.

'Well, it's very impressive,' I said, my curiosity now outweighing everything else. His other googlewhack, Unicyclist Periscopes was also a fine specimen. 'So go on then, where do your googlewhacks take us?'

'Well, Unicyclist Periscopes takes you to the American Physical Society.'

'What's that?'

'They represent the interests of physicists in America. They're based in Washington DC.'

He knew I was more interested in the other.

'And?'

'And Dauphin Gormandise leads you to a History professor at a Jesuit University in New York.'

We giggled a little more.

'Washington and New York?' I said.

'Yeah,' said David, the glint returning to his eyes. 'So … are you tempted? To go for it? Ten in a row?'

I was falling into his trap once more, seduced by the sheer bloody-minded whimsy of it all. My tongue pushed against my lower teeth, my mouth widened, my lips tightened and I inhaled slightly, ready to pronounce the very beginnings of a 'yes' when I suddenly caught myself. I relaxed briefly and took a deep breath. The tip of my tongue moved to the roof of my mouth instead.

'No,' I said, firmly. 'I am not about to get on a plane to New York or Washington! I've told you; I'm writing a novel. I don't have the time for those kind of shenanigans.'

'Yeah. You're right,' said David. He stood and walked to the doorway again. 'But maybe you should tell them that they're googlewhacks, eh?'

I looked David in the eye, wary that this might be some kind of trap.

'I liked hearing that I'm one,' he explained, 'you liked hearing that you're one...'

It seemed to make sense. It did seem to be the kind of fact people enjoyed learning about themselves. I *was* online. I *was* sending and receiving emails so it's not like I'd have to make any great effort. What harm could it do?

'You should at least tell them they're googlewhacks...' said David again.

*

I sent two emails to let the new googlewhacks know of their 'whack status. Then I carried on working my way through my inbox. About forty minutes later I'd done everything I needed to do but made one final check to see if any new emails had arrived in the meantime. There were two.

One told me that my email to the History professor at the Jesuit University in New York had not been delivered. It had been bounced back to me on the grounds that the address no longer existed. (I assumed this meant he'd left that job but that the website hadn't been updated, leaving a defunct email address hanging about in the ether but pointing nowhere in particular.)

The other came from someone called David Harris who worked for the American Physical Society in Washington DC. His email said that he'd heard of googlewhacks before and that it was lovely to turn up for work in the morning and get something so refreshingly odd sent to him. Then he shared his thoughts as a physicist on googlewhacks but, not being a physicist myself, I didn't really understand them. I think words like *nodes* and *networks* and *interconnectedness* were mentioned. While I didn't understand everything that was written, he came across as a charming and polite fellow so I sent a reply that hopefully adopted a similar tone of voice and left things at that.

*

I had a nice time in France. David drove us out to Les Auberges des Cascades where we communed with nature, sitting awestruck watching powerful waterfalls in action. We visited a nearby rural market where I bought some *produce Provençal* which I knew would make good Christmas presents for random elderly relatives. We ate well, we drank well and we laughed a lot. On my last night we sat up late, drank absinthe and put the world to rights.

'You know you said you'd changed?' said David

'Uh huh.'

'I think you're right. I really look forward to seeing your novel.'

It was a happy time.

When I returned home my head felt like it had been successfully cleared and I was ready to take control of life once more.

Christmas was quiet but lovely, spent with family back in my home town of Stafford. After a few days of home-cooked goodness I travelled back down to London taking a pleasantly circuitous route in order to visit those relatives not yet seen during the festive season. Back at home I made an early New Year's resolution: I resolved to have more resolve. As soon as the New Year was upon us I would begin work on my novel and there would be no stopping me. It was time for a new year, a new broom; a new me.

This determination gave me licence to enjoy New Year's Eve and I threw myself into the celebration with gusto. I met up with a large group of friends in Soho. So large in fact that this time there were two Geoffs and three Chrises. We moved from venue to venue, drinking, talking, drinking, dancing and of course, drinking. In the early hours of the morning there were maybe ten of us left and we didn't want the party to stop. We piled into a couple of black cabs and headed back to my flat.

Things were mellow now. Looking around my front room I could see nothing but friendly faces. The music was low and we sat around in a large circle telling stories and reflecting on the passing year. There were three girls and seven boys – odds that combined with alcohol and testosterone to inject a competitive edge into the proceedings. Everyone was polite and all were allowed to hold court for a while but each of us wanted to top the story that had just been told. Everyone wanted to tell the most entertaining tale of the night.

One of my friends, Duncan, did well with a story from his Spanish holiday. While walking up some Andalucian mountain or other he'd bumped into his next door neighbour from Peckham. The story won gasps of disbelief from the group.

'Isn't that the most amazing coincidence!?' asked Dunc, milking it for all it was worth.

'No,' I said, a competitive fire in my eyes. 'No, it isn't!'

'It is!' protested Duncan

'It is not!' I said, perhaps a little too forcefully.

The room fell silent. I suppose I *was* being a bit heavy-handed. Instead of backing down, I steamrollered on. If the game was Coincidence Poker, life had recently dealt me a very strong hand.

'*This* is the *most* amazing coincidence,' I said, and began to tell the room my story.

I told them how a one in three billion chance named Marcus had sat in that very room. And how that one in three billion chance had taken *another* one in three billion chance and landed at someone I knew. Someone I knew and who was also called David Gorman! There were some gasps along the way but when I came to the end of my story there was nothing but a shocked, awe-full silence. It was eventually broken by a lone voice:

'*That*,' said Zena, 'is the most amazing coincidence in the world!'

I smiled. Duncan scowled. In this particular bunch of gorillas, I was the silverback and he was still the young pretender.

'What happened next?' came a question.

'Nothing much. Well, I went to France to see David.'

'And then what?' asked another voice.

And so I told the room all about my trip to France. I told them about David's challenge and it was with a certain pride that I told them of my grown-up refusal.

'So,' said Duncan, after a pause, 'when are you going to go to Washington?'

'Yeah!' chorused three or four voices at once.

'I'm NOT!' I yelled, surprising myself with the level of my drunken anger. 'Didn't you listen to that bit of the story? Didn't you hear the bit where I said I wasn't doing that kind of thing any more?'

'But we bet you can't get ten in a row as well! Don't we?' said Duncan, rallying the troops.

'Yeah!' came the baying response.

'NO!' I exploded. 'Look at me! Just because I've done some stupid things in the past it doesn't mean I'm some kind of performing monkey! It's all right for you, Steve, with your *proper job*! We can't goad you into ruining your own life because you've got *responsibilities*! Well, just because I have no responsibilities it doesn't mean I have to be irresponsible! I'm 31! I've grown a beard! I've got a publishing deal! If you were any kind of friends you'd be encouraging me to write a best-selling novel not trying to make me perform stupid tasks for your own amusement! I am a bloody grown-up! So why the hell am I having a temper tantrum in my own house on New Year's bloody Eve?'

It wasn't the most comfortable of silences that followed. The party was in danger of ending on a sour note. Somebody coughed. Most people looked at their shoes.

'I'm sorry, Dave,' said Duncan.

'No, mate.' I shook my head, 'I'm sorry.'

'I just got a bit carried away. I think we've all come to expect this kind of thing from you and ... well ...'

'I know,' I said, 'it's my own fault. I'm sorry I lost my temper. I don't want the evening to end like this. Come on, who wants another drink?'

The room approved of this idea. In the kitchen I found

myself looking at an array of empty bottles. There didn't seem to be anything else to drink! But then my eyes came to rest on my bottle of tequila. Dan's present. A reminder of past stupidity, a warning for the future. It had a note attached: *Only to be opened in case of emergency!*

I knew there were some lemons in the fridge and of course there's always salt. This would put the party spirit back in to the room. This was a bona fide emergency. I loaded up the tray and walked back into the room with a smile.

'Ladies and gentlemen: tequila!'

There were cheers. There were hugs. There was ceremony. There was *everybody ready? One, two, three, go: salt, lemon, tequila, gaaah! More, more, more! One, two, three, go: salt, lemon, tequila, gaaah! More, more, more! One, two, three …*

*

The main thing I remember was the warmth. I do remember other things, but they're just details: smiles, laughs, the smell of sweat on leather but my memory can't put them in order, I can't find the connections between them, there are too many pieces of the jigsaw missing, but the one thing I know that was with me consistently that night was the warmth.

And somewhere in the missing pieces of that jigsaw, dear reader, somewhere in the random, fractured smiles, laughs and the smell of sweat on leather, somewhere in the warmth, the fuzzy warmth, the slurry, blurry, furry warmth lies the story of how I came to be waking up in Heathrow Airport on New Year's Day with a ticket to Washington DC in my pocket.

PART TWO

WHAT HAPPENED BECAUSE I WOKE UP IN

HEATHROW AIRPORT ON NEW YEAR'S DAY WITH

A TICKET TO WASHINGTON DC IN MY POCKET

four

Unicyclist Periscopes

Unicyclist noun: one who uses a unicycle (a one-wheeled, pedal-driven vehicle).

Periscopes noun: plural of periscope; an optical device using mirrors or prisms that allows the user to view objects not in the direct line of vision.

I didn't want to go to Washington. But I had a ticket. The return journey was scheduled for one week later. I needed to think straight but I was in no fit state to do so. My head was thumping. My stomach was turning. A hot sweat of sickness and a cold sweat of panic were competing for control of my body.

'Excuse me,' I approached the ticket desk, 'I was very drunk when I bought this ticket. It's a mistake and I'd really like my money back.'

'I beg your pardon, sir?' asked the assistant with a smile.

She seemed unnaturally cheerful. In my opinion if you're at work on New Year's Day and you haven't got a hangover you should at least have the decency to be bad tempered about it. Anything else just isn't human.

'I was drunk when I bought this. I don't really want to go to Washington.'

'Where do you want to go, sir?'

'I don't want to go anywhere ...'

'Then why did you buy a ticket?'

'Because I was very drunk!'

'I'm afraid there's nothing I can do about that, sir.'

'But surely it's *illegal* to sell tickets to drunk people...' I said, desperation creeping in already.

'No, sir,' she was calm and straightforward, 'it isn't.'

'Not even to Washington?' I cranked the desperation up a notch.

'No, sir.'

'But the President of America lives there!' I said, following some kind of tortuous hungover logic. 'You can't sell drunk people tickets to see the President of America!'

'Washington is a very big place, sir,' she said with her more straightforward unhungover logic.

'But I've got a novel to write!' I yelled. I remained where I was but my words leapt across the counter and grabbed the lapels of her jacket.

'Yes, sir,' she said, loading sarcasm into her armoury. 'We get a lot of that.'

I paused. I turned away from the counter. I breathed. I counted to ten.

'But ...!' I started but I was still shouting. I paused again. I turned away again. I breathed again. Deeper this time. I counted to 30.

'Look' – that was better, I was trying to match her for calmness – 'I've got a ticket to Washington. I don't want this ticket. What can I do?'

'You can go to Washington?'

'Aaaaagggggghhhhhh,' I aaaaagggggghhhhhhed, abandoning calmness.

'I beg your pardon, sir?'

'Aaaaagggggghhhhhh.'

'If you continue to behave like this, sir, I have to inform you that you won't be allowed to board your plane.'

I screamed, 'But I don't *want* to board my plane!'

Hang on. Surely here was a plan. I breathed deeply, but not to calm myself down. This time I was filling my lungs, preparing myself for a full-on burst of travel-banning ferocity.

'Aaaaaagggggghhhhhh!'

'You won't get a refund, sir.'

'Oh.'

I didn't know what to do. I'd spent good money on this flight. Jake's money. You can't go throwing money away paying for airline tickets and then not using them, can you? There are people starving in Africa!

I'd paid for a week-long trip to Washington. It was a holiday I didn't want but it was also money I'd never see again. Then it hit me: the best thing to do with a holiday you don't want? Start wanting it.

'Right then,' I growled, my eyes wide with a new purpose, 'I'll go to Washington then! And just to spite you, Mrs Ticket Desk, I'm going to enjoy myself! I'm going to be happy! Yeah? How do you like *that,* huh? I'm going to have a holiday and you're going to be working here and I'm going to be happy and it's all your fault!'

Yeah. That showed her.

'Happy New Year, sir,' she said with a smile.

But I *was* going to show her. I was going to have a holiday. I was going to enjoy myself, I was going to take my hangover on an eight-hour flight so that I could breathe recycled air while having my kneecaps ground down by the seat in front. That would show her!

*

People use many different techniques to combat hangovers. I find a fry-up often does the trick, whereas some people swear by the hair of the dog. There is a rumour going round that says fresh air can aid your recovery while others prefer to stay in bed and make friends with the duvet. In the history of man-kind, no one has ever suggested that an eight-hour flight to

Washington might be an effective remedy. And now I know why.

We landed in Washington and my hangover was still raging; my head was throbbing and my body was gripped by a thousand tiny convulsions. I made my way, zombie-like, to the baggage carousel.

In the eight hours of sensory deprivation (*note to self: never, ever, ever set foot on another plane without a book to read*) I had whiled away some of the time by letting my imagination wander. My imagination had decided to go on a date with a girl sitting a few seats away and, as far as I could tell, my imagination had enjoyed the experience a great deal. Standing waiting for our luggage to appear, this seemed as good a time as any to introduce my real self. After all, I think the shaking, sweaty wreck look really works for me.

'Hi,' I said, adopting an air of nonchalance.

'Hi.' She smiled.

'So ... what brings you to DC?' I countered.

No, no, no! *DC*? Why did I say *DC*? British people can't possibly refer to *DC*, it just doesn't sound right. I sounded like I was affecting an appalling fake, transatlantic accent. I sounded like the most insufferable breed of local radio disc jockey. Luckily she didn't seem to mind.

'I'm on holiday,' she said with another smile. 'You?'

I ran through the options in my head:

'*I got exceedingly drunk last night and woke up this morning with the ticket in my pocket.*' No.

'*A man who shares my name has challenged me to meet ten googlewhacks in a row.*' No.

'*I'm an international spy.*' What?

Oh, I know, this'll do: 'Yeah. Me too. Holiday.'

We watched the parade of luggage crawl by in silence for a moment.

'My bag is always one of the last!' she said, rolling her eyes. She had beautiful green eyes.

'Tsk, yeah, me too.'

And then a horrible fact hit me. *I didn't have a bag*. What was

I doing? My case wasn't going to come round last because it wasn't going to come round at all. My case was sitting at home, unpacked, on top of a wardrobe. I'd just followed the herd to the baggage carousel because *that's what you do* in an airport. I was about to lose my nonchalant air. Is it possible to emerge with any dignity when you spend fifteen minutes chatting someone up at an international airport baggage carousel and then walk away empty-handed?

'Well, it's been nice talking to you,' I said, trying to sound bright and breezy but falling some way short.

'What?'

'Enjoy your holiday,' I croaked.

My throat was dry and I could feel myself starting to blush.

'Er ... thanks,' she sounded understandably confused. 'And you.'

But I'd already turned away. I was walking fast, strictly speaking too fast to be a walk, but not fast enough to be a run either.

As holidays go, it wasn't the best start.

*

It was early evening in Washington but late night according to my body. I needed sleep. I needed a change of clothes too. And something to eat. I explained my needs to a taxi driver and accepted his judgement on the best place to drop me. He explained that the city was broken into four quadrants, that he couldn't guarantee my safety if I went to the wrong one and then left me in the North West quadrant which, I hoped, was the right one.

My plan was simple: get myself a room for the night, then buy a change of clothes, then get a bite to eat before rewarding myself with sleep. Getting a room was easy. I just handed over my credit card and spent a few hundred words of a novel I had yet to write but the search for clothes and food seemed to be impossible.

It was New Year's Day and nothing within walking distance of the hotel was open. Naked room service seemed to be the best option for now. Clothes would have to wait until the morning.

'I'm sorry, sir, the kitchen is closed today,' said the voice on the end of the phone. 'It *is* New Year's Day, sir.'

'But you're a hotel,' I pleaded. 'People are staying here. They must get hungry. They have to eat.'

'It *is* New Year's Day, sir,' he said again, as if it made more sense a second time. 'There is an all-night garage nearby. They might be open.'

It's fair to say that as I sat naked in my room, eating a pot of instant noodles with a toothbrush I'd bought from reception, life seemed to have reached something of a low ebb.

*

I woke the next day and decided it was time for the tide to turn. I showered, which was a futile gesture given that I then climbed back into my dirty clothes. I'd worn these clothes all through the last day of 2002 *and* the first day of 2003. I'd been sober, drunk and hungover in these clothes; awake and asleep, hot and cold, sweaty and very sweaty. My first job of the day was to buy something clean to wear while not standing too close to any sales assistants who might smell me. With this achieved I scurried back to the hotel, showered and changed once more. I'd wash the dirty shirt but it was probably safer to burn the underpants.

My next job was to enjoy myself. Whatever had been on my mind when I was buying the airline ticket was irrelevant; I was clearly possessed by demons at the time. What was important was simply this: I was in Washington for a week and I had to make the most of it. Googlewhacking didn't come in to it; I was here for a holiday.

I walked up to the White House because that seemed like the obvious first port of call for an accidental tourist like myself. It's one of the most famous buildings in the world and I'm glad I've seen it but it's just not possible to spend a long time looking at it. I can stand and stare at an ocean for hours but whichever way you look at it, the White House is basically *a* white house and that's that. A short while ago it would have been possible to take a tour of the building but fear of a terrorist attack had put paid to that. I gave it a couple of minutes.

As I turned to leave I heard a voice behind me.

'Happy New Year!'

Instinctively I turned to see if this was aimed at me and discovered a young man meeting my gaze. He wore no coat, just blue jeans and a baseball shirt. It was a cold day and a light drizzle was falling.

'Happy New Year,' I said and continued on my way.

He came with me, matching me stride for stride. It was very deliberate and ever so slightly intimidating.

'Hey, where you from? You got an accent, where you from?'

'England.'

'Right. My name's Carlton. I'm half African American, half Cherokee Indian, half English, half Polish and half … um … er … Spanish.'

'Really?' I said while subtly trying to increase my pace. I was hoping to be fast enough to leave him behind (all five halves of him) without being so fast as to look panicked. He increased his pace too.

'You know I met my hero,' he said, the new subject arriving as abruptly as he himself had done.

'Really?' I moved to the kerb, ready to cross the road.

Carlton stepped into the gutter and faced me, blocking my path. He had a large scar that stretched down from his right ear to the collarbone on his left side. He stepped forwards, forcing me to step back.

'Sean Connery. He's a scotman.' He screwed up his face, he knew something was wrong with the word *scotman* but he couldn't figure out what. He tried it out again for size,

'Scotman? Yeah ... he's a scotman. Do you know why he's my hero?'

'No.'

'Because he's the eppy-tome of manhood.'

By the time I'd worked it out he meant the '*epitome* of manhood' Carlton was busy making another sudden conversational gear change.

'I do martial arts.'

If I was compiling a list of *sentences I-didn't-want-to-hear-from-intimidating-strangers-who-accosted-me-on-the-streets-of-foreign-cities* that would be right up there. I think it would be just above '*stand here and tell me if anyone's coming*' but just below '*I've got a gun*'.

'Really?'

'Yeah. I'll show you if you like: hold your right hand up like this.'

Carlton raised his hand as if he were about to attack me with an imaginary knife.

'No!'

'Why not?' he asked, his voice full of moral indignation.

I had a lot of reasons. Because he'd just told me he did martial arts. Because he clearly had a move he wanted to try on me. Because it seemed like a sure-fire way of getting hurt.

'Just because.'

'Go on. Come at me with your right hand like this,' he said raising his right hand again. I flinched.

'No!'

I stepped past him and started walking.

'Just pretend to attack me! Go on! Please!' he said following me.

If this was an attempted mugging it was the strangest, and in many ways the politest I'd ever seen. Did he only mug people in self-defence?

I walked a bit faster.

'Go on!' he pleaded, keeping pace.

I was being pursued by a man who wanted *me* to attack *him*! I stopped.

'Look,' I said sternly, 'No. N. O. No. That's it. No more.'

He looked at me with a sulky expression.

'I'm going to walk this way and you're not coming with me,' I continued. 'OK?'

'OK,' he mumbled.

'Good.'

I strode off feigning confidence and didn't look back. I'd walked 50 yards or so when I heard his voice in the distance.

'Hey, mister!'

I stopped and turned. He waved at me and yelled again.

'Have a good day!'

*

I walked beside the long reflecting pool that more than doubles the majesty of the Lincoln Memorial. It's a genuinely impressive sight. I walked up the steps, through the colonnade and into the Doric temple-inspired building to see the 20-foot marble statue of Lincoln. He looked pretty much as he had done when he showed up in *Star Trek*. Only taller. And more marbly.

Inscribed on the walls was the Gettysburg Address so I stood and took in the words and drank in the history, sharing the reverential silence with ten or so other tourists. I walked to the front of the building and looked out. It was amazing to imagine Martin Luther King standing on this very spot to deliver his famous 'I have a dream' speech.

A young couple stood a couple of metres to my left.

'Isn't it amazing!' she breathed.

'Yeah,' he said, his arm reaching around her shoulders.

I felt lonely and wished that I too had someone to share this moment with.

'Just think,' he said, giving her a little squeeze, 'Forrest Gump jumped in that very pool!'

*

At the Vietnam Veterans' Memorial I was moved, once more, to silence. 58,000 lives are remembered here, each name carved into a simple, black marble wall. It cuts a gash in to the green lawn, growing and diminishing in size to reflect the growing and diminishing numbers of lives lost as the war moved on.

The war ended in 1974. I was three at the time, so my knowledge of the conflict is scant, gleaned from Hollywood rather than textbooks or memory, but that makes no odds when confronted with something so sombrely moving as this.

I was lost in a mood of reflection when I felt a tap on my shoulder.

'Excuse me,' said the middle-aged American woman whose finger was doing the tapping, 'would you mind stepping aside a moment?'

Her husband and two young children were standing in front of the memorial; her camera was poised, ready to snap the family group. They were tanned and plump.

I apologised and absent-mindedly stepped out of frame, my mind still awash with thoughts on mortality. I was about to be shaken from this mood. It would take one word.

'Smile!' shrilled photographer-Mom. It came in a singsong voice, pronounced *Smi-yull.*

I stood aghast and watched the two kids beam their perfect American smiles while Mom pressed the button and preserved forever that happy moment; her family smiling in front of a backdrop of lost lives.

It was time to leave.

*

Washington didn't evolve, it was created. It's an entirely planned city, built to serve the purpose of government and as a result it felt anodyne, devoid of personality, especially at that time of year when Congress wasn't sitting. Without the politicians and their staff and hangers-on the city not only lacks a large part of its population but also its very reason for being. I felt like I was visiting Walt Disney's Democracy World. Out of season.

I wasn't happy. As much as I was trying, I wasn't enjoying myself and it didn't feel like a holiday. Every time I had an experience of any worth someone was on hand to diminish it with their clottish behaviour. I could cope with that if I had company. If I had someone to turn to who could share my mixture of wonder, horror, disgust and amusement that accompanied the discovery of the *Forrest Gump* fans or the ghoulish Mom and her smiling kids. But I was alone. I'd come on holiday by myself and to be perfectly honest I don't think I like myself that much.

I sat in my hotel room and looked at my return ticket, hoping the date would magically change. I had another six days here and I didn't think I could bear it. I craved company. I just didn't know anyone in this city. Except?

Except that googlewhack. What was his name? The man from the American Physical Society? He seemed charming and polite in his email. He wasn't a *complete* stranger to me.

Desperate times call for desperate measures: I found an internet café. Offhand I didn't remember his name, or the precise address of the website I was looking for but somehow the words from the googlewhack, Unicyclist Periscopes, had lodged themselves in my memory. I was confident that if it was still a 'whack, I could easily retrace my steps.

The internet is constantly changing, pages are added and removed and what might be a googlewhack one day can cease to be the next. (Who knows, maybe an online circus equipment company will launch a new range of underwater unicycles for the submariner unicyclist, complete with a selection of available periscopes. That would be a 'whack ruined right there.) But no, as luck would have it, Unicyclist Periscopes was still a googlewhack and I easily found the website, the name and the email address I was looking for.

I emailed David Harris. I reminded him of our correspondence from December and then I bared my soul a little. I told him I was in Washington, I was having a miserable time and I was lonely. I gave him the number of the hotel and I suggested that if he wanted a meal or a drink I'd be very happy to pay for it in return for some civilised company.

*

I was flicking through TV channels back at the hotel when the phone rang.

'Hello?'

'Hello … is that Dave Gorman?'

He had an accent I couldn't identify although I knew it wasn't American.

'Yeah. Speaking.'

'It's David Harris here. I got your email and just felt a bit concerned. Are you OK?'

I felt a sudden rush of embarrassment for exposing myself quite so much.

'Oh yeah, I'm fine … I'm sorry I sent that email to be honest. I was quite low earlier and … well, I'm here for a week and I don't know anyone and it's doing my head in a bit.'

'Look, we've all been there. It's a bit weird, but I'm in your part of town tomorrow morning, we can meet for breakfast if you like?'

We arranged to meet in Kramer's Bookstore. This seemed an unlikely venue to me as the name suggested it was more likely to sell books than breakfast but I turned up a little early and discovered it to be a real gem. It was a regular bookshop, but also a café and a bar, selling books, good food, beers, wines and spirits and boasting the slogan, *serving latte to the literati since 1976*. Even before David turned up, Washington had just got a bit nicer in my eyes.

On his arrival things got nicer still. David was accompanied by his wife Danielle. The accent I hadn't been able to identify on the phone was Australian, but it had been tamed by living overseas.

'I'm not surprised you don't like Washington,' said Danielle, 'it's horrible.'

'You're lucky you're only here for a week,' added David, 'we have to live here.'

I was feeling better already.

They unleashed all manner of vitriol about America as a whole and Washington in particular. They tore into politics, gun culture, car culture, exploitation TV and more besides. And they were hilarious.

To be fair it was clear there was plenty they liked about the country too. But a good moan is liberating, it's a great and guilty pleasure that should be indulged from time to time. I think my presence only served to encourage them as, much to my amusement, every gripe and moan they had to suppress in polite American company was let loose.

*

'Oh shit, I'm going to be late,' said Danielle suddenly. I looked at my watch. It was 11.30. It felt like we'd been chatting for thirty minutes but in reality it was two and a half hours and counting.

'I've got a pottery class,' she said by way of explanation. 'Look, if you're hanging around, why don't the three of us have lunch? One o'clock?'

Breakfast started at 9.00 and at 11.30 they were planning lunch for one o'clock! These were my kind of people and this was shaping up to be my kind of day.

David and I walked off our breakfast while he pointed out a few of the more obscure tourist sights, like a giant statue of Albert Einstein that appeared to be fashioned out of poo. Really.

And then it was time for lunch.

*

'I've got you a present!' said Danielle as she entered the restaurant.

She had her hands behind her back, and a smile on her face.

'Oh, you shouldn't have,' I said.

I was really quite touched by the gesture. We'd only met four hours ago and here she was with a present! She brought her hands out from behind her back and showed it to me.

'Oh … that's … that's …'

I didn't know what to say. I was looking at a tiny stuffed toy. While such things aren't really my bag I don't think I've ever seen a stuffed toy that didn't achieve an acceptable minimum level of cuteness. Until now. Whichever way you looked at it, it was ugly. She really, really shouldn't have.

This 'toy' was about three inches long, white, fluffy and vaguely conical. There were two flippers at the fat end while the front end tapered in to a pink beak so I assumed it was meant to be a bird of some sort. But then again it had no wings, so maybe not. Beady eyes lent it a sort of pinched expression. (To be fair, its eyes were beads, although particularly beady ones at that.) Whoever designed it had made no attempt to give it any semblance of personality, save for the fact that it was 'wearing' a small blue Santa hat but then surely we all know that red is the only acceptable colour for such a garment. Let me be really clear here: this was not *so ugly it's cute*. This was not the ugly duckling of the stuffed toy world. This was just ugly.

The stunning ugliness of this stuffed *thing* rendered me incapable of even feigning gratitude. I really did try, after all, I didn't want David and Danielle to think badly of me.

'That really is … isn't it? … You … eh? I can't believe you've … I mean, will you look at that? … Isn't it? … You know… eh? …'

I tried, but I failed.

I was floundering in a sea of meaningless words when I looked up and caught Danielle's expression. There was a glint in her eye and the hint of a smirk in her smile. She was enjoying my discomfort. I'd been had.

'I'm sorry Danielle, this … *this* is an unusually ugly piece of shit!'

'It is, isn't it?' she squealed with delight.

'Well, why did you buy it then?' I asked, my own voice

climbing several octaves on the way.

'Take a look at the label!' she said, excited by what I was about to discover.

I turned the toy over and was amazed to read the words: 'Teeny Christmas Google'!

'It's really weird. I came out of the pottery class and walked in to a shop,' she explained. 'I don't know why I walked in there really because I didn't want anything, I was just walking. Then I looked to my left and I saw a whole shelf of *these… things.* I thought to myself, *my, they're unusually ugly pieces of shit*, and then I picked one up. I didn't understand why I was in a shop I didn't really want to go into holding a stuffed toy I didn't like and then I saw the label…'

'Teeny Christmas Google!' I showed it to David in case he didn't believe me.

'Yeah! I thought, *that's amazing.* You got in touch with David because of Google, right? Then a few hours after we meet you, I find myself holding *a google*!'

'That is amazing,' said David.

'Amazing,' I agreed.

'It must be a sign,' said Danielle. 'I had to buy it for you. It was too much of a coincidence to ignore.'

And so googlewhacking became the subject of conversation once more. Even now I can't work out whether it was happening to me or I was making it happen. A googlewhack is by definition the unique coincidence of two words, so perhaps it's inevitable that, once you're aware of the phenomenon, coincidence will keep bringing googlewhacks back in to your consciousness.

Over lunch David exercised his scientific mind and theories about the googlewhacking world bounced around the table. I found it difficult to keep up with his speed of thought and his scientific analysis. There were those words again: *nodes, networks, interconnectedness … group theory, complex sets* and more. I was getting very confused.

'So … do you want to come with me then?' asked David.

'I'm sorry, I got a bit lost in that last bit,' I owned up. 'Come where?'

'I've got to go to the office for the rest of the afternoon, but we can get online and put my theory into practice if you like?'

'Right oh,' I said.

I didn't really know what I was agreeing to but I was enjoying myself and the idea of being alone in Washington held no appeal.

As we approached the offices of the American Physical Society, Danielle decided that rather than join us while we tested David's theory (whatever it was) she would go ice-skating.

'I'll leave you two boys to your science,' she said with fondness and a tiny dash of sarcasm.

*

David made me a coffee, and then, with profuse apologies, set about doing some work. He tapped away at the keyboard, all the while throwing conversational snippets over his shoulder. Just as it had at breakfast, time flew.

'I'm sorry about the mess,' he said, still working away. 'I've been really busy lately.'

'I'm exactly the same,' I said, 'My desk only gets tidy when I'm not working. Especially if I'm meant to be working.'

'Oh, I know displacement activity very well,' said David with a chuckle. 'If I was left to my own devices I'd be exactly the same.'

'It sounds like we have a lot in common.'

'What was that?' asked David idly.

'Oh, nothing,' I said, feeling guilty for distracting him.

'OK,' he said with a clap of his hands, 'that's the work done, now, let's see if Harris's First Theory of Googlewhacking holds water?'

Crikey. We really did have a lot in common.

David's theory didn't involve cryptic crosswords but it did involve word disassociation. He opened a textbook and looked for a suitable word on the page – seismic seemed to meet with his approval so he typed it into the Google search box. Then he looked out of the window and, seeing a pedestrian, typed in pedestrian as well. Two words, 13,800 hits.

I tried not to look smug, but I had an inkling as to whose theory was the stronger. David shrugged, looked back to his textbook and changed seismic to oscilloscope: 287 hits.

He shrugged again and then changed pedestrian to pedestrianize: 0 hits.

'Ach,' said David, his fist clenched.

'So close!' I said.

It was as if he'd just hit the crossbar in the final seconds of the FA Cup Final.

Still, 13,800 to 287 to 0 was a pretty impressive progression for three attempts. I had renewed respect for his theory.

He tried Laser Pedestrian next: 14,800 hits.

'Unbelievable,' said David shaking his head.

'I don't believe it,' I said, shaking mine.

He changed pedestrian to pedestrianize again but hesitated with the cursor poised over the search button.

'What do you reckon?' he asked, his voice slow and steady, like a bomb disposal expert asking me which wire to cut.

'Only one way to find out,' I said.

I saw his finger flick and … WHACK!

'Yes!' David's fist was clenched in triumph this time.

'Brilliant!' I said. And I meant it.

'So let's email them and let them know!'

'We don't have to,' I said, but I saw David's frown and knew that, of course, we had to do just that.

The website that Laser Pedestrianize led us to was the Official Record of Proceedings from a Hong Kong local government meeting that took place on 29 January 1997. There was no email address on the page and there was no clue as to who was really responsible for the 'whack.

'There's no one to tell,' I said with a shrug.

'But my theory works,' said David, 'so let's find another one instead.'

Coelacanth (from a textbook) Stapler (from his line of

vision) gave an impressively low 9 hits but his very next go, Coelacanth Sharpener gave us a 'whack. I was very impressed with David's googlewhacking abilities. If I'd been wearing a hat, I would have taken it off to him.

Coelacanth Sharpener was a much more approachable 'whack. It led to a website called Wallytown.com which, as you might have guessed from its title, is a humorous website, the particular page we found ourselves on being a spoof problem page hosted by an 'agony-uncle' called Uncle Eusebio.

Of course visitors to the site are encouraged to ask Eusebio a question and there's an email address provided to allow you to do just that. We didn't have a question as such, but David sent him an email explaining that his was the only website in the world to contain the words coelacanth and sharpener. With that done, we continued to chuckle our way around Wallytown.

Moments later, David's computer announced the arrival of a new email with its familiar ping.

'Sorry, that'll be work,' he said preparing to put his serious head back on. 'Oh no ... no it's not ... it's Uncle Eusebio!'

'Really?'

'Well, it seems his real name is Warren, but we've obviously caught him online and he seems a bit confused.'

'By what?'

'Take a look,' said David, sliding out of view of the screen.

Hi David and Dave,

Thanks for your email. I checked it out and you're right. A Google search for *Coelacanth Sharpener* does lead to *Wallytown* and nowhere else. Amazing! But I'm forced to ask: why did you search for those two words? What on earth were you *actually* looking for?

Warren

'What is a coelacanth?' I asked David.

'It's a prehistoric fish. They discovered them still living in the 1930s.'
'I see. So you wouldn't want to sharpen one?'
'Not really, no.'

Hi Warren,

Sorry if we weren't clear in our first email. We weren't looking for a coelacanth sharpener, we were looking *for a googlewhack*. They just turned out to be the two words we chose.

D&D

Hi D&D,

So I guess the obvious question is: why were you looking for a googlewhack?

W

So, I explained it all. As concisely as I could. Maybe I was too concise. Maybe I didn't make myself clear.

Hi Dave,

You have a strange tale to be sure, but I like it.

Would you like to come to a party at our house tomorrow? I live in Boston. You can stay over if you like.

Warren.

I turned to David in a state of shock.
'What am I supposed to say to that?' I asked. 'He's a

stranger I met on the internet! He's inviting me to a party! He's offering to put me up for the night! I'm sure my mum told me not to do that kind of thing!'

'Do you know what?' said David with a chuckle. 'I think you should go!'

'What? Are you crazy?'

'Look at it this way: Danielle and I are both busy for the rest of the week. It'd be nice to hang around with you but we can't so you're on your own if you stay in Washington.'

'OK.'

'Boston's a much nicer city than Washington. I bet a flight to Boston comes in cheaper than a night in a Washington hotel. He's offering to put you up, so you'll be saving money.'

'Yeah?'

'And, when you get there …' he paused for dramatic effect, 'party! Yeah? Everyone loves a party!'

He was right: I do. I like a party. And if I could get a cheap flight I would actually be saving money! That would be better than a 2p flight to France!

'Let's look up flights now…' said David, surfing his way to an appropriate website, his fingers typing faster than I could think.

'OK,' I said, carried along by his enthusiasm. Now *this* was a holiday. Now I was having fun. Now I was alive.

'And then let's go and meet Danielle for that drink. There's a bar nearby we should check out: R.J. Bentley's. According to *Maxim* magazine it's one of the twenty seediest bars in America!'

'Brilliant!' I said, because right there and then, *everything* – even one of the 20 seediest bars in America – was brilliant.

five

Coelacanth Sharpener

Coelacanth   noun: a primitive bony fish, having fleshy, limblike fins. Genus: *Latimeria*.

Sharpener   noun: device used to make another object (e.g. a pencil) sharp or sharper.

Even for a short hour and a half flight I was determined never to set foot on another plane without a book to read, so Kramer's Bookstore was the perfect place for my very early breakfast. I chose blueberry pancakes and, for the flight, *A Fish Caught in Time: The Search for the Coelacanth* by Samantha Weinberg.

*

Warren was in his early fifties. He was a thin man with thinning hair atop a thin face and a broad grin. I'm not sure why but I was expecting someone younger. It might have been something to do with the sense of humour he displays on his website. Then again, it might have been the simple fact that he *had* a website. (Sometimes it's easy to believe the internet is inhabited exclusively by skateboarders and thirtysomething graphic designers.) But mainly, I think it was the fact that he'd invited a complete stranger to a party at a moment's notice.

Surely that was the action of a party animal, a man prone to acts of youthful folly in pursuit of pleasure. After all, you don't invite complete strangers to join your intimate dinner party or sedate family get-together, do you? I figured a man that reckless was bound to be hosting a wild party and I was looking forward to it.

So, when I was picked up from the airport the first shock was Warren's age. The second shock came as we sat in his four-wheel-drive negotiating the hazardously icy roads on the outskirts of Boston.

'I think you'll like this party, Dave,' he said, expertly steering into the skid. 'We do it every year on the first Saturday after Christmas. It's my partner Ann's family. Sedate, but nice.'

Oh.

It seemed there *was* someone who'd invite a complete stranger to a sedate family get-together after all.

But what kind of person? I started to feel slightly un-comfortable. Warren *seemed* lovely but I knew next to nothing about him. What if I was being kidnapped? Maybe I was about to be inducted into some obscure cult. Maybe I was about to lose a kidney. Or worse, two!

I looked Warren up and down to see what kind of man he seemed to be. He was smiling a lot. But isn't that what cult-members do?

I was in the middle of nowhere. Hardly anyone knew I was in America, let alone the outskirts of Boston. Why had no-one in Britain called me? Did no-one miss me? If Warren wished me any harm there was nothing to stop him. After all, there was no realistic way of anyone connecting the two of us.

'*But Sarge, what if this Gorman chap had decided to put Coelacanth Sharpener into Google?*' is just one of the many sentences you don't expect to hear from an investigating officer.

As we journeyed on down the highway I worried more and more about my safety. I may have travelled a lot in the past but normally I'd travelled with a friend or two and only really met strangers in public places. Here we were, just me and Warren. I felt exceedingly vulnerable. It was a worry that would take a long time to shake. There were three-foot snowdrifts all around us ... a dead body could lie undiscovered for weeks in conditions like that.

'Penny for them?' said Warren suddenly.

'What?'

'Whatcha thinking about?'

'Oh ... it's nothing,' I said awkwardly, '... beautiful scenery.'

I looked up and was glad to see that the view really was beautiful.

'It sure is,' said Warren with pride. 'We're about twelve miles out of Boston. This is Wellesley, the only town in America of that name.'

All around fir trees seemed to droop impossibly under the weight of newly fallen snow. There were some handsome houses too. With their timber frames, simple porches and large icicles hanging from the gables we could have been driving through a Christmas card.

'And this is our street,' said Warren turning with care. 'It's a beautiful little street. Very safe. We have great neighbours, we really do. There's never been any crime here. Ever. No burglary, no ... no murder, nothing.'

'Not that anyone knows about,' I said, under my breath.

'I'm sorry?' asked Warren cheerfully.

'Nothing.'

*

'This is my partner Ann,' said Warren walking me through to the kitchen.

'Hi,' said Ann, 'Would you like a coffee?'

She smiled. Ah ha! The tell-tale sign of the cult.

'Yes please.'

I made sure I added my own milk and sugar in case she was tempted to slip in some kind of knock-out pill.

'The guests will be arriving any minute now,' said Ann and right on cue the doorbell chimed.

I heard mumbling in the hallway. Maybe Warren was giving a perfectly innocent explanation as to why a stranger was lurking nervously in the kitchen. But maybe it was something more sinister and they were plotting my ritual sacrifice.

'Hi, I'm Sue – Ann's sister,' said another smiler as she entered the kitchen.

'I'm Dave. I'm Warren's …' I paused, struggling to know how best to define myself, '… friend?'

'Yeah, we know. He just told us. That whole *googlewhacking* thing is really … um… *cool,'* said Sue.

'I'm Carl,' said a tall, bearded man who looked like the dependable next-door neighbour from an American sitcom. 'I'm Sue's husband. And this is our son, Jack.'

'Hi, Carl,' I said shaking hands. 'Hi, Jack.'

I offered my hand to Jack but he didn't shake it, preferring to hide behind his father's legs.

Maybe it was the natural shyness that all nine-year-olds experience when they meet a stranger. Or maybe at his young age he still had a natural human conscience and felt uneasy at making friends with someone whose blood he would soon be drinking.

'He's a little shy,' said Carl (but then he would say that, wouldn't he?), 'so, do you fancy a beer?'

'Oh, I'm all right for now,' I said wary of letting my guard down. There were four and a half of them and only one of me.

In the next half an hour there was a parade of similar exchanges. As well as Sue, Carl and Jack there was John and Joanne. There was Dick and Martha, Emily and Tom, Tim and Heidi and their kids Josh, Helena, Susannah and Nathan; there was Wendy, Emily and Jessica, Janet, Bob and Debbie. There was a babe in arms and there were octogenarians and there were most things in between. These were Anne's parents, sisters, cousins, aunts, uncles, nephews, nieces and oojits-twice-removeds. Of course, no one was anywhere near as removed as me.

'*I'm a googlewhack three times removed on Warren's side.*' I'd say and think of David, David and Marcus – Unicyclist

Periscopes, Unconstructive Superegos and Dork Turnspit – the links between us.

After a couple of hours in their company I was forced to admit that, on balance, the chances of this being some bizarre pagan, New Year ritual were slim. I was probably not about to be inducted into a cult and increasingly there seemed to be every chance of emerging not just alive but with all my internal organs in place. They may have been strangers but they were as welcoming and genuine as it is possible to be. I decided to relax and have a glass of wine. Or two.

As I dipped a nacho into something spicy I found myself talking to Ann's aunt, Janet, a woman of a certain age and a look I'd describe as librarian-chic.

'Have you travelled far?' I asked.

'I flew in from Washington DC a couple of days ago,' said Janet.

'I've just come from Washington this morning,' I said and then, adopting a conspiratorial whisper, 'to be honest I didn't think much of the place.'

'I know what you mean,' said Janet. 'There are some nice places if you look for them.'

'I suppose I did like Kramer's Bookstore,' I offered.

'Oh, I *love* Kramer's.'

'I can see you two are getting along,' said Ann joining us and topping up my glass. 'Would you like another glass of wine, Janet?'

Janet frowned in mock offence: 'Do I look like an old drunk?'

'Not yet,' I said before I realised quite what I was saying.

Luckily Ann laughed. Luckier still, so did Janet. It was the moment I knew I was completely relaxed in their company.

'Top me up, Ann,' said Janet offering her glass, 'I'll give this young man a run for his money.'

It wasn't the party I'd imagined by any means but there's no denying it *was* a lot of fun. All thoughts of danger had vanished from my mind and I'd completely lowered my guard.

'Hey you three, come through to the living room,' said Carl, popping his head round the kitchen door. 'It's time for the Yankee Grab!'

All of a sudden, my worries came flooding back. *Yankee Grab?* The Yanks were about to kill a Brit! What else could it mean? This was it! This was the ceremony! This was my end!

With trepidation, I walked through to the living room to find the whole family sitting in a large circle. A group of that size wasn't easily accommodated. Chairs had been brought in from other rooms and five pairs of buttocks were squeezed on to a three-seater sofa.

I felt some reassurance – the sight of an old lady in a bean bag does that for you – but nevertheless I still checked the room for ominous signs. No one was wearing a cowl and in the centre of the circle there was no altar, no pentagram, no candles and no goat. Instead, there was a coffee table laden with gifts.

Surviving the Yankee Grab involved no act of resilience, no plan of escape and no feat of derring-do because the Yankee Grab turned out to be nothing more than a present-giving game.

Each of the adults brought a gift-wrapped present, nothing too expensive, around $15 each, say. These were then arranged on the coffee table. Names were drawn out of a hat and people took it in turns to select a present. But it wasn't just a lucky dip. Oh no, there was a catch.

Because you didn't just get whatever you chose, you also had the right to steal other people's presents too. Say it was round seven of the game and it was your turn to pick. You unwrapped an ornamental candle and thought you'd much prefer the bottle of wine that was picked a couple of turns back. So you stole the wine and passed on the candle. Now the person who'd just lost the wine might not want the candle either so they could also steal somebody else's present and so on. You couldn't steal anything that had already been stolen in that round, so round seven would end when someone got the candle and preferred it to the remaining, stealable, presents.

Then it would be time for the next round so person number eight would unwrap a present and it would start all over again.

It was incredibly jolly. Some of the presents were nice, some deliberately naff and, who knows, some of them not so deliberately naff. Barbed 'who bought *that*' comments flew around the room, husbands stole from wives and somebody inevitably ended up with the present they bought in the first place.

'OK, Dave,' said John, Ann's father and master of ceremonies for the grab. 'It's your turn to pick.'

This was their family thing. As much as I was enjoying watching the game, joining in didn't feel right.

'I c-c-c-can't,' I said, developing a nervous stutter from nowhere.

'Your name's just come out of the hat, you have to,' said John.

'But... but I haven't put a ... present in,' I explained. 'I think I should just watch, otherwise you'll be one present short. Obviously if I'd known ...'

'It's OK, Dave.' It was Warren. He leaned in, his hand on my shoulder, 'I've put a present in on your behalf.'

I unwrapped a present. It was a book. A big book. It was the *Reader's Digest Bedroom Reader*. I could feel all eyes on me. I looked around the room. Somebody with a present they liked was nonchalantly trying to place their foot in front of it to obscure my view. I stood up and crossed the room. Janet had six miniature bottles of Scotch. I gave her the book and took the whisky.

There was a small cheer of approval from the room. I was able to steal from an old lady. I was now well and truly one of them.

I lost possession of the Scotch in the very next round. As the game moved on I had, variously, a souvenir mug, the *Reader's Digest Bedroom Reader* again, some Earl Grey tea (the possibility that I might return to England with some tea amused everyone greatly), a novel, the *Reader's Digest*

Bedroom Reader once more, a T-shirt and then, tighten up lines finally, the *Reader's Digest Bedroom Reader.* Janet ended up with her whisky too.

'Nice try, sucker!' she said.

In years to come I intend to make the Yankee Grab a part of every Gorman family Christmas.

*

It was the end of the evening. Most of the guests had left by now: they had long journeys to make in bad weather. Sue, Carl and Jack were still around and Jack was buzzing on that energy that nine-year-olds suddenly get when they have a late night.

Jack said he wanted to take me to the basement for a game of table tennis and I let him because I figured it would be nice if Warren, Ann, Sue and Carl could relax and chat for a while without dealing with hyperactivity.

Jack had been reluctant to talk to me when we first met but down in the basement he revealed himself to be a talkative and inquisitive soul. He was fascinated by the fact that I was English, seemed surprised that I didn't sound like Austin Powers … and wanted me to explain the rules of cricket. I don't know much about cricket but I made up some rules and he seemed happy enough with that. If you ever meet an American kid who thinks the batsmen are in, the bowlers are trying to get them out while the fielders have to shake it all about, that's probably Jack.

'Dave!' a voice echoed from above. It was Warren. 'Come upstairs, I've got something to show you.'

'I can't right now,' I yelled. 'I'm playing table tennis.'

'It's really important! I'm in the study!'

'OK,' I said, apologising to Jack and putting my bat down reluctantly. I reckon if I'd had one more game I could have beaten him.

I walked into Warren's study. I wouldn't have thought it possible for Warren to seem happier than normal but somehow he'd managed it. The perma-grin was set to maximum.

'I've done it!' he beamed.

'Done what?'

'I've found you your two googlewhacks!'

'What?'

'You want to get ten in a row and everyone you meet is allowed to find you two more googlewhacks, right? You said that was part of the challenge ...'

'I also said I hadn't accepted the challenge!' I said, aghast.

'What?'

'What on earth makes you think I am trying to meet googlewhacks?'

'Oo, I don't know, Dave,' said Warren, an uncharacteristic trace of scorn in his voice, 'maybe it's the fact that *you're in Boston*!'

That rather took the wind out of my sails.

I *had* explained it all when I was emailing Warren from David's office in Washington but still I had to admit that, from an outsider's point of view, it must have looked like I was *trying* to do this. When a man tells you a story in which he accidentally travels from London to Washington to Boston, it doesn't really *sound* like an accident.

I sat down, put my head in my hands and took a deep breath. There was a very long pause.

It was longer than the pause you just imagined.

'So ... do you want to see my googlewhacks?' asked Warren tentatively.

There's a question.

'Let's see what you've got, Warren,' I sighed. I have to admit I *was* interested.

He'd found Ammonite Googolplex and Bamboozled Panfish, which certainly bamboozled me.

The first website declared itself to be the 'Global Source for Space Rock Exploration'. Space rock, by the way, is a genre of music but I'm not quite sure how to define it. The site says that space rock includes 'psychedelia and related electronic music' but also adds 'we love the more avant-garde, experimental and adventurous forms of jazz and progressive rock'. I can't say that leaves me any the wiser. At a guess, I'd say that if most people don't like a genre of music, it probably qualifies as space rock.

From a cursory glance at the site it was obvious that both the artists and record labels involved liked to stretch their vocabulary when choosing names. I wouldn't be at all surprised to discover there are hundreds of googlewhacks to be found in aural-innovations.com where you can find out the latest news on Upsilon Acrux and their song 'In the Acrux of the Upsilon King' or Friends of Mescalito with *Nagual Music for Tonal People*. Here there are record companies called Slutfish Records and Vas Deferens Organization and who wouldn't want to know more about the Detroit improv duo Intuitive Tesseract? It must be a veritable googlewhack heaven.

The second of Warren's 'whacks also led to a music-based website. It was a Japanese page listing hundreds of releases from the peculiar canon of Frank Zappa. Did you know that the two CD set *Anyway the Wind Blows* has the product code *Panfish CRCL-7506/7*? Or that his *Tinsel Town Rebellion* album contains the track 'Bamboozled By Love'?

You do now.

'Warren, as interesting as these are, I'm not really trying to meet these people. I'm not about to travel to Japan to meet some Frank Zappa fan just because you found Bamboozled Panfish.'

'But I...'

'So please,' I implored, 'don't ask me to email them?'

'Ah.'

'What?'

'I already have.'

'What?'

'I emailed to give them the good news.'

'What good news?'

'That they're googlewhacks!'

'And ...'

'And I haven't heard back from Bamboozled Panfish yet, but ... but ...' Warren looked away.

'What Warren? But what?'

He took a deep breath.

'But Ammonite Googolplex is about to ring ...'

'What do you mean he's about to ring?' I said, desperately trying to keep a lid on my temper. I knew exactly what he meant but I didn't want to believe it.

'We've exchanged a couple of emails and he said he was going to ring,' explained Warren. 'That's why I had to interrupt your game of ping—'

Rrrring rrrring.

I looked at Warren. I looked at the phone. I looked at Warren again.

'You might as well get that, Dave,' he said. 'It's for you.'

Rrrring rrrring.

'What's his name?'

Rrrring rrrring.

'Ammonite Googolplex.'

Rrrring rrrring.

'No, Warren! What's *his bloody name*?!'

Rrrring rrrring.

'Jerry. His name's Jerry.'

Rrrring rrr—

'Hello,' I squeaked, 'is that Jerry?'

'Hey there, you must be Dave!' the voice was energised. It made me feel like I was taking part in a radio phone-in.

'So ...' I started, '... you're Ammonite Googolplex then?'

'Yeah. Cool huh? So, do you wanna come meet me?'

'Um ... well ... not really ...'

'What?' he asked, the energy falling away.

'I don't really want to ...'

'Right. So you wanted to meet the others...'

Was he sulking?

'Well no, not really. I *have* met the others, but I didn't necessarily *want to*. It's different. I mean, I don't even know where you live, Jerry ...'

'I live in Columbus.'

'I don't know where Columbus is.'

'It's in Ohio.'

'Jerry I don't know where Ohio is' I said, because I didn't. I covered up the mouthpiece and turned to Warren, 'Where's Columbus, Ohio?'

'Well ...' Warren gave it a lot of thought. He squinted and looked up as if he had a secret out-of-focus map of America mounted in the top corner of the room. '... It's *kind* of ... on the way back to Washington.'

'Really?' I was suspicious.

'Well, it's nearer to Washington than we are here. You do have to go back to Washington to get your flight home, right?'

'Right.'

'Well it *would* make sense,' said Warren convincingly.

I thought about it for a couple of moments. Warren had clearly already given it some thought. He leaned forward and pulled a couple of sheets of paper from his printer tray.

'I looked up a couple of flights,' he said, 'and there's a very reasonable hotel in Columbus ...'

Resistance was futile. I removed my hand from the mouthpiece. 'Jerry, I'm coming to Columbus, Ohio. I'm looking forward to meeting you Mr Ammonite Googolplex.'

'Great!' said Jerry with so much energy I think Tony the Tiger would have been impressed.

Why did I say I'd do it? Well, this was an accidental holiday, but I had to admit it had only become fun since I started meeting googlewhacks. My time alone in Washington was thoroughly grim and unpleasant. But from the moment I met David and Danielle life became enjoyable and I had just had a remarkably lovely day in the bosom of a Boston family and ... well, maybe being a googlewhack means you're likely to be interesting and fun to be with. Maybe the people who use language in a way that no-one else uses it on the Web are, by definition, worth meeting. And I could think of a lot worse ways to spend a week.

On top of all this my international fridge magnet collection was coming on in leaps and bounds.

*

In Warren and Ann's spare room I looked at the few possessions I had with me. The clothes I'd bought since I'd arrived in America, a toothbrush, a book about the coelacanth and not much more. I fumbled inside my coat pocket looking for my mobile phone, curious as to why I'd had no calls.

My hand found two miniature bottles of Scotch wrapped up in a piece of paper. It was a note, from Janet, that said simply, 'Enjoy!'

I went back into my coat and pulled out my phone and soon discovered the reason I'd had no calls. The battery was dead. I wandered back in to the study.

'Warren, your cell phone isn't a Nokia, is it? My battery's dead, I need a charger.'

I had 17 messages. There were a few *'Happy New Years'* from friends and family, a couple of concerned *'Where are you, the last thing we knew you were getting into a minicab and heading to Heathrow!'s* and lots and lots of messages from Rob and Jake.

Rob wanted to know where I was because Jake was asking him and he said it was embarrassing not knowing when he was supposed to be my agent. Jake wanted to know not only where I was but, more importantly, where the first couple of chapters were. I'd promised to deliver some writing at the start of the New Year. Shit.

I turned my phone off, got in to bed and read a bit more about a prehistoric fish.

*

There's a famous painting titled *American Gothic*. You may not know the name, but you'd know it to look at. It features a man and a woman standing side by side. She has her hair tied back while he is bald and holds a pitchfork. They wear buttoned-up high collars, he stares straight ahead while she is looking to one side but both have looks that could curdle milk. It's an austere and mournful look at a bygone age and it's become something of an American icon.

I mention it because, as I came downstairs the next morning I found Warren and Ann preparing breakfast. They turned to face me. They were standing side by side, Warren was holding a spatula and for a split second, they formed a perfect parody of this classic image. If they were thinking of entering fancy dress competitions I bet they could have won prizes with this look. Of course, to be truly authentic they'd have had to stop smiling and I'm not sure they'd be capable of that.

'I'll give you a lift to the airport later if you like,' said Warren.

'Thanks,' I said. 'You've both been wonderful.'

'We have time to see one thing in Boston first if you like?' said Warren, checking his watch. 'But I really do mean *one* thing. Is there any one place you'd like to see?'

I thought about it carefully. In American terms, Boston is steeped in history. It dates back to the seventeenth century and was for many years the largest city in the States. It was the home of the revolutionary movement that led to independence from British rule and there are many museums and monuments to this time such as the Boston Tea Party Ship and Museum and the site of the Boston Massacre. Harvard University lies on the other side of the Charles River and again sites of interest abound. So much to choose from, so little time.

'Could we go to the bar they based *Cheers* on?'

'You got it!'

six

Ammonite googolplex

Ammonite   1. noun: any extinct marine cephalopod mollusc of the order Ammonoidea (or the fossilised shell of the same).
2a. noun: an explosive, such as TNT, consisting mainly of ammonium nitrate.
2b. noun: a nitrogenous fertilizer made from animal wastes.

Googolplex   noun: a very large number written as 100,000,000,000,000,000,000,000,000,00 0,000,000,000,000,000,000,000,000,000, 000,000,000,000,000,000,000,000,000,00 0,000,000,000,000,000.

What can I tell you that will best sum up the city of Columbus? I could tell you that it is surrounded by miles and miles of rolling farmland. I could tell you that it's Ohio's largest city, state capital and home to the massive Ohio State University. Or I could tell you that, in spite of its size and importance, it somehow manages to feel small and homely. All of which is true. All of which, in some way, shaped my experience of the city. But somehow that doesn't really sum it up. No, from my brief stay there, what sums it up is this: Columbus appears to be the Mullet Capital of the World.

From the moment I arrived at Port Columbus International

Airport I was amazed by the abundance of short-on-top-long-at-the-back hairstyles on view. The airport was crawling with mullets. There were mullets arriving and mullets departing. Mullets were there to wave other mullets off and mullets were there to welcome other mullets back. And there were mullets working too. If you wanted to buy something, anything, be it food, drink, newspaper, book or fridge magnet the chances were you'd have to deal with a mullet. Officially there was no time difference between Boston and Columbus, but if the hairstyles were to be believed Columbus was at least seventeen years behind.

I had been a little worried about the standard of hotel I'd be staying in. The deal seemed too good to be true and seeing as it *was* true, I assumed that meant it must be too true to be good.

Warren had booked it online on my behalf and he'd assured me it would be comfortable enough. But, unless I'd mis-understood the exchange rate, it was going to cost me less than £30 a night so I really wasn't expecting any great sense of luxury. Or a roof. But if my suspicions were correct and I'd travelled seventeen years back in time en route to Mulletland, Ohio, then I'd be looking at things a little differently. After all, at 1986 prices I reckon thirty quid would buy five-star, four-poster, jacuzzi-style splendour and probably an in-room stereo to boot. (Although, obviously, the in-room stereo would only play vinyl and cassettes.)

The truth was somewhere in between. My mulleted taxi driver dropped me at the hotel where a mulleted receptionist checked me in. I took the lift to the 15th floor and there I discovered the biggest hotel room I've ever seen.

It wasn't a four-poster but the bed itself was bigger than my entire bedroom back in London. I lay down and stretched out as far as I could but no part of me could reach the edge of the bed in any direction. In this room, if there were ten in the bed and the little one said 'roll over, roll over', they'd all roll over and none would fall out.

I sat in the middle of the bed and flicked channels for a while, waiting for the hotel phone to ring. Jerry and I had arranged to go to a gig this evening, presumably to hear some space rock, and he was going to come by the hotel and pick me up when he'd finished work.

Eventually a phone rang. But it wasn't the hotel phone, it was my mobile. The caller display gave me no clues as to who it was. My first thought was one of panic. What if it was Jake? That was a call I didn't feel ready to deal with. I did some mental arithmetic and realised that, whatever year it was here, it was nearly ten o'clock in the evening back in London. It was long after office hours so I safely dismissed the possibility of an angry Jake and took the call.

'Hello?'

'Hi, Dave. It's Jake.'

He sounded angry.

'I've been trying to get hold of you for days,' he continued. 'Is everything ... all right?'

'Um ...' I knew that 'everything' included the novel which meant that *everything* was not all right. 'Yeah,' I lied.

'So ... er ... Happy New Year, glad everything's OK and ...' Jake paused, we both knew that the pleasantries were now over, we both knew what was coming next, '... and ... well, I was wondering why you haven't sent me any chapters yet?'

'Chapters? By which you mean chapters ... of the novel?'

'Yeah.'

'I've ... um ... I've taken a slightly ... different ... approach ... to the novel ...'

I was floundering.

'Dave. Have you written anything?' asked Jake, sensing the chase and cutting to it.

'No'

'No?'

'A bit.'

'Really?'

'No.'

I was the last to speak so I waited a while, expecting Jake to take his turn next. He didn't seem keen. I heard him sigh awkwardly. Was that a turn? That's not a turn is it? Sighing? I waited another couple of beats but no, it was definitely up to me to break the silence.

'The thing is, Jake, I'm … I'm …' What? What could I possibly tell him? 'I'm … researching things?'

'Dave, this is ridiculous! What do you mean? What are you doing? Where the hell are you?'

It was time to own up.

'OK, Jake. I'm … in America.'

'What?!'

He sounded furious. Maybe it wasn't time to own up after all? If I wasn't going to tell him the truth I needed to think of something good. And quick.

'OK, Jake. You know the novel is about a new colour?'

Jake let out a suspicious, 'Yeah …?'

'Well, the thing is … I wanted to back it up with some real science, you know, make it seem convincing … so … I … went to Washington to visit a scientist from the American Physical Society …'

'Really?'

'Yeah,' I said surprised at my own resourcefulness. Who'd have thought it? There I was preparing to tell a full-blown lie and instead a convenient half-truth just fell out of my mouth!

'Isn't there someone in England you could have spoken to?' asked Jake making an annoyingly good point.

'Er … they're … not as good,' I said pathetically.

'So,' said Jake testily, 'what have you found out then?'

'Well … you know I told you that the character goes in search of this colour?' I said, trying to give myself time to think.

'I remember it well,' said Jake, 'I wrote it down. You said he swims the deepest oceans, and penetrates the densest rainforests in search of obscure flora and fauna, hoping to find his mysterious hue …'

'Right. Well …'

I didn't know where I was going with this. Oceans? Rain-forests? Obscure flora? And fauna? Yes! I had it. There was one example of obscure fauna I knew quite a lot about …

'Well …' I continued with growing confidence, '… this scientist told me about the coelacanth!'

'The seal of what?'

'The coelacanth. It's a prehistoric fish. People thought it was extinct until one was caught off the coast of South Africa in 1938. So I thought our character could go to the same waters …'

'Which are?'

'The Indian Ocean, between Madagascar and Africa. He goes diving there to see if there might be another undis-covered species of fish … a new fish that might display this *new* colour.'

'I like it …'

My recent bedtime and aeroplane reading had armed me with a whole host of coelacanth facts and I spared Jake none of them. The more detail I gave him, the more reassured he sounded. My prehistoric fish tale had him hook, line and sinker and before long the whole conversation was suffused with calm.

'OK, Dave. I am disappointed that I haven't got any writing to look at but I am impressed that you're taking it so seriously,' said Jake. 'Just so long as you're not ignoring it. You'd be amazed at what some authors are like!'

'Really?' I said, my half chuckle sounding half-hearted. 'Amazing.'

'Next time you want to go off on a research trip just let me know,' said Jake. 'Keep me in touch with what you're doing.'

'OK. Sorry, Jake.'

'So … when do you get back from Washington?'

'I'm flying back tomorrow.'

'OK. I think we should have a meeting when you get back. I'm away from the office right now so I haven't got my diary to hand but I'll give you a ring tomorrow morning your time and set something up …'

'Ah … the thing is, the battery on my mobile is almost dead …'

'OK, just give me the number of the hotel.'

'Ah ...'

'What?'

'The thing is ... I'm not in Washington any more ... I'm ... in Ohio ...'

'What? *Why?*'

'Because I'm meeting ...'

I didn't know what to say. Why, in the name of research, would I be in Columbus, Ohio? I tried to think of something to say but my mind was blank.

'I'm meeting ... I'm ... I'm meeting ... a world expert in space rock ...' I said weakly.

I almost flinched as if I expected Jake's palm to emerge from the phone and slap me. It didn't happen. His reaction, however, certainly caught me by surprise.

'Brilliant!' said Jake with a squeal of excitement. 'Space rock! Of course, if anything's going to turn up with a brand new colour in it, it's rock from outer space! Brilliant!'

'Oh!' I said and then tried to say it again without sounding quite so surprised. 'Oh.' (That was better.) 'Thanks Jake. I'm glad you like where I'm going with it ...'

I gave him the number of the hotel. I agreed that we would have a meeting on my return to the UK. I promised to show him my research notes, storylines and as much actual writing as I could. And I wondered how much it was possible to write on a flight from Washington to Heathrow.

*

A phone rang. This time it was the hotel phone. I assumed it would be Jake checking up on me, making sure I'd given him the right number. I picked up.

'Hello?'

'Hey, Dave! It's Jerry!' exclaimed Jerry.

Everything Jerry says comes with an exclamation mark.

'I'm in reception!'

*

Jerry's little jeep crept slowly through the streets of Columbus.

'We're gonna go to a great venue tonight!' said Jerry.

'So, what are we going to see?' I asked. 'Is it space rock?'

'Hmmmmmmm? Well? Well? Weeeeellllll?' said Jerry. When he thinks, it's like he's coiling up a spring, when he comes to his conclusion it gets released. 'Not really!'

'So it's ...?'

'It's kind of like an improvisational, experimental night!' said Jerry, enunciating ev-ery sy-lla-ble. 'It should be good!'

'OK ...' I said, barely able to conceal my concern.

In the performer's lexicon, *improvisational* and *experimental* are generally by-words for *bad*.

'I mean there *might* be some space rock kind of stuff. You never know,' said Jerry, and then, realising he hadn't said it with his usual force, he said it again. 'You never know!'

'I certainly don't,' I said, which was at least honest. 'So ... what's the venue?'

'Little Brothers! It's a great place! In a district known as the Short North! Used to be a red light district!'

'Great!' I said and realised that my Wandering Accent Syndrome was kicking in.

Jerry could make a fortune in advertising, his voice is perfect for sentences like *'All stock must go!'* and *'Hurry, hurry, hurry!'* but it does make it a very easy accent to slip in to. *Very easy indeed!*

The Short North is the cool, hip part of town. The further in to it we travelled, the fewer mullets there were to be seen. Here there were funky boutiques, secondhand record stores and individual little coffee shops.

We were a little early for the gig so Jerry took me to the Coffee Table first. He told me it was mainly known as a gay hangout, but it had a relaxed atmosphere, enormous windows, comfy wooden booths and great coffee which made it a fine place to chill out and kill some time. I suppose I should mention that there was one mullet on display but I'm not sure it really counts as it was being worn ironically by a lesbian.

(Before anyone accuses me of jumping to conclusions I should point out that her T-shirt bore the legend, 'Yes, I'm a lesbian. And?')

Over coffee Jerry talked enthusiastically about Aural-Innovations.com. He'd started it as a paper fanzine but the cost of printing and posting it to people all over the world had proved prohibitively expensive. When he realised that more people were logging on to the associated website than subscribing to the 'zine he'd decided to make it into an entirely Web-based project instead.

Now, as well as editing (and largely writing) a monthly online magazine, Jerry also hosted his own space rock radio shows and these too are broadcast on the Web.

The more he talked, the more I understood Jerry's passion and commitment to his website. I once saw a football referee interviewed and he was asked why he had taken up such a thankless profession. His answer, basically, was that he was a football fan who got to spend the whole 90 minutes of an FA Cup Final on the pitch at Wembley, a privilege that his limited playing abilities would never have afforded him. I think something similar can be said for Jerry. A fan of a particularly niche area of music, his site has put him close to the heart of that niche. As a result, he's met and interviewed many of the artists involved. What more could a fan want?

'ID?'

We were at the entrance to Little Brothers and the doorman was requesting some identification.

Jerry nonchalantly flashed his driver's licence while I fumbled for my wallet. It was a pointless gesture. I didn't have any ID on me. Why would I?

'I've got a credit card ...' I offered weakly.

The doorman, a young, scrawny indie-kid, smirked.

'You need picture ID,' he said.

'Why?' I asked, genuinely confused. Did they need to know the names of everyone who attended?

'To prove you're over 21,' came the matter-of-fact reply.

'But I'm 31,' I said, bemused. 'I'm *clearly* over 21. Any idiot can see that.'

The doorman bristled.

'Not that I'm calling you an idiot,' I added hurriedly. 'This guy's an idiot!' I whispered to Jerry.

'Dave!' said Jerry stepping in between us. 'The show isn't going to start for a while, I'll give you a lift back to the hotel, you can get your passport and then we'll come back. Yeah? We'll come back!'

'I'm not sure that's wise,' I said.

'Why not?' asked Jerry.

My mind flashed back to New Year's Eve, the last time I got drunk in possession of my passport.

'Oh, it's a long story. I'll explain it on the way back to the hotel.'

And that's what I did. On the way to the hotel I told Jerry all about the email from Stevo, finding Marcus, my trip to France and, of course, New Year's Eve. On the way back to Little Brothers I told him all about my time in Washington and Boston. Basically, I told him the whole googlewhacking story.

'So, this is it, huh?' he said as we got out of the jeep. 'A little adventure to start the year, but tomorrow you head back to London and that's that?'

At last! I was finally with someone who understood my peculiar situation, someone who wouldn't be forcing a googlewhack agenda on me.

'That's right. It's back to reality tomorrow,' I said with a sigh. A sigh that gave me pause for thought. Was it a sigh of regret?

We flashed our ID at the doorman and this time he let us pass. There was a small cover charge to get in but instead of issuing tickets the venue used a rubber stamp to mark our hands. The doorman used the stamp on Jerry's hand with a nice, gentle rolling action. I placed my hand on the desk in front of me expecting the same treatment but instead he brought it down with force. It was the kind of stamp a library book gets in the hands of a repressed and angry librarian.

The venue was huge and open-plan but divided into two defined spaces. The first was the bar area with a long bar running down one side of the room. There were odd artefacts attached to the wall here and there, an old-fashioned oil painting, a stuffed animal head and so on, but mainly the room was decorated with its own history. The walls were covered with posters for previous shows, all slapped on at different angles, overlapping each other and creating a rich tapestry of colours.

The other space was the performance area. There was a high and deep stage and enough space for a few hundred audience members. I looked around and I reckon there were less than twenty of us in that night. Oh well, I thought, I'm sure they can still perform for twenty people. If the rest of them are as enthusiastic as Jerry it's probably equivalent to playing in front of 200 Brits.

The first performer stood up. Rather than take to the stage, which would have put a huge distance between her and the audience, the wise decision had been taken to perform at floor level. It felt more intimate that way, something the numbers demanded. I realised that the girl strumming her guitar on stage was one of the twenty people I'd assumed to be the audience. I looked around the 'crowd' again and saw a number of guitar cases propped up among the chairs. In my new estimate, the paying, non-performing audience probably numbered eight.

I was preparing myself for a difficult and embarrassing night out. But it never came. What could have been small and awkward became small and supportive instead, almost special.

Despite my initial misgivings regarding the improvisational and experimental nature of the evening, it has to be said the entertainment was good. Certainly good enough to make me forget the throbbing sensation in my recently stamped hand.

The music ranged in style from acoustic folk through to avant-garde electronica. There were thin and sallow young

men with too many badges who looked at their feet while
singing gently, and there were theatrical, over-the-top perform-
ances from strident and eccentrically dressed people of
indeterminate sex.

The strangest group were saved for last. Two men stood
with their backs to the audience while a third faced us but
fixed his gaze on his own fingers. He played guitar, by which I
mean he held the guitar and strummed it occasionally, while
stubbornly refusing to let anything that resembled a tune
escape. One of the other two was playing with a laptop while
the other fiddled with a piece of electronic equipment that I
didn't recognise but strongly suspected was making the sound
of an unhappy dolphin.

While this trio was on Jerry leaned in to speak. 'What do you
think then?' he whispered.

'I've really enjoyed it,' I whispered back. 'To be honest, this
is the only act I've struggled with.'

'Yeah. These guys are kind of challenging!'

'It's so wilfully odd and …' I was struggling to find the words
'… you can't really tap your toes to it, if you know what I
mean?'

'Yeah!' said Jerry, nodding his head.

He obviously didn't agree with me; I looked down and saw
that his toes were tapping.

*

In deep sleep that night I found myself in a strange and vivid
dream. It took place in and around the Lincoln Memorial
where, bizarrely, it was introduced by Martin Luther King.

'I have a dream!' he cried in familiar full flow. '*You* have a
dream, we *all* have a dream, *this* dream is the dream of Dave
Gorman.'

Given the impact the original 'I have a dream' speech has
had on the modern world and the regard in which Martin
Luther King's legacy is so rightly held, it might seem offensive

to take words of such import in vain. But, hey, it was my subconscious thinking and whatever you want to read in to it, I don't think you can take it as any indication of my conscious thoughts. I once had a disturbing dream involving Princess Anne and a bridle and she's never done a thing for me in real life.

As the dream went on I realised that what looked like the Lincoln Memorial had been transformed, in my dream, in to the David Gorman Monument. Not a tribute to me, but to David Gorman who lives in the South of France. The marble statue in the centre of the monument was no longer Lincoln sitting in an upright chair but a crude simulacrum of David on his sun-lounger. The Gettysburg Address wasn't inscribed on these walls. Instead I read the words David had spoken to me that December day in Provence: *If you personally find no more googlewhacks, but every googlewhack you meet finds you two more, I bet you can't get ten googlewhacks in a row before your 32nd birthday.*

I'm standing at Martin Luther King's shoulder and looking out at the long reflecting pool. The masses haven't assembled to hear him speak this time. No civil rights march has taken place earlier today in dreamland. Instead there's a sparse crowd, a gathering of familiar faces. I walk down the steps and wander among them.

There's Jerry, tapping his toes. There's Warren and Ann and all of Ann's family from the party. I wave at Janet and yell out some thanks for the Scotch but she can't see or hear me. No one can. There's David and Danielle. To be honest I'd have been disappointed if they weren't here. It's easy for them because the dream's in Washington. Everyone else has travelled. Does Danielle have a dog on a leash? No … it's a giant *Teeny Christmas Google*! That explains why Marcus is standing so calmly beside them. A woman and a dog might have set his pulse racing but a woman and a giant *Teeny Christmas Google*? Pah. And there's David and Eillen. Is it big-headed of him? Coming to look at his own monument? There's the girl I fancied on the flight to Washington and there are all my friends from New Year's Eve and there's Princess Anne … no … no, no, no she isn't there, that's better, it isn't her, it's Carlton, the man who wanted me to attack him here in Washington and … and why is Forrest Gump jumping in the pool?

Martin Luther King is introducing a band now. It's the strange trio from Columbus. Two of them face the marble-Dave on his sun-lounger, the guitarist faces the crowd and they start making their tuneless, atonal noise. Jerry starts dancing. One of the trio is using a laptop and I can see the screen. He's not using it to play music, he's online, he's looking at Google. The guitarist plucks a string but instead of a note, a word rings out.

'Candelabra.'

The man with the electronic equipment I don't recognise hits a button. Instead of the sound of an unhappy dolphin another word rings out.

'Telescopic.'

The laptop man dances, types the words, hits the search button, shakes his head and the audience all 'Ooo' in shared disappointment.

'Dave Gorman has a dream!' sings Martin Luther King, who's now doing unofficial backing vocals.

The trio repeat the process using different words:

'Forensics.'

'Tea towel.'

A shake of the head and the audience all 'ooo' as one.

'Dave Gorman has a dream!'

'Wainscoting.'

'Conquistador.'

A shake of the head. 'Ooo.'

'Dave Gorman has a dream!'

'Conch.'

'Scintilla.'

A shake of the head. 'Ooo.'

'Dave Gorman has a dream!'

'Francophile!'

'Namesakes!'

The headshaker turns to the crowd but this time he's nodding.

He yells, 'We have a whack!'

Martin Luther King joins the celebration: 'People, we have a whack!'

The audience roars their approval.

'Whack! Whack! Whack!' they chant, 'Whack! Whack! Whack!'

'Aaaaaaagggggghhhhhh!' I woke with a start. The sheets were clammy. I looked at the clock. It was morning. Jake hadn't yet called. It was time to check out.

*

I took a taxi to the airport and from there I flew to Washington DC. My plane landed at Ronald Reagan Washington National Airport which, as the name suggests, isn't where I needed to be for my international departure so I took a bus across town to Dulles International Airport where I checked in with plenty of time to spare. Plenty of time to relax, to think, to consider what had just happened to me.

I was sitting in the departure lounge, flicking through a free promotional airline magazine when I found myself looking at a map of the world. A series of red parabolas marked the different routes it was possible to fly and a chart gave the distances from city to city. I totted it up and worked out that, by the time I landed back in London, my round trip, including my jaunt to France in December, would total 10,364 miles! All that to meet Marcus, David, David, Warren and Jerry!

Five googlewhacks in a row and I hadn't even been trying! It seemed to me that everyone else had done all the trying. Everyone else *wanted* me to meet the next one, everyone else *wanted* me to meet the 'whack *they'd* found. Now it was about to end. Now the journey was over. I found myself sighing again, the same sigh I'd sighed back in Columbus. It wasn't a sigh of relief; it *was* a sigh of regret. There were times when I'd turned the next corner, made the next trip because I felt harassed, press-ganged even, by events. But now that outside pressure was evaporating I realised it left a part of me exposed. The part that *wanted* to do it. The part that realised five in a row was – gulp – half way.

I shook the temptation from me and focused on the reality of the situation. I had an eight-hour flight ahead of me and nothing to read. I went in search of the nearest bookstore.

As I browsed my mind continued to wander through my predicament. I knew when I got back to London I would have to meet up with Jake. I needed to explain myself which was going to be difficult because I didn't have an explanation. He wanted a few chapters of a novel I hadn't written, a novel I might not even be able to write. Failing that, he wanted to see some research notes on coelacanths and space rock – the wrong sort of space rock – based on meetings with experts I hadn't met. If he found out the truth I was in trouble. More importantly, I was in breach of contract. If Jake wanted his money back, he had every right to it. But I'd already spent a fair chunk of the money and Rob, as my agent, had already taken 15%. He'd done his job; if I now failed to do mine that was no concern of his. I simply couldn't afford to tell the truth and there simply wasn't time to come up with enough work to back up my lies. I had to find a way to avoid that meeting.

Inspiration came when I found myself holding a copy of *The Adventures of Huckleberry Finn.* I'd never read it before and thought it might be a good read for the flight. I started to read the inside jacket.

'Mark Twain (real name Samuel L. Clemens) wrote most of his books in a cabin at his sister's farm in upstate New York. His family were not allowed to disturb him here, giving him the peace he needed in order to write.'

Ah ha! If I told Jake I was going to a retreat to write I could buy myself some time without incurring his wrath. Of course if that was my story I really ought to actually go somewhere. No point being at home unless I wanted to be found out. But where should I go?

I had a plan. I picked up my mobile and scrolled through to the Js. Jake and Jerry's numbers nestled side by side.

'Hi!'

'Hi, Jerry. It's Dave. This is going to sound a bit odd. I need you to find me *two* googlewhacks.'

'That is odd! I got in last night and I was thinking about this whole googlewhacking thing. I had a couple of drinks, got online and found three!'

'That's fantastic, Jerry. Drunk is clearly a good tactic. So, can you give me the first two?'

'But … I found three …' he said, his usual ebullience disappearing suddenly.

'I know, Jerry, I heard you. But I just want the first two.'

'I … found … three …'

The words of David Gorman echoed through my mind: *If you personally find no more googlewhacks, but every google-whack you meet finds you two more, I bet you can't get ten googlewhacks in a row before your 32nd birthday.*

'Jerry,' I said firmly, 'I only want the first two—'

'But I fou—'

'You have to have rules, Jerry.' I was getting short with him now. 'Give me the first two.'

'OK. OK. I need to go to my computer to find them—'

'Look, I'm about to get on a flight to London so why don't you email them to me? I'll get them when I get back.'

'OK!'

I would go wherever the next 'whack took me. Maybe I'd stay there and write the novel, actually use it as a retreat, try and catch up with the job. No, I was kidding myself. I knew the truth. I was going to carry on googlewhacking. I *wanted* to get ten in a row. After all, success was only five googlewhacks away. It hadn't taken long to get to five in a row *without* trying, imagine how easy it would be to collect the next five if *I actually tried.* It shouldn't take me more than a couple of weeks.

I wanted to do it. I wanted to prove David Gorman wrong. More importantly, I wanted to run away from Jake. From trouble. From responsibility. Just as the teenage mum who's drowning in debt knows that signing up for another credit card is not the solution to her problems so I knew that I was getting myself deeper into trouble. But it put it off for now and it felt good.

I picked up the phone again.

'Bonjour.'

'Hi, David, it's Dave,' I said.

'Hey, happy New Year namesake!' said David G. 'How's it going?'

'It's going great. I've got five in a row!' I gabbled.

'What?' asked David, clearly confused.

'Five *googlewhacks* in a row. I'm going for it. Number five is sending me his two 'whacks right now. I'm going to get to ten.'

My heart was racing. I was excited. I knew that in making this call I was also making a commitment.

'You're kidding me?'

'No!'

'You're kidding me?'

'No!'

'You're kidding me?'

'No!'

'You're not kidding, are you?'

'No.'

'Well … what can I say?' he said. 'Good luck to you.'

'Thanks. I'll let you know how I get on.'

'You know … when I challenged you … I wasn't … really …' David paused uncomfortably.

'What?' I asked.

'Nothing. Good luck, Dave. And enjoy.'

*

I had less than an hour before my flight left for London. I felt buoyant and giddy, high on the recklessness of it all. I couldn't wait to get home, check out Jerry's email and find googlewhack number six. I tried to break *Huck Finn*'s spine but I was too excited to concentrate. I looked at the page but my eyes refused to focus on the words. There was something far more appealing to be seen out of the corner of my eye: a computer.

It was a laptop and it was sitting on top of a rather shapely lap but it wasn't the lap that drew my attention. It was the fact that, in spite of no obvious connection to a phone system, the computer appeared to be connected to the internet.

There's a well-known website called eBay that operates online auctions. Anything and everything is put up for sale and people from all over the world can take a look at the website and bid for the lots.

Well, the laptop that had caught my eye was currently connected to eBay. The laptop's owner was an attractive but starchy looking businesswoman. She was in her early thirties, her hair was scraped back from her face, she wore the odd combination of pinstripe suit and sneakers: red Nikes with a white flash. Her red shoes suggested she was lively. She appeared to be bidding to buy a hairdryer fashioned in the shape of the cartoon dog, Snoopy. I was fascinated.

'Excuse me,' I said with a cough, 'are you *actually* online?'

'Uh huh,' she said without looking away from the screen.

She was concentrating so hard her tongue was poking out. She looked like a child trying to colour in a picture without going over the outline.

'But there're no wires. How does it do that?' I asked.

'It's Wi-Fi,' she said tersely. I was obviously an unwelcome distraction.

'Wi-Fi?' I asked. 'What does that mean?'

'It *means* there are no wires,' came the matter-of-fact response.

'But then how does…'

'*This* is a hotspot,' she snapped.

'I don't understand.'

'Will you please just shut up for a minute,' she said. 'I'm in the middle of … here we go … and … yes!'

She punched the air with excitement.

'What happened?' I asked but she ignored me.

'Come to Mommy!' she said, speaking to no one in particular.

'What?'

She looked up from the screen and for the first time our eyes met. She was weighing me up which is only reasonable seeing as she was a lone woman and my attentions were wholly uninvited. I tried my hardest to look reassuringly innocent. I smiled. I realised that my smile was probably a bit unsettling so naturally I stopped smiling. But I stopped too soon. I didn't have a back-up expression ready, and now I didn't know what to do with my face at all. I started to feel horribly self-conscious and became uncomfortably aware of a suddenly sweaty brow.

I think I probably ended up with the universal expression of guilt that takes every innocent man as he passes through customs but amazingly it was enough for me to pass muster.

'Hi. My name's Christa,' she said offering her hand.

'Dave,' I said, shaking what had been offered.

'I was in an online auction. It was about to end. I wanted to make sure I got it.'

'*It* being a Snoopy hairdryer?'

'Uh huh,' said Christa, with a smile. 'I *love* Snoopy.'

'Really?' I asked. 'You don't really look the sort.'

'What does *the sort* look like?' she asked sarcastically.

'Like Charlie Brown,' I said. 'Y'know, yellow T-shirt, black zigzag stripe …'

She laughed. 'He wouldn't want a hairdryer,' she said, 'he's only got one hair!'

I laughed. 'Only one hair? That must be tough to deal with for someone so young,' I said, keeping the rally going.

'No wonder he's always visiting the psychiatrist!' said Christa, rewarding herself with a little chuckle.

I chuckled too. Then I realised that I didn't understand the joke and had no idea what I was chuckling at.

'I'm sorry,' I owned up, 'you've lost me there.'

'You know; *Lucy's psychiatric booth?* In the comic strips? No?'

'No. Sorry. I'm not really a fan.' I tried to look apologetic for the fact.

'That's OK,' she said. 'I do talk to people who don't like Snoopy!'

'Good,' I said.

There was an awkward pause before I remembered what had drawn my attention in the first place.

'So, your computer is able to connect to the internet without a phone line?'

'Yeah. It's Wi-Fi' she said and then, seeing the look of confusion on my face, added, 'It stands for *wireless fidelity*; it's a high-speed, wireless connection.'

'Technology is amazing, isn't it?'

'It sure is. And I'm using it to buy a hairdryer!'

'I don't want to be cheeky, but could I have a go?'

*

From: Jerry Kranitz
To: Dave Gorman
Subject: My googlewhacks!

Hey Dave,

I know you only wanted the first two, but number three is a doozy!

Alligator Peristyles.
Jeremiads Conifer.
Dingdong Larvas.

Best of luck, and remember, if you're ever in Columbus...

Jerry

'What the hell is that about?' asked Christa, reading over my shoulder.

'Googlewhacks' I said staring intently at the screen. It was my turn to concentrate.

'What?' she asked.

'Words,' I said, which didn't help her much but I was busy opening a new mail. My tongue was poking out.

From: Dave Gorman
To: Jake Lingwood
Subject: Hugh's Hue.

Hi Jake,

I know you wanted to meet up soon but I'm not really going to be around for a while. London's just so full of distractions so I've decided to get away from it all. That way I can really concentrate on the writing. In the meantime, I've attached a few documents for you to look at.

I'll be in touch with more soon,

Dave

'Ahem.' It was Christa. 'I know *I'm* reading *your* mail, but this is *my* computer. What documents were you thinking of attaching?'

'Can I open a new Word document?' I asked.

'Sure. You just do ... this,' she said, leaning over me and pressing a few buttons.

A big empty white page stared at me. I saved it and called it chapter1.doc. I saved another as storyline.doc and a third as notes.doc. Then I went back to the mail programme and attached all three documents to the mail.

'Erm ... those documents are blank. When this Jake character opens them, he'll just get blank pages,' said Christa, censoriously.

'I know,' I said, 'I'm being very naughty. There won't be anything there, but he'll think there's been a mistake. At least he'll *think* the documents exist.'

'I'm not sure I should let my computer be used for this kind of subterfuge!'

'You don't have a choice,' I said, pressing send.

'Have you finished now? I should be on my way,' said Christa, looking at her watch.

'Not yet,' I said. 'If I could just ...'

I opened a new window and connected to Google.

'You wanted to know what a googlewhack was?' I asked.

'Yeah.'

I typed in the words alligator and peristyles and hit the search button. Almost immediately the page came up with just the one hit.

'That,' I said, grandly, 'is a googlewhack.'

'What?'

'One hit. Now, let's take a look at this one.'

I clicked on the link and the home of the Alligator Peristyles 'whack opened up. It *seemed* to be the pages of something called *East West Magazine*. The website contained three volumes of the magazine all written between 1925 and 1928 so I'm guessing it wasn't originally written for the Net.

The article containing the googlewhack was entitled 'My Travels in India'. Most of the articles seemed to concern Buddhism, meditation and the Indian subcontinent although there were one or two on an Egyptian theme too. But I wasn't interested in the content. I was interested in the author and on that subject there was precious little information. I could find no contact details on the site either for the author – who might well have passed on by now – or for the webmaster. It was a dead end. I wasn't too concerned because, of course, I still had Jeremiads Conifer to save me. I returned to Google.

'I'm sorry, but I really am going to need my computer back,' said Christa with growing urgency.

I'd forgotten she was there. I typed in the words for Jerry's second 'whack.

'Where are you flying?' I asked as I pressed the search button.

'London,' she said as the googlewhack appeared on her screen.

'So am I,' I said, clicking the link, 'which flight?'

She showed me her boarding card. Business class.

'You're on the same flight as me,' I said, 'only nearer the front of the plane. Can I just have a few more seconds?'

She shrugged her shoulders.

I was looking at the website of Integrity USA, an organisation that bills itself as 'A witness of God's inclusive love to the Episcopal Church and the gay, lesbian, bisexual and transgender community'.

I'm none of the above but it certainly gave the impression that they were a welcoming bunch so I was sure they'd be perfectly agreeable to the idea of a meeting.

I looked further around the site, seeing if I could find out in which part of the USA they practised their integrity.

'Oh my God! Oh my all inclusive, gay, lesbian, bisexual, transgender God!' I said.

'What?' asked Christa.

'I might not be taking this flight,' I said, my fingers darting around the keyboard, locating an email address.

'What? Why not?' asked Christa.

'Because I might be staying in Washington!' I explained. 'I might be meeting someone from the Episcopal Church for the gay, lesbian, bisexual and transgender community.'

'You don't look the sort.'

By the time she'd delivered her quip I'd already emailed Integrity USA.

'Dave, I really do *need* my computer now.'

'They haven't called our flight yet! *Please* let me at least check this out. I need to know if I should stay or go!'

'You've got one minute. Max.'

I looked at the screen. It was bad news.

'I don't need that long.'

I slid the computer round to show Christa the evidence for herself. My email had bounced straight back.

'So I guess you are flying to London then?' said Christa.

'Yep,' I said. I couldn't see any other option.

I sat and stared at the screen. If Jeremiads Conifer was a dead end then the whole chain died with it. I wasn't trying to meet any old ten googlewhacks; it had to be ten googlewhacks *in a row*. It had to be a chain, each googlewhack responsible for finding the next. Jerry – Ammonite Googolplex – was the fifth link in the chain. He'd found Alligator Peristyles and Jeremiads Conifer. If they went nowhere that was the end of that.

For a few moments I considered looking up Dingdong Larvas but deep down I knew there was no point. The rules were clear: *every googlewhack I met could find me two more*. If I followed up Jerry's third find I'd be cheating and there could be no satisfaction there. Besides, Christa was starting to tut.

'Tut,' she tutted. See what I mean?

Was that it? Could my googlewhack adventure end that simply? Without trying I'd cruised to five in a row and then the moment I actually applied myself to the task I encountered nothing but failure. It didn't seem just.

I couldn't let it end now. I'd told David I was going for it. I'd made my excuses to Jake. I was committed. But if the chain was dead what else could I do?

I was shaken from these thoughts by Christa wresting her computer from my clammy palms.

'I have to run,' she said, deftly folding the computer up and slipping it into its carry case. 'So I guess you need to do the same.'

I looked at my watch. I was supposed to be sitting on a plane. I looked up and saw that Christa was already several yards away. She was running. I started to run after her and my longer stride and lack of luggage meant that I caught up with her pretty quickly. As I was responsible for her lateness it seemed impolite to overtake.

'I'm sorry,' I panted.

'You will be,' she wheezed.

'Do you want me to carry that bag?' I said.

It's quite hard to sound gallant when you're sprinting.

'No … you might stop and get online. You're obsessed.'

That seemed a bit rich.

'Snoopy lover!' I said, the spirit of the playground alive and well.

'Googlewhacker!' came the retort.

Just then the airport PA system crackled into life.

'Ladies and gentlemen, we regret to announce the delayed departure …'

It was our flight. It was delayed by two hours. We stopped running. We looked at each other. We were ridiculous, panting, purple-faced wrecks. We started to laugh. It was a giggle at first but it grew rapidly, my laughter feeding on hers and vice versa and pretty soon we were, in the truest sense of the word, hysterical.

*

'Well, obviously you need to try and pick up the chain part way through,' said Christa sipping her cappuccino.

I call it a cappuccino but to be honest that isn't what I heard her order. When she ordered it she must have employed twenty words I've never heard used in relation to coffee before. It might as well have been a skinny-mocha-choca-supa-cali-frag-ilistic-expiali-ccino as far as I was concerned but I'd said, 'I'll have the same please', and mine looked, smelled and tasted pretty much like a cappuccino so that's what I'm calling it.

We were killing the time together and I'd explained my situation. Most importantly I'd explained my distress at the chain falling apart after only five links.

Christa, who described herself as a business analyst, whatever that is, had immediately seen a way through the problem. As I'd explained the situation she sketched a diagram to show me the connections between the different googlewhacks. It showed not only the 'whacks I'd met, but the 'spares' along the way:

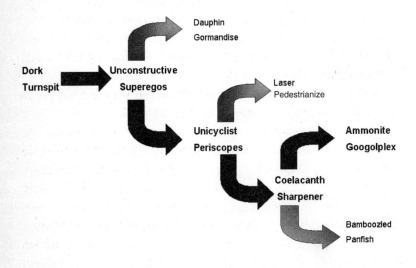

'Your best-case scenario would be to meet Bamboozled Panfish,' she said; 'that way you're meeting a number five. Failing that, Laser Pedestrianize gives you a four and Dauphin Gormandise, three. If none of them are possible you have to start again and find yourself a new first-place googlewhack.'

'That's against the rules,' I said earnestly. 'David made it very clear: *If you personally find no more googlewhacks, but every googlewhack you meet finds you two more, I bet you can't get ten googlewhacks in a row before your 32nd birthday.*'

'So, how many had you found before he said that?' asked Christa.

I had no idea what a business analyst actually did for a living but on this evidence I suspected she was very good at it.

'I found three others,' I confessed. 'In a crossword.'

'Do you remember what they were?' she asked.

'Yep,' I said. They were indelibly burnt into my memory.

'Termagant Holbein, Varsities Bonnets and Rarebit Nutters.'

'You're very, very strange,' she said, looking at me in disbelief.

I smiled back as 'normally' as possible.

'Well, we need to take a look at all these spares and email them all. There's no point waiting to discover you can't meet Bamboozled Panfish; we need to attack on all fronts at all times, keep as many irons in the fire as we possibly can,' said Christa, demonstrating exactly why her employer pays for her to fly business class.

In the time before our flight we made our way to a Wi-Fi hot spot, fired up the computer and went to work.

I emailed the Japanese Frank Zappa fan responsible for Bamboozled Panfish. I took another look at the minutes of a six-year-old local government meeting in Hong Kong but there was still no way of identifying or contacting Laser Pedestrianize. I revisited the site of the History professor from the Jesuit University in New York and even though I explained to Christa that my earlier email to that address had bounced she insisted I try it again just in case. I did. It bounced straight back. In pursuit of Termagant Holbein I emailed a Canadian school, chasing Varsities Bonnets I emailed a surfing-mad student in South Africa while the hunt for Rarebit Nutters led me to email a group of Mini fanatics based in North Wales.

'If this was work I'd be charging you a $2000 consultancy fee,' said Christa, packing the computer up once more.

'I'm glad it isn't work then,' I smiled. 'I'd love to buy you dinner in London if you like. As a thankyou.'

'No thanks,' she said. 'It's been fun, but when we board the plane, I'm turning left and you're turning right and that will be that. I really don't like beards.'

*

For the first time that year I was awake, sober and in my own living room. I checked my email, eager to see which of the googlewhacks had come back to me. The results weren't good. Every single one of my requests for meetings had bounced back or been ignored.

But I was committed now. And I had a plan ...

seven

Rarebit Nutters

Rarebit   noun: a traditional Welsh dish that is, essentially, cheese (sometimes with milk and or seasonings) on toast.

Nutters   noun: plural of nutter; a British slang term for a mad or eccentric person.

If my career ever takes a peculiar turn and I end up in the signwriting trade I think I'll probably move to Wales. There must be twice as much work there for signwriters as almost everything is written in both Welsh and English.

Personally I'd prefer it if it was all in Welsh because I enjoy feeling like I'm in foreign parts when I'm driving around. It feels more like a holiday. Besides, how stupid are you if you can't work out that *Wrecsam* is Wrexham and the *promenâd* is the promenade? If you can't handle signs like that you probably shouldn't be driving and I recommend you take a tacsi.

Anyway, if you happen to be a signwriter, take a tip from me: move to Wales and do a special offer – two 'L's for the price of one – and you'll soon have the lion's share of the market. Or the *llewod* share of the *marchnad*, if you prefer.

These thoughts were going through my mind as I pulled into the potholed car park of the Fairview Inn in the tiny Welsh town of Llanddulas and parked my Vauxhall Corsa, somewhat conspicuously, on the end of a long row of Minis. I was there to attend a meeting of the Welsh Rarebit Minis, the bunch of Mini enthusiasts responsible for the googlewhack Rarebit Nutters. These people were my only hope.

*

As Christa had made clear, my best-case scenario was to meet Bamboozled Panfish. But all I knew about him was that, along with 125 million other people, he lived in Japan. Without a reply to my email there was clearly no way of tracking him down.

I had even less information for some of the others. I had no email address for Laser Pedestrianize while a defunct address for Dauphin Gormandise meant I had no way of knowing whether or not he was still teaching history to New York Jesuits.

With those three googlewhacks out of commission I had no choice but to start a new chain and that meant I had only my three crossword 'whacks to go on.

Emails to Termagant Holbein and Varsities Bonnets yielded nothing and I had no other way of contacting the people responsible. I'd had no reply from Rarebit Nutters either, but some investigation of their website had provided a glimmer of hope.

Because the Welsh Rarebit Minis had *public* meetings and there was nothing to stop me, a member of the public, attending.

As far as I could tell, every member of the club was equally responsible for the appearance of the googlewhack (it appeared in one sentence: 'Hi fellow Mini *nutters*, *we* are Welsh *Rarebit* Minis') so all I had to do was persuade *one* of them to find me two new 'whacks and the ball would be rolling once more.

So there I was in Llanddulas, about to enter the Fairview Inn and meet my Rarebit Nutters. I wasn't really expecting to like a bunch of Mini enthusiasts because … well, because they're Mini enthusiasts. On a sliding scale of hobbies, isn't Mini enthusing somewhere between stamp collecting and trainspotting?

Not that it mattered because, of course, I wasn't there to enjoy myself; I was there to find my next googlewhack. I certainly hadn't enjoyed very much of the day that far.

I had thought accommodation would be easy to find in an out-of-season seaside town but I was wrong. The B&B next door to the Fairview Inn had been my first port of call but no one was in. I'd asked a passer-by for another suggestion and he'd directed me to the Dulas Arms, a hostelry that was, frankly, as dull as ditchwater. They told me they were full but the empty car park (and the time of year) led me to believe this was slang for 'can't be bothered'.

I could find nothing else in Llanddulas (I told you it was small) so I drove on to the adjacent town of Old Colwyn, as depressing and unwelcoming a place as I've been in many a year although at least I managed to find a small hotel that would put me up for the night.

As I checked in, a cleaning lady was pouring her wages into a fruit machine and dropping fag ash on the carpet. The owner explained that a single room was usually £39. The luxury of my sub-£30 Columbus room was still fresh in my mind and it must have shown in my expression because I was instantly offered a £10 discount. Maybe if I'd paid the extra tenner I would have got a smile.

What I did get was a kettle, a teacup, a bed that was positioned on an angle because, even though it was tiny, it was longer than the wall it tried to abut, and a John Smith's Bitter ashtray that the previous occupant had chosen to ignore, preferring to leave an inch-high pile of cigarette ash on the skirting board beneath the window. I say the previous occupant, maybe it was the occupant before that. The air smelled stale and the bathroom, sorry, shower room, was the kind of windowless, dank space that left you feeling dirtier than you were when you went in. It wasn't so much a hotel room, more a Young Offender's Institute but without such a modern TV.

With several hours to kill before the meeting I'd gone for a walk round Old Colwyn. As I left the hotel the cleaning lady was on her knees by the fruit machine sweeping up the fag ash, a bleak demonstration of futility if ever I saw it. She makes a mess. She cleans it up. They pay her. She puts the money into the fruit machine. She makes a mess. She cleans it up and on and on and on it goes.

On the *promenâd* I discovered a disused pier, some public toilets and not much else but nearby Eirias Park promised pedaloes, pitch and putt and the prehistoric pleasure of Dinosaur World. Maybe Old Colwyn was older than I thought? I walked up to discover the green, pitch and puttless, the lake, dry and Dinosaur World, closed. A fibreglass T-Rex poked his head over the fence apologetically, his expression seemed to say, 'I'm sorry I'm not very lifelike but it's your own fault, you came to Old Colwyn, you loser.' Or was I reading too much in to it?

I suppose it's the same for many seaside towns; they don't really serve a purpose out of season. You'd think the people who live there might disagree but Old Colwyn in January feels like a 17-year-old boy waiting to sup his first legal pint. Being in Old Colwyn in January is like putting tinsel up in June. It's a shame we can't put the town in the attic for most of the year and fetch it down when it's useful.

*

I stepped into the back room of the pub and slid quietly into a chair at the rear of the room while avoiding any eye contact with the 15 or so folk there. I wanted to gauge the room first, to work out how and when to best broach the subject of googlewhacking.

'You'll need one of these,' said a voice to my right.

I looked up and found a few sheets of paper being thrust in my direction. The thrusting hand belonged to a skinhead. A shaft of light bounced off his facial piercing. I looked at the paper and saw the word *'agenda'* written across the top.

'It's an agenda,' explained my skinhead friend in a reassuring whisper.

He said it as if he were talking to a five-year-old and I realised I had a look of shock on my face that must have made me look more than a little simple. Then I realised that he also had a look of shock on *his* face, which seemed odd because it didn't match his tone of voice. It took me a few seconds to notice that his startled expression was permanent – the result of having no eyebrows.

I studied the agenda as intently as I could. There weren't many items and I gathered from the main conversation that we were approaching the end of business.

'So, well done everyone who took part in the charity toy run,' said a jolly woman who seemed to be holding court.

'We filled a load of Minis with toys …' whispered Mr No Brows helpfully, '… delivered them to Barnardo's.'

'We had a really fun day,' continued Mrs Jolly. 'The kids really appreciated it, so well done Gwyn and Gina for organising that.'

There were murmurs of approval all round and a few nods of acknowledgement from a shy couple I took to be the two Gs.

It was obviously a lovely thing to have done but I couldn't help thinking that the kids would have liked it even more if it had been the Range Rover Enthusiasts who'd filled *their* cars with toys. Or the Articulated Lorry Enthusiasts for that matter.

'And finally,' Mrs Jolly was back, 'a big hand for Pete who raised £125 for Children in Need by shaving all his hair off!'

A little ripple of applause went through the room. I turned to Mr No Brows with a new understanding of his startled-rabbit expression.

'You must be Pete,' I said.

'I even waxed my legs,' said Pete with a conspiratorial wink, before lifting a trouser leg to prove it. All of a sudden he was the least threatening skinhead I'd ever met.

That appeared to be the end of the meeting and the group broke down into three or four little conversations instead, just a bunch of mates down the pub. And me.

'You're new, aren't you?' asked Mrs Jolly, sliding into the chair next to me.

'Er ... yes,' I said.

'Well, we're all very friendly so make yourself at home,' she smiled. 'I'm Ems.'

'I'm Dave.'

'Oh, *that's* another Dave,' said Ems, pointing across the room. The other Dave looked up and Ems beckoned him over.

'Dave, this is Dave,' said Ems. 'Dave runs a company called *Autopetite.* He fixes and builds Minis so if there's anything wrong with yours he's worth knowing.'

'What year is your car?' asked Dave.

Ah... they were about to discover that I wasn't a Mini enthusiast.

'Umm ... it's a ... W reg.'

'So that's ...' Dave's internal calculator whirred and clicked a bit '... 1981?'

'No ... it's ... um ...' my internal calculator whirred and clicked a lot, '... 2000? I think.'

Suddenly the whole room fell silent and all eyes were on me. Disapproving eyes. You'd think I'd just confessed to some heinous crime involving cute animals and a blender.

Ems was the first to speak.

'We don't like the *new* Mini.'

'It's a *German* car,' said Pete.

'They're owned by BMW now,' said Dave.

'All our cars have stickers saying "100% free of BMW parts",' said Ems.

'We like *proper* Minis,' said Pete.

'No, you don't understand,' I said, trying desperately to recover the situation.

The idea that I had a modern BMW designed Mini sitting in the car park clearly made me persona non grata and I knew that meant I was likely to end up as persona non googlewhack.

'It's not a modern Mini …' I said, eager to set the record straight. 'It's a Vauxhall Corsa!'

There was silence. I winced, expecting the worst. The silence continued so I continued wincing. Eventually Ems spoke.

'A Vauxhall Corsa?' she laughed and I unwinced. 'Ooooh, that's all right then!'

'Why didn't you say?' asked Pete.

'If you're thinking of buying a Mini I can do you a good deal,' said Dave passing me his Autopetite business card.

'He's brilliant,' said a new voice, eager to extol Dave's virtues.

'I built Kelvin's Mini from bits,' said Dave.

'I'll take you for a drive in it if you want,' said Kelvin.

'I'd love to!' I lied, determined to do whatever it took to fit in.

*

'Aaaaaggggggghhhhhh!' I screamed.

'Am I going too fast?' asked Kelvin, going too fast.

We were hurtling along a dark country lane in a tiny metal box. It hummed and whirred and even screeched the way cars do in the movies but it also clunked and clanked and boinged the way cars do in the circus. I knew Dave had assembled it from bits but I didn't understand why Kelvin seemed quite so determined to shake it apart again. Especially as I was in danger of disintegrating with it.

Kelvin took the novel approach of not slowing down for the bends, but he was conventional enough to still speed up on the straights so we didn't have to travel far down this windy lane before the car was clearly at its limit. It was at this point that Kelvin put his foot down a bit more and discovered a new limit that must have been hiding behind the last one.

I looked at the dashboard for information and found none. Not only no information, but no dashboard. I'm used to seeing four or five dials on an average car, but here there was only one, sitting alone in the centre of the car. I tried to take in exactly how fast we were going but everything was shaking too much. The car was shaking, the speedometer was shaking, I was shaking and my eyeballs were shaking in their sockets. I reckon that being unable to read the speed is probably proof that you're going too fast.

'Aaaaaggggggghhhhhh!' I screamed again.

It wasn't just the speed that made me feel unsafe, it was the lack of protection afforded by such a small and seemingly flimsy car. Getting into it hadn't felt like getting in to a car at all, more like putting on a slightly starchy overcoat.

'We'll turn round here,' said Kelvin, hitting the brakes for the first time. 'We don't want to go in to Abergele.'

He turned the car round on a sixpence and revved the engine, preparing for the sprint back.

'Did you enjoy that?' he asked.

'Yes.'

'Really?'

'No.'

'Oh.'

'Look, the thing is, I'm not really interested in Minis,' I blurted out. 'I came because of a googlewhack.'

Kelvin shuffled uncomfortably in his seat, his turn to be frightened.

'A google ... what?' he asked.

I explained. I told him what a googlewhack was. I told him I was trying to get ten in a row. I told him that the Welsh Rarebits were number one in a chain. I didn't tell him I'd spent most of the year so far in the States in case that made me look a bit eccentric.

'So,' said Kelvin, 'you're not from North Wales and you're not into Minis?'

'No.'

'And yet you came to a North Wales Mini club?'

'Yes.'

'Because of a googlewhack?'

'Yes.'

'And you think *we're* strange?' Kelvin seemed incredulous.

'Well … when you put it like that …'

'Oh … the others are going to *love this*,' he said, putting the car in gear.

We hurtled back at a speed I think I recognised as Warp Factor Nine. Kelvin steered round the car park's potholes – a wise move, as some of them were bigger than a Mini. Back in the pub, Kelvin took great delight in telling everyone that he'd not only driven me to Abergele, he'd also driven me to tell him the truth.

Kelvin was right; the others did seem to love hearing this tale and instead of resenting this strange non-Welsh non-Mini-admiring gatecrasher they greeted Kelvin's retelling of my tale with confused laughter.

'So it was *you* that sent that email?' asked Ems.

'Yes,' I said. 'You got it then?'

'Yeah … but I just thought it was a wind-up. I can't believe you've actually come all this way just for a … whaddayacallit?'

'A googlewhack'

'Yeah. A googlewhack. They must be *impossible* to find.'

Concern dripped from every syllable Ems spoke. She obviously had no obligation to try and find me a googlewhack but she was evidently a kindly soul and it probably wasn't in her genes to say no when someone asked a favour.

'I think it probably seems harder than it is,' I said as persuasively as I could. 'I really want you to find a couple if you can.'

'I work on a computer all day,' said Kelvin. 'I'll have a go if you like.'

Ems breathed a sigh of relief.

Now that Kelvin had volunteered to be the group's googlewhacker I relaxed. I was confident that he would try to find me the 'whacks and there was nothing I could do to ensure his success. I'd just have to wait and see.

And now that I was relaxed I started to enjoy myself and I started to enjoy their company. I met John who was described by the others as 'a bit clumsy' (he held up a hand with only four and a half fingers on it by way of proof), I met another John who was a vicar which delighted me because we all know there should be a vicar in every group of hobbyists and I met a third John who stood out from the crowd because he had no distinguishing features of any kind.

I enjoyed hearing them plotting their next daytrip and their next charitable venture and I really enjoyed it when they started bitching about other Mini clubs: *'The Cheshire Cats are really stuck up. You know, they trailer their cars to shows! We drive our cars. They're car cars, not show cars; cars are for driving. Honestly!'*

I told Ems and Pete where I was staying for the night and they mocked me roundly for my choice.

'I hope your car is still there in the morning,' said Pete dryly. I chuckled.

'No. I mean it,' said Pete. 'There's loads of crime round here.'

Suddenly the gentle trickle of conversation became a raging torrent with everyone in the room competing to tell me how much crime there was in this seemingly quiet part of North Wales.

'I've had six cars stolen in the last twelve months. The police have done nothing.'

'Our car got sprayed with gold paint and the police said they couldn't do anything because the kid who did it was only nine!'

'We just wish he'd sprayed the whole car.'

'The police station had its windows put through the other day.'

'You never see a policeman on foot any more. You see 'em in cars, but they're more interested in you doing 32 mph in a 30 zone than if you've been burgled.'

'To be fair, I saw one on foot the other day. He was on the promenade.'

'That was probably a strippogram.'

Laughter.

'No, he'd probably had his car stolen!'

More laughter.

'It's the drugs, you see.'

The laughter stopped.

'All round Colwyn Bay is known for it. Heroin. It's Bag City round here and *they* don't do anything any more.'

*

As I drove home the next day, alone with my thoughts, I realised that the Welsh Rarebits weren't really about Minis. Yes they all drove them, yes they all liked them, but really the club was just an excuse to hang out together because hanging out together is fun. If it wasn't Minis I'm sure they'd find something else to talk about. If I lived in Colwyn I'd join the Welsh Rarebits and I think I'd be welcome in any car. As long as it wasn't one of the modern Minis.

*

I got home to find an email from Kelvin. I was delighted to see that he'd come up with the goods in the shape of Bushranger Doublespeak. It was just the one googlewhack but it was a start and Kelvin assured me that he was looking for another.

I looked up Bushranger Doublespeak and it filled me with hope. It led to the homepage of a man called Ken Fussichen. A brief glance was enough to show me that Ken was American. But whereabouts in America was he based?

When I found out I was amazed. If I was a betting man I'd have put money on Ken Fussichen having a mullet.

A few days ago I didn't even know where Columbus, Ohio was. Now I was hoping to return.

From: Ken Fussichen
To: Dave Gorman

Hello Dave,

No one has ever asked me permission to come to the US before. It gives me quite a rush, a sense of power that I could get used to. OK. You can come, but be sure to wipe your feet on the mat when you get here.

Keep smilin'

Ken

Columbus, Ohio – here I come, again.

*

I didn't know what lay beyond Columbus but it would prove to be the start of a very strange and exciting time in my life. Before the next three weeks were over I would travel a further 30,922 miles taking my total googlewhacking mileage to 41,286. I would cross the Atlantic Ocean five times and I would meet many more googlewhacks. Rarebit Nutters had led me to Bushranger Doublespeak but from there I would travel to Hippocampi Wallpaper, Bibliophilic Sandwiched, Dripstone Ingles, Verandahs Plectrums, Psychosomatic Rambunctiousness and Pomegranate Filibusters. And all of that before January was out.

That's a lot of travelling and a lot of googlewhacks. Eight googlewhacks if you're counting. You might be sitting there, in your armchair, in your bed, on that train, wherever you are, dear reader, and you might be thinking, *'Eight! That's eight in a row! Come on, Dave, only two more to go and you've done it!'*

Alas, it's not that simple.

As the next few chapters will explain it wasn't eight in a row at all. That may be the order in which I met them. But it isn't the way they were connected to each other. Those eight googlewhacks were split into two chains and with Christa's advice ringing in my ears ('*attack on all fronts at all times, keep as many irons in the fire as we possibly can*') I had pursued every available lead as and when it presented itself, flitting from chain to chain, keeping both alive for as long as I could.

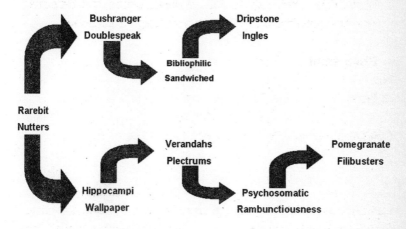

But less than three weeks later, with all that travelling behind me and all those 'whacks met, it still amounted to nothing. I was at stalemate. I had four in a row and five in a row but I had two dead ends.

My life was in turmoil.

Less than three weeks later ...

I am asleep. Now I'm not asleep. But I'm not yet awake. I'm in the twilight zone somewhere in between; no longer dreaming, not yet conscious. The synapses of my brain are just beginning to fire up, sensations drip, drip, dripping into my central nervous system, each drip bringing me closer to reality.

I pull the covers to me for warmth. Drip. Not yet prepared to open my eyes, not yet ready for the world. Drip. My head aches, my body aches, if I can stay in the land of nod I can delay these unpleasant sensations. I try to rewind the dream to delay the inevitable but the video of my mind has broken and the dream is not only over but gone. Something to do with an anchor, but maybe not. No. Forgotten. Lost without trace. Drip. My hands start to wander, a scratch here, another there. Drip. Nothing untoward going on – it's just that certain things need to be checked, counted, rearranged. Drip, drip, drip. Yep, one of those, two of these. OK. Best to just shift everything to the left like so. Drip. What's the last thing I remember? Drip. The bouncer. The noise. The neon lights. The music. Drip, drip, drip. My passport. Drip, drip, drip, drip, drip. Bourbon. Passport. Me. Shit. Where am I? Think. Drip. Think. Drip. Nothing. Blank. Oh well, I need to work this out. I need more information. I have no option, I'm going to have to open my eyes and let reality in. Drip. Here goes.

Eyes open.

Drip, drip, drip. But the drips become a flood; information overload leading ultimately to relief. I'm in a hotel room in Austin,

Texas. I haven't gone anywhere, I'm where I'm supposed to be. And I'm in bed.

I'm half dressed. Or half undressed, depending on your point of view. My coat is on the floor by the door to the room, I'm wearing my shirt, I've tried to kick my trousers off but they're hanging on to my ankles, turned inside out like some kind of magic trick. On the bedside table there's a glass of water. I must have been very pleased with myself last night; drunk, yes, but sober enough to bring a glass of water to bed. Too drunk to remember to drink any of it though.

I prop myself up on the pillows, reach for the glass and down it all in one gulp. I'm sure my insides are supposed to contain hundreds of miles of small intestines through which everything must travel before leaving my body but less than five seconds after drinking the water it seems to have completed its journey and is bursting to get out. It feels quite urgent.

I leap out of bed and run towards the bathroom. My trousers are still clinging to my ankles, dragging me back, slowing me down as the corduroy grips the nylon carpet, reducing me to a pathetic flappy waddle. This is useless. I stop, tread on the left leg with my right foot and yank my left foot free. I should remove the right leg also but the need to pee is growing more urgent still. I put my right hand inside my shorts and grip, hoping to stem the flow and try to run once more.

Only one leg is being attacked by the trouser monster now, but as I kick my right foot out the monster comes to life and rotates all the way around in front of my path like a demented game of swingball. I try to jump over it but as my right leg is the pole around which it's swinging it jumps up with me and wraps itself around my left leg bringing me tumbling down.

'Aagggghhhhhhh … oof … ow … gah.'

I try to break my fall but the waistband of my underpants traps my right hand. My left wrist is forced to take more than it should before the right-hand side of my face comes cracking down on the rough carpet. My right hand lands with a crunch too. Given what it's holding, it's better than the alternative.

I want to cry.

I don't know what I notice first. The sound of a lock turning, the sudden triangular shaft of daylight, the rush of brisk cold air or the voice.

'Room service.'

My body won't move but I turn my head to see an Hispanic cleaning lady standing in the doorway. She's tiny. She seems to have the body of a nine-year-old. Chewing gum, with one hand on her hip and the other resting on the door frame, she looks like a youngster bored in the middle of 'I'm a Little Teapot', but the lines on her face reveal her to be a world-weary, hard-done-by, minimum-wage fifty something.

'I'm sorry, sir,' she says, still chewing, 'I didn't know you were busy.'

Busy? I'm lying on my front, trousers round my ankles, arse in the air, my hand in my underpants staring helplessly back at her with a carpet-burn graze on my forehead and she chooses to use the epithet 'busy'!? I look like I've been sexually assaulted by a jumble sale!

I look at her, my face contorted by embarrassment, pain, incredulity, shock and yet more embarrassment. She shrugs her shoulders, a silent, pitiful but somehow reassuring 'Don't worry, sir, I've seen it all before' shrug and moves on, swinging the door closed behind her.

I've had better mornings.

I pull myself to my feet, rip my trousers from my leg and hurl them angrily at the door.

I get to the bathroom and take aim. Despite the urgent sensations, nothing happens for a good while. My body, taking revenge for the stresses and strains of last night, is clearly determined to play tricks on me this morning. But then ... then it comes, a long, luxurious pee. A Sssssssssssssssssssssss ssssssssssssssssssssssssssssssssssssssssssssssssssssssssssssssssssssssssssss ssssssssssssssssssss breathe 2, 3, 4 sssssssssssssssssssssssss ssssssssssssssssssssssss... ss...ss... s kind of, ssssssss, pee.

I stand in the bathroom and look at myself in the mirror. My loser's eyes stare back at me, daring me to face the facts. Not yet.

I examine my graze. Nothing too serious; it'll heal soon enough. A disposable razor sits by the basin, and next to it, a notepad full of drawings of differently bearded faces. I remember.

I'm in the midst of a very strange hangover. I've never had a hangover quite like this before. My head is aching a little, but not the constant, low dull thud I would have expected. My stomach feels a little fragile but not the queasy, washing machine spinning stomach I would have expected.

No. No, most of the hangover appears to be in my arm. I've never had a hangover in my arm before. I don't understand the sensation. A throb, a dull ache, a ... well, a hangover in my arm.

I lift my sleeve to see what's going on. I see a bandage, a thin, papery bandage held on with what looks like masking tape. What? What have I done? Tentatively I pick away at the edge of the tape and peel back the bandage. What the ... ?

Maybe in the room next door the tiny old cleaning lady lets her imagination run wild, when she hears my screams.

What the hell have I done? Information is flooding back into my brain faster than I can take it in. Last night. The walls, awash with colours, the dentist's chair, the needle, the pain, the pain, the pain, the anger, the walking in the street, the screaming, the tattoo. The fucking tattoo. The tattoo on my left arm – of a driver's licence!

What have I done? What have I done to myself? What's going on? How could this happen? I have a Texas driver's licence tattooed on my upper left arm. In my name. With a face. My face? Is that my face?

A passport-photo-sized face with a red beard stares impassively back at me. From my arm! Every line, every detail of the licence is a wound. A hundred wounds. A thousand tiny raised wealds, some weeping slowly, a pathetic, thin, watery blood.

I'm very confused. Scared, even. I look back at my arm. At the poor rendition of me, at my tattoo face. I'm hoping that he will be able to explain the situation to me. Instead, he stares back at me, emotionless, curious, still.

I'm running round my room screaming because I don't know

PART THREE

HOW I CAME TO WAKE UP IN A HOTEL ROOM IN

AUSTIN, TEXAS WITH A DRIVER'S LICENCE

TATTOOED ON MY LEFT ARM

eight

Bushranger Doublespeak

Bushranger   1. noun (*Australian*): a robber or escaped convict who lives in the outback.
2. noun (*US*): a backwoodsman, someone who lives away from civilisation.

Doublespeak   noun: evasive or deliberately ambiguous language, often associated with bureaucracy.

Packing for Columbus was difficult because it wasn't *just* a trip to Columbus. Beyond that it was a journey into the unknown. If Ken found me a new googlewhack – and I hoped he would – then the chain would continue and so would my travels. I had no way of knowing how long I would be away or what climate I would be meeting so how could I know what clothes to pack? Or how many?

Eventually I decided to leave my suitcase on top of the wardrobe and take a small backpack that I could carry on board in its stead. I packed a few shirts, a pullover and three or four days' worth of underwear. If I was away for any length of time I would simply have to wash things by hand or buy new clothes along the way. In most cities in the world it's cheaper to buy a new pair of socks than it is to pay a hotel laundry to clean them.

Besides, my earlier, less planned, luggage-free jaunt to the

States had taught me the huge benefits of travelling light. If you don't have a suitcase you can afford to check in later than normal and when your flight lands you can waltz straight through the airport at the other end. I reckon washing your own smalls is a small price to pay for that kind of convenience.

I threw in a toothbrush, a couple of good books and music in the form of my iPod. I was about to put my mobile phone in too when I had second thoughts. My phone would be a way for Jake to get in touch with me and I really didn't want that.

I flew to Columbus via Cleveland and once there I headed to the one hotel I knew for some more cut-price luxury. I'd arranged to meet Ken for lunch the day after my arrival so I had an evening to spare. My mind and body craved sleep but I knew if I was to conquer jetlag I had to stay up for a few hours at least. I called Jerry.

'Hello?' asked a woman's voice.

'Hello,' I said. 'Is Jerry there?'

'I'll just get him,' she said. 'Who can I say is calling?'

'Dave Gorman.'

There was a pause, the sound of a palm on a mouthpiece, some distant mumbles and then the 10,000-volt voice.

'Hey, Dave!'

Yep, that was Jerry.

'So you got my googlewhacks, right?' he asked excitedly.

'I sure did,' I said. 'Unfortunately they were both dead ends.'

'Both?' asked Jerry, 'What about the third one?'

I didn't really want to explain the two 'whack rule again so I just ignored the question and carried on.

'But … while they were both dead ends I started a new chain and—'

'Cool! Hey, where'd it take you?'

'To Wales.'

'No shit!' he said.

Jerry was so surprised by this development he managed to

climb several octaves in only two syllables. I shouldn't think anyone's ever been that surprised by Wales before.

'And then,' I continued, 'the Welsh googlewhack *also* found one—'

'So where you heading to next?' asked Jerry champing at the bit.

'I'm already there?'

'Where?'

'Columbus.'

'*No shit!!*'

This was clearly much more surprising than my Welsh news and Jerry's pitch scaled new heights accordingly. If I had a greater surprise up my sleeve I think glassware would shatter and only Jerry's neighbourhood dogs would be able to hear him. Mind you, I expect they'd be confused by the strange voice in their heads telling them not to shit.

When Jerry's voice returned to its normal register he invited me to join him and his wife for dinner at theirs.

'I'd love to,' I said, reaching for a biro. 'Where do you live?'

'Are you kidding?' he replied. 'I'm comin' to pick you up!'

*

I was surprised by just how normal Jerry's apartment was. I was expecting to find a shrine to space rock, all lava lamps, incense and psychedelia but instead I found myself in a modern, spacious, elegantly decorated front room. It could have been a show home if it wasn't for the reassuring presence of a few family photos dotted about the place and boxes of toys for visiting nephews and nieces.

'Hi, I'm Debbie,' said Jerry's wife with a smile, 'would you like a beer?'

'That'd be great,' I said, although I could feel tiredness taking me already.

We sat down at the dining table and tucked in to a gorgeous casserole.

My eye was drawn to a framed poster on the wall beside us; the one nod to space rock in the whole room. It featured a sort of pot-bellied alien in an ethereal landscape and it was advertising a gig by a band called Mr Quimby's Beard.

'I helped promote that show!' said Jerry with pride. 'Have you heard of them?'

'Heard of them?' I chuckled. 'I'm sorry, Jerry, I'm not a space rock aficionado.'

'You should look them up!' said Jerry. 'They're from England!'

'Mr Quimby's Beard?' I asked incredulously.

'Oh yeah!' said Jerry. 'They're from Sunderland!'

He said *'Sunderland'* as if it might be the crucial fact required to trigger my memory, as if it was possible to forget the name Mr Quimby's Beard, but remember where they came from. Maybe there's a Middlesbrough band called Mr Beardby's Quim and people sometimes get the two confused. Excuse my language.

'I'm afraid I've never heard of them,' I said.

'They used to be a punk band called S.A.D!' said Jerry, still hoping to jog my memory. 'Then they discovered Hawkwind, Pink Floyd and drugs and became 21st Century Module... obviously that was a few years ago before it *was* the twenty-first century!'

'Obviously.'

'Then they became The Amazing Professor Tribbly And His Awesome Filling Machine ...'

'I expect they'd discovered some more drugs around then ...' I said.

'Probably!' agreed Jerry. 'And then finally they became Mr Quimby's Beard!'

'That's amazing,' I said, shaking my head, as amazed by Jerry's power of recall as I was by the band's ever-changing name.

'They're great!' said Jerry. 'They played a really long show too. *Really* long!'

'But they *were* still called *Mr* Quimby's Beard when they finished,' added Debbie with a wry smile.

'I'm really glad they came over!' said Jerry clearly relishing the memory. 'Sometimes you need to *educate* an audience, show them what's out there!'

I wondered if Debbie was one of the people Jerry was trying to educate. I guessed she had to be either a space rock fan or a space rock widow.

'I like some of it,' she said brightly. 'The festivals are fun.'

'Oh, *you'd love Prog-Day*!' said Jerry growing more animated by the second. 'We drive up to North Carolina for the Labor Day weekend; there are loads of bands on and hundreds of prog rock fans; it's heaven!'

'I don't know my American geography,' I confessed. 'How far is North Carolina?'

'Oh ... it's about ... a nine-hour drive!' said Jerry. 'But it's worth it!'

I looked at Debbie, expecting to find a more cynical point of view.

'It is great fun,' she said with a smile.

'It seems an awfully long way to travel to see some music,' I said.

'Yeah ...' Jerry scoffed, '... and that's coming from a man who's travelled all the way to Columbus, Ohio to meet a googlewhack!'

I was a little stung and started to defend myself.

'Yeah but—'

'Twice!' said Jerry making the case against me watertight.

'Well ... it's complicated,' I said pathetically.

Jerry just laughed. Debbie laughed. I knew my behaviour was ridiculous so I laughed too.

Debbie raised her glass and proposed a toast.

'To googlewhacking.'

The three of us clinked our glasses.

'To googlewhacking!' Jerry and I said in unison.

We all took a sip of cold lager and began laughing again but I had a toast to propose too.

'To space rock!'

'To space rock!

*

I woke up late.

My mind was fuzzy from oversleep and last night's beer so the hotel room wasn't immediately familiar to me and I experienced a tiny moment of heart-stopping where-am-I panic before it all made sense. I lay back, relaxed in the gargantuan bed and picked up the remote control.

On the TV, one of the many American talkshow hosts that fill the moral vacuum between Oprah Winfrey and Jerry Springer was holding court. The theme of the show was something along the lines of *Help! I Get Teased about my Wild and Crazy Hair!* I sat, dumbstruck, watching a high school girl whose hair was certainly both wild and crazy in that there was more of it than there was of her.

She explained, through floods of tears, how her hair made her a target for bullies and was ruining her life but she just didn't – sob – know what to do – wheeze – about – hyperventilate, sob, wheeze – it.

Once she'd cried enough, the sensitive, caring host offered her the remarkable solution of – wait for it – a haircut! She was whisked away but returned after the break with a new hairstyle that is probably best described as *tame and sane*. There were more tears but this time they were tears of joy. She declared all her troubles over and promised that she would now aim to 'get good grades and get in to college'. The studio audience whooped and hollered their approval. I didn't share their sense of joy. If someone can so spectacularly fail the multi-choice question:

If you don't like your hair should you call:

A: A hairdresser or B: A TV show

I don't hold out much hope for them on the exam front.

The phone rang.

'Mr Gorman?' said the receptionist. I had no way of knowing, but I was sure he had a mullet. 'I have a … Ken *Bushranger Doublespeak* Fussichen waiting in reception for you?'

Lord only knows what code he thought Ken and I were using, but it made me chuckle and when someone makes you chuckle before you meet them, it's normally a good sign.

Ken was a big man. A very big man. He had a dark moustache flecked with grey to keep his smile warm and, while he was wearing a baseball cap, there was no sign of a mullet. He looked slightly dishevelled but in that comfortable way, like when a favourite cushion bursts but you prefer it that way.

'So, where do you wanna go eat?' he asked.

'This is your town, I'm in your hands,' I said. 'I'll go wherever you like.'

'OK … well … I think we should head out of the city centre because what I like most of all is free parking,' said Ken with a laugh.

He had a big laugh to suit his big frame, a hearty, head thrown back, *hyuk hyuk* of a laugh.

We climbed into Ken's big four-wheel-drive with a Stars and Stripes flag flying from the back and started to drive out of the city. The landscape was sprawling, flat and featureless. We passed industrial estates, parking lots, small clusters of retail outlets and not much else. Here I was, alone in the company of another stranger, driving into the unknown once more, but this time the situation held no fear. I'd given up on the idea of being frightened when I'd committed myself to this challenge. I wasn't frightened of strangers any more, least of all my googlewhacks. I wasn't frightened of anything or anyone. Except Jake.

When we pulled up we were in a car park shared by several identical, modern, low-rise buildings, each offering something cheap and cheerful to eat. As far as I could tell there was nothing else for miles around this wasn't a place to grab a bite while you were shopping, say. No, as odd as it seemed, this was supposed to be a destination in itself. Ken selected the Chinese restaurant because he reckoned their buffet was second to none.

Inside there were several counters, each containing maybe twenty, stainless-steel trays loaded up with one Chinese dish or another. We piled our plates high, filled enormous paper cups with syrupy cola and sat down. The food looked the way it does in commercials. The broccoli was the most vibrant green, the peppers the purest red and the mushrooms were bigger and more symmetrical than they should naturally be. Odd. If I was drawing up a list of desirable qualities for foodstuffs, I'd probably put 'natural' above 'symmetrical'. Not that it stopped me tucking in.

'So, what do you want to know about me?' asked Ken.

The honest answer would have been 'I want to know if you can find me two googlewhacks' but it didn't seem polite to bring it up just yet. That'd be like asking a girl to sleep with you on a first date. The start of a first date. Before the wine list. Honestly, darling, I want to get to know you for who you are. I'm not just interested in you for your googlewhacks!

'Well,' I said, 'just tell me about yourself. Fussichen's an interesting name ... do you know where it comes from?'

Every American I've ever met knows where their family hails from so I figured this was a subject he'd be happy to run with. I wasn't wrong.

'It comes from Southern Austria originally,' said Ken, 'although I know my grandfather spent some time chasing pretty girls in Italy, *hyuk, hyuk;* he came to the States in 1920.

'I was born and raised in New York,' he continued, 'but I've been kicked out of a few states. It's a family tradition. *Hyuk, hyuk.* The Fussichens have been kicked out of a lot of countries in our time.'

I liked hearing Ken talk; it was strangely hypnotic. Like so many New Yorkers he has the non-stop, scattergun delivery of a sassy stand-up comic and the turn of phrase to match.

To be honest it didn't really matter what he was saying, I would have been happy just to sit back and let the rhythm and the tone hit me. Bada-boom-bada-boom-bada-boom ... *hyuk, hyuk, hyuk.*

'One thing I've learnt along the way, Dave, is that God has quite a sense of humour. You think you're doing OK then He says, "So let's see how you handle *this*", and then He sits back laughing: Ha ha ha ha!'

Ken mimicked a big, boomy cartoon-God laugh that melted into his own genuine laughter.

'Really?' I asked, wanting him to expand mainly because I preferred the sound of Ken's voice to my own.

'Oh yeah!' said Ken. 'Take me for example. I've got more personal life than anyone knows about ... *hyuk, hyuk.*'

I paused, chopsticks poised at my open mouth. Ken was laughing but I had an uneasy feeling about where the conversation was going. Maybe as an Englishman I'm just genetically programmed to tense up at the mere mention of a *personal life*, but what did he mean by having *more* of one? Was he about to confess to having an affair?

'Really?' I asked nervously, '... wh-wh-what do you mean?'

'I mean I have nine kids,' said Ken.

Once again the chopsticks remained frozen in mid-delivery. Nine kids! My imagination was running wild but I didn't want to know how many wives, girlfriends or significant others were involved!

'I shouldn't be asking these kind of questions, Ken,' I said hurriedly. 'You don't owe me any kind of explanation ...'

''s OK,' he said with a shrug. 'Originally we planned to have four. Two biological and two adopted. So we had a kid, Matthew. When he was young he got ill ... quite ill ... and the upshot is that he's severely disabled.'

Oh. I put my imagination on hold and listened to the words instead. The '*hyuk hyuk*'s had stopped but I looked into Ken's dark eyes and they were positively shining. I put the chopsticks down.

'He's a good kid,' Ken continued, then corrected himself. 'He's a *great* kid. It's all going on up top, it's just physical. Then we had another boy, David, then two girls. They're all grown-up now, David has a great job and the girls are at Ohio State University.'

'You must be really proud,' I said, and we were only four kids in to a nine-kid story.

'I am,' said Ken, his chest swelling, 'but the thing is, when they moved out, Matthew started to lose some of his lustre. You see, he lives vicariously through others. When David came home from school and said he'd made the football team, that's what made Matthew come to life. And all of a sudden he didn't have that any more.

'We didn't know what was wrong for a while, but we missed having the kids around the whole time too, so after a while my wife and I started thinking; "What about Plan A? What about adopting?"

'The long and the short of it is: we adopted twin boys. Don't get me wrong, I'm not saying we're perfect people. I know I'm not. I've made mistakes and I know I'll make some more, but I gotta lot of love.

'Anyway, when the twins were the right age, we'd go out and tell them, "Matthew's in charge", and they all know there's nothing Matthew can *really do*, but they all get along, and everyone understands the situation and that boy, *that boy*, just started to blossom again. He just came back to life.

'And we've adopted three more. Nine kids and let me tell you, we're one *real* big, happy family.'

'What can I say?' I said, because it was the only thing I *could* say.

'I'll be honest,' said Ken, leaning forwards, 'there was a time when I thought I was the world's greatest dad. Now I know I'm not. I learn more from my kids than I can ever teach them … the only reason I have nine is because I'm a slow learner, *hyuk, hyuk, hyuk*.'

All of a sudden, for a brief moment, the conversation was

back *bada-boom-bada-boom-bada-booming* along.

I'd never met anyone like Ken before. I'm not sure there are that many people like Ken out there to meet. Not only was I impressed by what he'd said, but also by the fact that he'd said it. There's a vulnerability that goes with a story like that and it's not often I find myself in a Chinese restaurant with a vulnerable giant of a stranger.

Suddenly the idea of introducing googlewhacks into the conversation seemed somewhat crass. Ken seemed to be working on a higher plane to me. Now it would be like asking a girl to sleep with me on a first date when she's just told me how she's raising money for sick puppies with a charity celibate-athon. How could I expect Ken to find my need for two googlewhacks important?

But it *was* important. It was the only reason I'd come to Columbus so I had to ask him. But it couldn't come from nowhere. I had to find a way to steer the conversation towards the trivial.

We cracked open our fortune cookies.

'What you got?' I asked.

Ken looked at his fortune.

'You achieve great peace of mind when you talk to an old friend,' he said. 'Ha, I'd say it looks like the fortune cookies have promoted you to "old friend"! What about yours?'

I looked at my fortune and read it silently to myself. 'Be calm when confronting an emergency crisis.'

'It says, "Don't be afraid to ask a stranger for a favour",' I lied.

'So I guess you'll be wanting me to give you a ride back to the hotel?' laughed Ken.

'Yes please,' I smiled. This was my chance. I'd just go for it. I'd ask a man with a full life to waste his time putting random words into a search engine.

'Ken … you know how you're Bushranger Doublespeak …'

'Oh yeah; the googlewhack thing, I was wondering when you were gonna bring that up.'

'Do you think you could find me two new googlewhacks?'

'Sure!' he said. 'I'll have a go. Could be fun.'

It was as easy as that.

On the way back into the city I explained the google-whacking rules and Ken seemed confident that he'd find what I needed.

'D'y'know, I don't have a job right now,' he said as we pulled up outside the hotel, 'and in American society that makes me a loser. We live in a society that values material things, Dave, but I know there are more important things.'

We shook hands.

'I can think of nine,' I said, although I waited until Ken had driven round the corner before I said it.

At the start of our meeting I think I was guilty of prejudging Ken. My English sensibilities saw he was a flag-flying, cap-wearing, 'tache-sporting, four-wheel-drive-driving, man-of-a-certain-size and I thought I had him pegged as a particular kind of American. Probably the kind of American you see hollering in the audience of a *Help! I Get Teased about my Wild and Crazy Hair!* TV show. But I was wrong. Ken wasn't one of the crowd. He was no more an American stereotype than I was an English stereotype.

I went up to my room and made a nice cup of tea.

*

I'd only been back at the hotel for a couple of hours but I couldn't resist the temptation to get online and check my email. After all, in the time that had passed Ken could easily have found me a 'whack by now.

There was no email from Ken. But there was another email from Kelvin.

From: Kelvin (work)
To: Dave Gorman

Hi Dave,

I hope things have worked out with Bushranger Doublespeak. You said that every googlewhack could find you two others so I figure I still owe you one more. Here it is: Hippocampi Wallpaper.

All the best from all of the Welsh Rarebits ... or as you probably call us, the Rarebit Nutters.

Kelvin

nine

Hippocampi Wallpaper

Hippocampi   noun: plural of hippocampus, being

1. a sea horse; a marine teleost fish with a horselike head and a bony-plated body.
2. a mythological sea creature with the front legs of a horse and the tail of a fish.
3. part of the brain, that, in cross section resembles a sea horse.

Wallpaper   1. noun: paper designed for pasting on to walls or ceilings.

2. verb: to apply wallpaper (1).

This is a list of the things I knew about Seattle before I went there. It is the home of:

- The grunge music scene and its patron saint, the late Kurt Cobain.
- Anti-capitalist protests as witnessed by the World Trade Organisation Conference of 1999.
- The 1993 Tom Hanks/Meg Ryan romantic comedy, *Sleepless in Seattle*.
- The sitcom *Frasier*.
- The Space Needle. (A structure that looks like the space-age cartoon family *The Jetsons* might live there and that I only really recognise because its silhouette features prominently

in the opening titles to *Frasier*.)
- Lisa, Tom and Jonelle Edwards.

I'm slightly embarrassed, however, to reveal that I didn't know *where* Seattle was. It was (and indeed still is) in the North West of America in the State of Washington, which borders Canada to the North and the Pacific Ocean to the West, and which is completely different to the *city* of Washington, which isn't really in a state at all; it's in the *District* of Columbia. You probably knew that already.

Travelling to meet Hippocampi Wallpaper didn't advance my chain of googlewhacks any further. It was another second place 'whack just like Bushranger Doublespeak but the words of Christa were ringing in my ear: '*We need to attack on all fronts at all times, keep as many irons in the fire as we possibly can.*'

She seemed to possess great wisdom, Christa, and I respected her opinion. Except when it came to beards. And Snoopy. But I'd already had one chain fall apart at five in a row, halfway to victory, so I knew how easy it was for it all to go wrong. I was confident that Ken – Bushranger Doublespeak – would find me two googlewhacks and if I could persuade Hippocampi Wallpaper to do the same I would end up with four potential third place 'whacks. If they all came good, I would have eight potential fourth place 'whacks, which could lead to 16 potential fifth place 'whacks and, who knows, 512 potential tenth place 'whacks. The more chains I could keep alive, the better my chances of getting to ten.

So, when I read Lisa's email: '**We (we being my husband, Tom, 15-year-old daughter Jonelle, and I) are very amused by your quest and would love to be a part of it. It sounds like fun!**' I'd headed straight for the airport.

*

I looked at the door. A sign said 'No salesmen or peddlers.' It didn't say anything about googlewhackers so I rang the bell.

The door opened and Lisa, a big smile framed by frizzy black hair, was there to greet me: 'Hey! You must be Dave; come in!'

The first thing to strike me when I stepped into their front room was Mickey Mouse. There were Mickey Mouses all over the place. Or should that be Mickey Mice? Every spare inch of wall had been given over to a framed Disney print, large glass cabinets contained frightening amounts of Mickey Mouse memorabilia and three, two-foot tall Mickey figurines stood guard over the sofa. This was a shrine to Mickey Mouse. I swear I've been in Disney shops with less stock.

Maybe I should have expected this kind of Mickeyphilia; after all, the website that had led me there had featured Lisa's very thorough review of Tokyo Disneyland but no, it took my breath away. To be honest, even if someone had told me I was about to step into the living room of the world's biggest Mickey Mouse fan, I would still have been surprised by the amount of Mickey paraphernalia that confronted me. As you read this, I hope you're imagining a house full of the stuff. I promise you, there was more of it than you are currently imagining. Double it. You're still not there. I was shocked.

'You look shocked,' said Lisa with a giggle; I clearly wasn't the first person to react like this.

'It's just so … so … so … *Disney*!' I said.

'This?' said Lisa, her arm sweeping around the room, passing approximately 3542 images of the cartoon rodent. '*This* is nothing. I've seen people's houses with much more than *this*.'

'Yeah,' agreed Tom, a big, broad-shouldered man with a long blond surfer-dude's ponytail. 'I've seen places much worse than this.'

'What do you mean "much *worse*"?' asked Lisa.

'I mean *better*,' Tom corrected himself hurriedly. 'Not worse. *Better*.'

I must have looked a little sceptical because Tom was quick to add more.

'Some people make their house really plain and boring,' he

explained, 'but we think: "Fill it with stuff we like. It's just fun."'

Bless him, I thought, how sweet of him to understand and accommodate his wife's obsession.

'Why don't we head upstairs,' said Tom leading us in a procession. 'We can sit down and chat about this google-whacking thing.'

'OK,' I said, filing in on the end of the line.

Every step up brought the eye to a new Mickey portrait.

'The thing is,' said Lisa, 'if it wasn't Disney it'd be something else.'

'Like what?' I asked.

'Like *Star Wars*,' said Tom standing aside at the top of the stairs to usher me into their upstairs room.

'Oh my God!'

It just slipped out under my breath as I took in the more than liberal sprinkling of *Star Wars* paraphernalia.

'Oh my God!'

It happened again when I saw the TV screen.

In front of a comfy array of sofas was the biggest flat-screen TV I've ever seen. It must have been six feet wide. I guess most Americans would call this room a 'den'. Most Brits would call it a cinema.

'Nice, isn't it?' said Tom beaming with pride.

'Oh my God!' I said because the needle in my head had stuck on the phrase. 'That is an amazing telly!'

'Like I say,' said Tom, 'we fill our house with stuff we like.'

'So *you* like Disney,' I said to Lisa and, turning to Tom, '*you* like *Star Wars*.'

'Yeah,' they said in unison.

'So there are two obsessions fighting for control of the house?'

'Well, Jonelle loves *Beanie Babies*,' added Lisa, straight-faced.

'Three obsessions?'

'Yeah,' said Tom.

'But we all like each other's obsessions too,' said Lisa.

'When I die, I want all my Lego and *Star Wars* stuff to make a funeral pyre.'

'And I want to be cremated and sprinkled in Disney theme parks.'

'What does Jonelle want?' I asked.

'She thinks that's all a bit morbid,' dead-panned Lisa.

'So, tell us more about *your* obsession?' asked Tom.

'Well, I did once get a bit obsessed with my namesakes,' I confessed, 'but that was a while ago now and I'm over it—'

I stopped. I could feel the confusion filling the room and I found myself looking at two very blank faces. I saw Tom and Lisa exchange a quick glance of uncertainty.

'I think Tom was referring to your googlewhacking thing,' said Lisa.

'Oh *that*! I'm not obsessed with *that*,' I said, chuckling at the very idea. 'No. I just *need* you to find me a couple of googlewhacks, that's all.'

'Why don't we go to the computer and you can show us what you mean?' said Tom, standing.

Moments later we were at the computer and with R2D2 watching over us, I gave them a googlewhack demonstration.

'So, if I type in, say, bushranger and doublespeak like … so,' I said, 'and then I hit search …'

I hit the button and 0.2 seconds later Google was showing us the 'whack.

'Cool,' said Tom.

'Funny,' said Lisa.

I think they were suitably impressed. I pointed out the important features, the dictionary.com underlining and so on and then explained the process once a googlewhack had been found.

'So, if you visit this site, it takes you to a website belonging to …', I pressed the link and the site opened up, '… a certain Ken Fussichen, so as far as I'm concerned, Ken Fussichen *is* Bushranger Doublespeak.'

'And so then you go and *meet* him? Right?' asked Lisa,

feeling her way round the facts.

'Right,' I nodded.

'Cool,' said Tom.

'Funny,' said Lisa.

'Only I've already met him,' I explained. 'I'm just using Bushranger Doublespeak as an example. Obviously I'm hoping you two will find me two *new* googlewhacks.'

'OK.' Tom shrugged. He was obviously confident it wouldn't be a problem.

'When you find a 'whack all you need to do is email it to me,' I said. 'I check my email using mail2web.com, like … so,' a few deft keystrokes and I was there, '… and…'

I paused. My inbox was looking really full, but in the list of senders, one name stood out above all others. It wasn't Jake, although I could see his name a few times.

'What's up?' asked Tom.

'This might be a better example than I originally thought,' I said.

My heart started to beat a little faster as I clicked open the email from Ken Fussichen. Tom and Lisa leaned in to read over my shoulder.

From: Ken Fussichen
To: Dave Gorman

Hello Dave,

Well... I did it. I have two googlewhacks for you. I'm not sure how useful they're going to be, but here they are. Reticulated Soymilk and Bibliophilic Sandwiched.

Keep smilin'

Ken

I typed back a hasty 'thank you' and then went to work, checking out the two new prospects. Reticulated Soymilk was intriguing. It led to a very long address that began with www.rdi.ku.ac.th. The 'ac' told me that it was an academic site while the 'th' told me it was based in Thailand.

Further investigation revealed that it was *The Official Journal of Kasetsart University (Natural Sciences Dept.)* and that it was based in Bangkok. Intriguing.

I whizzed through the pages and discovered it was full of dense scientific facts. For example, there were several pages concerning 'histochemical detection of glycoconjugates in colonic epithelium of the goat', which is a scary sentence given that I don't understand many of the words involved and even more so because two of the words I do recognise are 'colonic' and 'goat'. There wasn't much in the pages of this journal that I understood and more annoyingly, there was no sign of an email address.

I sighed anxiously. I heard Tom and Lisa do the same. Reluctantly, I gave up and shifted my attention to Bibliophilic Sandwiched instead.

In bright red letters against a black background I found the following warning:

**THE MATERIAL ON THIS PAGE IS NOT SUITABLE
FOR EASILY OFFENDED PEOPLE OF ANY AGE, OR
MINORS. ALL CONTAIN REFERENCES TO, OR EXPLICIT,
MALE/MALE ROMANTIC SEXUAL INTERACTIONS.
DO NOT READ FURTHER IF YOU ARE LIKELY TO BE
OFFENDED BY SUCH MATERIAL OR IT IS ILLEGAL
FOR YOU TO VIEW IT.**

'This *is* legal in Seattle, right?'

'Uh huh,' came the reply.

Tom turned R2D2 round; there was no need for him to see this. I ploughed on. Seconds later I found an email address. I didn't bother looking further into the site. I hadn't seen any romantic interactions of any kind but I didn't need to; I'd found what I was looking for. A few seconds more and an email was winging its way to someone called Tritorella.

'You've got a lot of emails in your inbox,' said Tom. 'Feel free to spend some time online if you like.'

'I might delete a few from a guy called Jake,' I said.

I was about to do just that but, as I returned to my inbox, I was distracted by the presence of a freshly arrived email.

'Oh my God!'

It came from Tritorella. I clicked on the mail.

'Oh my gosh!' said Tom and Lisa together, leaning over my shoulder and witnessing, for the first time, the immediate results of a successful googlewhack.

Tritorella was 'happy to meet me.'

'Oh my good God!'

Tritorella lived in London.

Tom chuckled, 'I'll give you a lift to the airport if you like.'

'OK,' I said, beaming at him. He'd got the hang of it. 'Let's go!'

ten

Bibliophilic Sandwiched

Bibliophilic   adjective: descriptive of someone who is a
bibliophile; a lover of books.

Sandwiched   transitive verb: for one thing to be inserted
tightly between two others.

I didn't manage to get on a flight out of Seattle until around
eleven o'clock that night which meant I had to spend several
hours hanging around at the airport which meant that I could
now add the following fact to the list of things I knew about
Seattle: its airport smells of cinnamon. In fact, I'd go so far as
to say that it smells more of cinnamon than any other airport
in the world.

My flight took me first to Chicago where I made a
connection to Washington and then to Heathrow. None of
these airports had the faintest sniff of anything even remotely
spicy about them.

When we landed in London it was about ten o'clock at night
but which night I couldn't work out. The length of the flights
and the four different time zones involved were all too much
for my addled brain to calculate. Was it a day later or two? Or
had I just gone back an hour? It was all too confusing.

There was no point travelling all the way across London to
get to my flat, especially as the next 'whack was based in
Richmond. It would be easier to travel there from out west

than it would be to cross London twice. Besides, I didn't *feel* like I'd come home and I didn't want to trick myself into feeling that way by actually going there. I checked in to a Heathrow hotel instead. As far as I was concerned this was just the next leg of my journey and it just happened to be in London.

I may have been physically exhausted and mentally confused but I was very much awake. And I was very clearly focused on my goal, the next googlewhack.

As I checked into the hotel I looked up and saw seven or eight clocks telling the time in various cities around the world: LA, New York, Tokyo and so on. No doubt these were there to help keep the international businessmen who pass through the hotel in tune with the global marketplace or something like that. More importantly, they probably make the odd small-time sales rep feel like a bona fide international businessman.

My eye ran along the display trying to see which clock my body agreed with most. It didn't *feel* like it was any of *those* times in my world. I was no longer operating on anyone else's time frame. I'd started to exist in a time zone all of my own. From here on in I was on GMT: Gorman Manic Time.

Nevertheless I had to force myself to fit in with other people and I had a lunchtime appointment for the next day so I forced myself to go to bed. But no matter how hard I tried, sleep wouldn't take me and at 4 am I could be found still wide awake and staring blankly ahead at the bland hotel wall. I decided to use the time wisely instead. All I knew about my next googlewhack was that his website contained 'explicit, male/male romantic sexual interactions'. Wouldn't it be polite to take a proper look around the site, find out a bit more about the man I'd be meeting? I pulled on a pair of trousers and a T-shirt and made my way downstairs to the hotel's business centre.

As Tritorella's page was opening up I was startled by a polite cough. I turned to find the night porter standing in the doorway. The only light in the tiny room was cast by the computer screen which only served to make his elderly, craggy face look all the more craggy. He wore the shirt and tie of the hotel uniform but the corporate identity was undone somewhat by the faded, home-made tattoos that adorned the back of his liver-spotted hands. I didn't like to look at his hands; the thought of the needle puncturing his skin over and over and over again made my skin crawl.

'I'm sorry, sir,' he said, his voice as rough as sandpaper, 'I just heard a noise and came to see who it was. We don't normally have people using the computers at this time.'

'Well, I've got some very important business to attend to with … em … some clients,' I lied, 'in … em … somewhere.' Badly.

'Right you are, sir,' he said with an air of world-weary cynicism. He knew I was lying but he also knew it was his job to let me. 'Can I just see your room key, sir?'

I showed him my key, he thanked me and went on his way. As he left I stood and closed the door behind him. I turned back towards the computer and immediately saw that the words on the screen were clearly readable from this distance. They stood out somewhat, being big and bold and red.

THE MATERIAL ON THIS PAGE IS NOT SUITABLE FOR EASILY OFFENDED PEOPLE OF ANY AGE, OR MINORS. ALL CONTAIN REFERENCES TO, OR EXPLICIT, MALE/MALE ROMANTIC SEXUAL INTERACTIONS. DO NOT READ FURTHER IF YOU ARE LIKELY TO BE OFFENDED BY SUCH MATERIAL OR IT IS ILLEGAL FOR YOU TO VIEW IT.

I had no doubt that the night porter had been able to read this warning. Perfect. The man with love etched into the back of his right hand had doubtless gone away thinking I was about to make love to mine.

Without thinking I found myself striding through to reception, desperate to explain away what he'd just witnessed.

As I approached the desk the night porter put down his newspaper, raised his eyebrows expectantly and asked, 'Can I help you, sir?'

'Umm, I just wanted to say it's not what you think,' I said, unwisely choosing the one phrase guaranteed to make him think 'it' was precisely the thing he'd been thinking. 'Not that I know what you think, but I know what I'd think if I were you and it isn't that. So unless you were thinking it was a wholly innocent situation, which I admit it doesn't really look like, then you were wrong. Because it is. Innocent I mean. There's nothing untoward going on, you know, not that you'd …'

'It's OK, sir, I understand,' he said misunderstanding. 'You've got a lot of *"important business"* to attend to with *"some clients"*…'

His words positively dripped with meaning that didn't belong. I knew what he thought and it wasn't true. I would have to try a little harder to persuade him otherwise.

'No, actually, that was a lie,' I said. If my lies were making it worse I would go with the truth instead. 'I'm not conducting important business at all.'

My sudden rush of new-found honesty seemed to startle him.

'I think I knew that, sir, but you really don't need to tell me …'

'And I'm not in there to do *that* either,' I said firmly.

'Oh,' he said, confused, clearly unable to fathom another possibility.

'If you must know,' I said, '*all* I am doing in there is researching my next googlewhack. OK?'

'Yes sir.' He was still confused. 'You're *"researching"* your next *"googlewhack".*'

He spoke tentatively, placing the words carefully to see if they sounded like they belonged. He thought he knew what I'd been up to in the business centre and he wanted the words to make sense so the only way was to try and lend the words 'researching' and 'googlewhack' the euphemistic quality he thought they deserved. It didn't sound quite right and a look of confusion crept across his gnarled face.

Like a teacher wanting a student to get it right, I repeated the sentence but with the correct pronunciation. I placed no undue stress on any syllable. No word was quite so deliberately placed; it was clear that the sentence was a single entendre, if that:

'I'm researching my next googlewhack.'

This time he copied my intonation as well as my words.

'You're researching your next googlewhack,' he said, and knowing he'd got it right this time he gave himself a big smile.

'That's right,' I said. 'I'm glad we've got that clear.'

'Yes sir. Clear as day, sir.'

*

I was in a leafy suburb in a relatively affluent part of London, although the number of doorbells on each doorway gave away the fact that most of the big houses had long ago been converted into flats. I got out of the taxi and rang one of those doorbells.

I was a little nervous about meeting this latest 'whack. In fact, the more I'd seen of his website the more nervous I'd become. I was about to meet a writer of 'Highlander Fan Fiction'. That is, he was a fan of the *Highlander* TV series, so, using the pen-name Tritorella, he'd written a series of short stories using the show's characters. Oh, and there was quite a lot of gay sex involved.

I've never seen an episode of *Highlander* so I suppose it's possible that the TV show has that element of gay sex in it as well but somehow, I doubt it. I'm assuming the TV show is not too dissimilar to the *Highlander* movie, which I have seen – it stars Christopher Lambert as an immortal Scotsman while the immortal Scotsman Sean Connery plays an immortal Spaniard. I don't remember the two of them getting it on, but I did go to get popcorn part way through so you never know.

As it was, in the story I'd read last night at the hotel there had been quite a lot of that sort of thing. In just over 50 pages I read about the characters Duncan, Methos, Caspian and Kronos having sex in different pairings, none of which I can imagine making it on to American network television.

And all of this added to the unease I felt about meeting Tritorella. It wasn't the nature of his sexuality that made me nervous; it was simply the fact that I knew more about him than I care to know about a stranger. I'd have felt just as concerned if I'd looked at his website and found the message: *'Hello, my name's Brian and I like to make love with my wife in the missionary position. We do this three times a week, which I think you'll find is the national average.'* It's just too much information.

So, what kind of person would Tritorella turn out to be? I heard footsteps approaching the door and knew I was about to find out. The door opened and I found myself looking at a conservatively dressed man with sandy, ginger hair, glasses and a pair of white towelling house slippers.

'Hi, Tritorella?' I said, offering my hand.

'No. I'm her husband, Greg.'

He shook my hand and I made a rapid mental adjustment. None of my gay friends indulge in that kind of husband/wife role-play but each to their own.

'You must be Dave,' he said. 'Come in. Tritorella's upstairs getting lunch ready.'

We were halfway up the stairs to their flat when the peace was shattered.

'Oh, for fuck's sake!' screamed a voice from above and a procession of equally colourful words was quick to follow. The voice was loud, Australian … and female.

'That's her,' said Greg with a wry smile and a roll of the eyes.

Oh.

There I was wondering what kind of man spends his time writing stories about someone else's fictional characters having gay sex and the answer turns out to be a happily married, 40-year-old Australian woman who curses when she discovers her lasagne dish is too big for the microwave.

Once the dish/microwave issues had been resolved we sat down to a gorgeous vegetarian lasagne that came with unnecessary apologies from Tritorella: 'I don't think the leeks are cooked; we'll all be farting later!'

I think brash is the word.

The living room was painted the same bright yellow as my own and everywhere I looked there were similar touches. They even had the same curtain rails as me allowing them to hang two sets of curtains, the first a thin gauzy cotton just like my own. And like me, they'd had to make the best use of limited space. There were shelves wherever shelves could go and the living room had been pressed into service as both an office and a dining room too.

'Aha, trying to avoid going home,' said life, 'well, I'll do my best to remind you all the same.'

We were joined for the meal by Simone, a friend of Tritorella and a fellow writer of fan fiction. The two of them told me everything there was to know about the world of fan fiction, or fan-fic as it's inevitably known to aficionados.

There are three types apparently. *Gen-fic* is just simple, straightforward story writing. The other two types involve material of a sexual nature. *Het-fic* involves straight sex, and *slash-fic* involves gay sex. So if you wanted to write *Starsky & Hutch* fan-fic (and I'm reliably informed that hundreds of people do) then, if gen-fic is your thing you'd probably write a basic detective story starring the two all-action cops. If slash-fic is your bag you could have the two of them solving crimes while making out, but if you're more of a het-fic type you might have to get them double dating *Cagney & Lacey*. Slash-fic was the chosen genre for two of my dining companions. Greg, on the other hand, was a zoologist.

Beyond these three simple divisions there seem to be endless variations. Most people write about characters from the screen, others write about characters from literature while a small number write about real people too, maybe actors or members of bands.

'There's an awful lot of 'N-Sync fan-fic, for reasons I just *cannot* understand,' said Simone with a withering shake of the head.

The idea was clearly preposterous to her, which might seem a bit rich seeing as she writes stories in which the young Clark Kent and Lex Luther get jiggy.

'Yeah,' I agreed, 'weird!'

'Most people who write fan-fic, even slash-fic, tend to be women,' said Tritorella.

'Really?' I asked, bemused.

'Oh yeah. And highly qualified too,' added Simone.

'I've got three degrees,' said Tritorella and it took me a moment to realise she was talking about her qualifications not writing some girl on girl on girl action for the Seventies singing sensations.

As the conversation moved on Greg passed the odd insightful comment but mainly Tritorella and Simone held court. They were witty, they were articulate and with their enthusiasm they made the world of fan fiction make sense.

As far as I could work out it wasn't a sexual thing to either of them, although Tritorella explained that she had used her writing partly as a way of dealing with her own feelings towards a friend's sexuality. I'm not sure why she chose *Highlander* as a vehicle for this exploration. I can only presume that her friend is an immortal Scottish swordsman.

As Simone was handed the task of slicing the chocolate cake that followed, I explained my travels so far and the need for two more googlewhacks. Tritorella moved quickly to the sofa, placed her laptop on her knees and started conjuring up some unlikely words.

After a little while and a few near misses – each marked with an innovative new cuss – Tritorella suddenly declared, 'I've got one!'

I moved to the sofa to take a look and there it was: Actaeons

Wordplay. Both words were underlined and there was only one hit.

Actaeons wordplay led to another academic site, this time from a German university and the page, written in English, concerned the work of Elizabethan playwright Christopher Marlowe. The author of the page was named and an email address for the site's editor was listed. After the long distances I'd been travelling recently a trip to Germany would be child's play so I was eager to pursue it.

But I knew it was only fair that I allowed Tritorella to find googlewhack number two first. She was a talented 'whacker and it didn't take long before Dripstone Ingles showed its face and an email address was found.

Tritorella slid the laptop over to me and I clicked into my mail account. Immediately my excitement grew. There waiting for me was an email from Tom and Lisa in Seattle. I opened it up and yes, they'd found me their two googlewhacks.

All of a sudden I had four potential 'whacks on the go. As well as the German academic responsible for Actaeons Wordplay, Verandahs Plectrums meant there was a distinct possibility of a trip to Holland to meet the author of 'an ever-evolving site that is chock full of lesbian literature'. Dripstone Ingles, however, would take me back to the States to meet a creationist scientist while if Catnips Gargoyle came good it would test my resolve; the man responsible, a player of the dice-rolling fantasy game, Dungeons & Dragons, lived in Australia!

In an instant my googlewhacking world had become a world of many possibilities. I sent all four emails and hoped that one or more of them would yield a result.

Actaeons Wordplay bounced. But the other three did not.

I left Tritorella and Greg's home full of hope and lasagne. I took a taxi to Heathrow figuring that, whatever happened next, I would be taking a plane somewhere. I checked my email regularly, keen to know where I would be heading next. For several hours there were no replies. I started to worry. Was this it? Was it all over? Early that evening a reply finally came. Dripstone Ingles was on.

I'd missed the day's last flight to San Diego so I checked back into the Heathrow hotel from the night before. It was a cold January night, but the bed was warmed by my constant farting. Tritorella had been great company, but I think she was right about the leeks.

eleven

Dripstone Ingles

Dripstone noun: the form of calcium carbonate that exists in stalactites or stalagmites.

Ingles noun: plural of ingle; an archaic or dialect word for a fire in a room or fireplace.

With so many hours of air travel behind me I had somehow managed to acquire a sort of Zen-like calm about the whole flying experience. Lack of legroom had ceased to be uncomfortable, the air had stopped tasting stale and other people's elbows were no longer the enemy. Being on a plane wasn't odd any more; it had become the norm. I put my headphones on, closed my eyes and zoned out. I might have walked on to a 747 but once there I ascended to an astral plane all of my own.

Long after the plane had landed I too returned to planet earth. Today, I was in the sunny climes of San Diego. By rights, I should have been mentally and physically wiped out by the rigours of travel but instead I felt energised and focused. Adrenaline was coursing through my veins; I was feeding on the energy of the task itself.

A dollar and fifty cents bought me a bus ride from the airport to the city centre. From there I took the tram, or trolley as it's known to the locals, past trailer parks full of cheap homes and expensive cars, out to the small town of Santee, home of the Institute for Creation Research and therefore the home of Duane T. Gish, PhD, aka Dripstone Ingles.

Santee is at the end of the line and the trolley deposits you at what is basically a big out-of-town shopping complex; a cluster of warehouse-size shops and an enormous parking lot. I was a little early for my appointment so I took the chance to slip into a branch of Old Navy and buy some clean underwear. (By the way, Old Navy is a regular high street clothes store in the States, selling things at the (exceedingly) cheap and (quite) cheerful end of the market. I don't want you to think I was buying used underpants from retired sailors.) I dumped my dirty underwear in a nearby litter bin. It didn't seem quite right but I wasn't taking them with me and I didn't know what else to do with them.

I rang the offices of the ICR to ask for directions and was pleasantly surprised when I was put through to Dr Gish himself who then offered to come and pick me up in person. He spoke slowly and deliberately, his voice reedy with the sibilant whistle that comes with old age.

I'm not sure why, but I hadn't expected him to be particularly old. I was already expecting this to be a difficult encounter. I wasn't expecting to share much common ground with Dr Gish and now, in discovering the generation gap between us, I knew there was even less.

Normally when meeting a googlewhack my expectations would be shaped by the emails we'd exchanged. There might be only one or two but it would be enough for me to glean some kind of insight into their personality. I'd had no direct contact with Dr Gish at all; what contact I'd had was with his secretary.

No, my expectations of Dr Gish were based on one simple fact. I might not have known what he was like as a person but he was a senior figure at the Institute for Creation Research, so I knew that I fundamentally disagreed with him.

As you might guess from the name, the Institute for Creation Research is a creationist organisation. This means they argue *against* the theory of evolution, preferring to believe that the earth was created by a supernatural being. At least that's how they phrase it when they try to present it as a scientific argument rather than a fundamentally Christian one – because essentially it always seems to boil down to a particularly zealous and literal interpretation of the Bible. They believe that mankind was created, that we are the great grandchildren of Adam and Eve, not Bobo the chimp.

In parts of America there is a powerful lobby group in favour of creationism and alarmingly, they have won some victories. Some American schools have banned the teaching of evolutionary theory. I find it impossible to believe that the children affected have not had their education harmed as a result.

But of course I would say that, wouldn't I? Because I'm a product of an education system that teaches evolutionary theory. Like anyone else who's been through the British school system, Darwin's ideas on evolution are lodged in my brain as incontrovertible facts. Just as I know that William the Conqueror invaded Britain in 1066, the Great Fire laid London to waste in 1666 and Miranda Mcleod would put out on a first date (OK, one of these might have been specific to my school) so I know that, in nature, the fittest survive and they pass their winning attributes on to their children and so, over several millennia, species evolve.

The theory of evolution is placed so firmly in our consciousness that anyone who doesn't believe in it inevitably appears to be a crank. Of course, if you take a suspected crank and serve them up with a side salad of religion, not unnaturally, the world tends to recoil.

I'm no expert, but insofar as the arguments have trickled down to mainstream media this would be my understanding, complete with the prejudices of my education, of the two points of view.

Evolutionists say: this is our theory to explain the way the world is. We've got a lot of fossils, we've done a lot of carbon dating and it all fits in with our theory. Cool, huh?

Creationists say: my, the world is an amazingly beautiful place, isn't it? Look at how well it works. And *we're* here! Aren't we great: people? I mean there's no way any of this *just happened* is there? It can't have done. No, no, no. Someone pretty special must have come up with this. Evidence? You want evidence? Oh … right … well, look, it must be true, it says so in the Bible.

What strikes me as particularly odd about this is that, to my mind, the two views don't seem quite so incompatible. I'm not a religious person myself but plenty of eminent scientists have a faith in God so presumably, somehow they manage to square the two. All you really need to do is accept that the Bible is a piece of literature and, as such, is full of poetry, allegory, metaphor and so on. People often forget that Charles Darwin himself was a theologian.

If memory serves, the Bible says it all started with God saying 'Let there be light' while the conventional scientific view says there was a Big Bang. I don't see any argument there. Big Bang? Check. Lots of light? Check. Yup, everything seems to be in agreement so far.

Now, according to the Bible things were created in this order: water, land, plants, fish, animals, man. I think that's pretty much what evolution says too. All you have to do is find a poetic interpretation of the word 'day' so that *'on the second day'* reads as *'and then what happened is'* and the two camps seem to agree on quite a lot of the broad strokes. If anything this serves to make the Bible seem *more* real to me, not less. If I wanted to make a case for religion I'd be pointing out how thousands of years after the Bible was written, scientists using the latest technology have proved what the good book was saying all along. Instead the creationists seem to be throwing their toys out of the pram because it turns out creation probably didn't happen in only six days.

All this was running through my head as I stood at the Santee Trolley Station waiting for Dr Gish to arrive and, as you can see, I had some preconceptions, ill-informed prejudices if you like, about his beliefs and therefore about him. I thought creationism to be narrow-minded, wrong-headed, dogmatic poppycock. But I didn't care, *as long as he found me some googlewhacks.*

To that end, I had a plan. Presumably his secretary, Mary, had explained the reason for my visit so he would have a rudimentary understanding of my googlewhacking needs. If we had to get into a discussion about creationism I would try to ensure it happened *after* the googlewhacking had been completed. If we talked about it beforehand and I revealed my own views on the subject we might fall out with each other and if that happened he might not even be prepared to try and whack his Google for me.

I carefully eyed every car that pulled into the parking lot, looking for the kind of car that would be owned by an elderly, narrow-minded, wrong-headed, dogmatic poppycock believer. When his car did eventually roll in I somehow knew that this was my man. The car seemed to be as big as a house. It was so long that the front end had turned through 180 degrees before the back end had left the main road. It drove directly towards me and for a moment it looked as if no one was driving but as it got a bit closer I could see a pair of eyes peeping over the steering wheel like a little chipmunk. Here was a very small man in a very big car.

'Ah, Dr Gish I presume?' I presumed as the car pulled to a halt.

People have been presuming aloud about doctors for a long time now and I don't like to buck the trend.

'Mister Gorman?'

As we cruised down the big, straight, wide Californian roads it became clear that either Mary had failed to pass on the nature of my visit or Dr Gish had failed to take in the details. Either way, it was obvious that he thought I was there for the specific purpose of learning about creationism. I guess that's what most people who visit him do and at 81 years of age it's no surprise that he assumed I was there for the same reason.

'So, what first got you interested in the subjick of creation?' he asked, his breath whistling through his teeth.

With his diminutive stature, chipmunk eyes and whistling, teeth-clacking speech I remember thinking he was kind of cute. But creationism had just landed on the agenda and my plan was flying out of the window so I didn't have time for thoughts like that.

'To be honest,' I said, scrabbling to steer the plan back on course, 'I'm not really here to learn about creation. I came because you wrote an article on your website that contained a googlewhack and I was hoping you'd be able to find me a …'

I'd lost him. At the mere hint of my lack of interest his brow furrowed. At the mention of googlewhacking his chipmunk eyes clouded over with confusion. This wasn't what he expected. I was speaking googlewhacking gobbledegook and the data just didn't compute. Just as my computer sometimes freezes when it's confused, so Dr Gish seemed to freeze at that moment. His head was cocked at a slight angle, his expression was unchanging and he said nothing for an uncomfortably long time. Luckily the road was straight and wide.

'I mean, obviously, I am interested in the subjick of creation as well,' I said, hurriedly abandoning honesty. 'It's just that I only encountered the subjick…' (damn that wandering accent, stop it, stop it, stop it!) '… when I saw your website recently.'

That seemed to do the trick. Dr Gish's head straightened up, his brow unfurrowed and his eyes cleared. I'd successfully rebooted my host. Just in time too, as the entrance to the ICR arrived moments later. We cruised in and parked up.

I sat in a comfy chair in Dr Gish's book-lined office and he sat across the table from me. Several books authored by my host were placed on the table in front of me and Dr Gish set about extolling the virtues of creationism. I had no choice but to revert to plan B. I would allow Dr Gish to teach me his views on creation. And I wouldn't argue. I would listen to it all with wide-eyed innocence, I would nod, I would agree, I would take it all on board. I would do this for as long as it took. Later on, when I was convinced that Dr Gish regarded me as a friend, I would segue the conversation into googlewhacking. That way, I figured, we would both go away from the encounter with our desires fulfilled. He would go away believing that another mind had been persuaded to his cause and I would go away knowing that this chain of 'whacks continued.

Dr Gish began by explaining his background (he's a highly qualified scientist with a doctorate in biochemistry from the world-renowned University of California in Berkeley) and while he talked I picked up one of the books in front of me. It was face down, but I read the opening paragraph of the back-cover blurb with delight.

This sequel to Dr Gish's influential book, *Evolution: The Fossils Say No!* (first published in 1973), is now bigger and better than ever!

What a fantastic title that is: *Evolution: The Fossils Say No!*!! It seems more reminiscent of a 1950s B-movie than an academic textbook on the subject of creation. Say it aloud to yourself, say it in a big booming Orson-Welles-playing-God voice and it sounds fantastic. I liked it. It displayed a sharp mind and a common touch that I found endearing. I was still convinced that the message contained therein was cock of the poppiest variety but I had to admire the man who could package it in such appealing terms.

I looked up at Duane T. Gish and did a bit more nodding as he explained his beliefs further.

'... if the Big Bang is true and we all start off as hydrogen gas and by natural processes the universe has evolved and life formed by evolution and so forth and so on then who needs God you see and many people conclude there is no God. Well, I was convinced otherwise and I believe that the teaching of evolution as a fact in our schools and colleges has had a profound effect on American society because it has changed tremendously in the last 60 years ...'

I looked back down at the book in my hands. The *sequel* to *Evolution: The Fossils say No!* If the original had such a compellingly brilliant title, what had he called its sequel? I was excited to find out.

'... since that time I've lectured in 49 of our 50 states, most provinces of Canada and about 40 different countries. I've had about 300 debates with evolutionists mostly held on university campuses or schools or auditoriums, sometimes in churches ...'

I turned the book over to see the title. It was brilliant.

'... I've spoken all over the world and in my own country on the subjick...'

EVOLUTION: The Fossils STILL Say NO! A small snicker escaped my lips but I managed to pass it off as a bit of a cough. It was brilliant; quite, quite brilliant.

'... We're not a theological organisation, we are scientists...'

I could barely contain my glee. *The Fossils STILL Say NO!*! A stroke of genius to be sure! This man had asked the fossils in 1973 and they'd told him evolution hadn't happened. Years later he's gone back and the fossils have said, 'Look, we told you last time!' I was in the presence of genius. Cuddly, old, wrong-headed genius maybe, but genius nonetheless.

'... We are depending upon our scientific facts for our strength for our position. We are a Christian organisation but I've been invited to Turkey to speak to Muslims. Our main thrust is scientific ...'

As Dr Gish moved from explaining his background and into the scientific theory both for creation and against evolution, I picked up a copy of another one of his publications. If I was to keep myself from laughing I had to find something else to look at. This time I held a small pamphlet, around three by five inches in size and about 30 pages long. The front cover was bright orange and featured a drawing of six heads progressing from a chimp at the far left to a man at the far right. But in case you think the pamphlet was suggesting this journey had taken place, the title begged the question: 'Have You Been

The Agent, Rob (left) and the Publisher, Jake (below). I suspect this was the first literary deal ever agreed on the basis of the author's facial hair.

Cheers!

Warren (back row in white roll-neck) and the Boston nice party

A woman and a dog

Dave Gorman (left), meets Dave Gorman (right).

David, Danielle – my saviours in Washington.

A teeny Christmas google.

With Nene and Corrie in Holland – exactly as the wishbone had predicted.

Ken

Jerry

Tom and Lisa. And Mickey and Goofy.

Seattle
Space
Needle

Dr Duane T. Gish.
'Smile please'

Julie, my Los Angeles angel.

Byron Reese.

What the ..?!

In a hut near Memphis, a brilliant new boy band is formed.

China.

Being licked by
Cang Xin, Chinese
performance artist.

China. By a wall.

Happy, happy birthday to me. By the Sydney Harbour bridge.

Brainwashed?' The back revealed it was published by Gospel Tract Distributors and that a copy could be ordered for only 25 cents. (If you're interested in spreading the word yourself, you can bulk buy a hundred of them for the bargain price of $15.) This was publishing more interested in spreading the word than making money, more interested in prophets than profit.

I opened the pamphlet to see it was laid out in comic book style and took in the first few frames. Some young, attractive, clean-cut students at the University of California were thinking of attending a lecture on the subject of creation vs evolution.

'I think it would be a good idea. I've really been confused on the subject of evolution,' says one, no doubt reflecting the voice of American youth. In the bottom right-hand frame the visiting lecturer was concerned about whether or not there would be a crowd. The name of the visiting lecturer? Dr Gish.

Brilliant! He'd written a cartoon pamphlet starring himself! Not that I recognised him from the pictures. The Dr Gish before me was considerably shorter than my five feet nine inches, he had a small pot belly and a round, cuddly face. Yet in his cartoon incarnation he had strong, rugged good looks, broad shoulders and an impressive jaw. He appeared to have cast Ben Affleck as himself. I stroked my beard as if fascinated. I rested my index finger on my bottom teeth and bit down hard on the knuckle. It was the only way I could stop myself from laughing while maintaining a dignified, 'interested' presence.

The pamphlet was making me laugh so I looked at Dr Gish instead. I stared intently at him and his neatly coiffed hair but found myself having to bite down harder on my knuckle when, through his grey thatch, I swear I could see the stretched fabric that gave it away as a wig.

The rugged Gish of the pamphlet and the rug-ed Gish before made me think he was a man of great vanity. Which shouldn't have surprised me because the creationist viewpoint seemed to be one of great vanity too. The world, it said, was so beautiful, things were so perfect and all this has been given to *me*! This must be the work of God!

It's like a lottery winner thinking it was bound to happen to him, when the truth is, it was bound to happen to *someone*.

But that's what Dr Gish and his creationist literature seemed to be telling me. Underpinning it all was an inability to see oneself as *part of* the chance and randomness. Yes, the chances of life evolving as a result of a big explosion that spilled hydrogen and helium into the universe are billions upon billions to one. But the universe is infinite. How many billions upon billions upon billions of such explosions have occurred? Besides, just because something is a squillion to one chance it doesn't mean it can't happen. I should know because a one in three billion chance called Marcus once sat in my living room and took a one in three billion chance that led to a man called Dave Gorman. If that can happen, surely anything can!

In spite of my cynicism for the subject, I am alarmed to say that Dr Gish was an incredibly persuasive speaker on the matter. He explained that billions of fossils for sophisticated life forms were found in rock from the Cambrian period but that no fossils for simpler ancestors were found in Pre-Cambrian rocks. Essentially, he explained that there was no fossil record showing a transitional animal, part way between one simpler and one more complex life form. If there's no evidence to show these creatures had ancestors, does it not follow that they must have arrived on this earth fully formed? Were they created? It was a powerful argument and I could feel myself falling under his spell. Perhaps the fossils had indeed said 'No'!

I turned a few more pages of the pamphlet and saw a picture of a fish and a lizard. I read the accompanying text: *'Evolutionists claim that it took perhaps 50 million years for a fish to evolve into an amphibian. But again there are no transitional forms. For example, not a single fossil with part fins, part feet has ever been found.'*

Was that possibly true? What about the coelacanth? The

book, *A Fish Caught in Time* was still fresh in my mind. The coelacanth was a prehistoric fish. It had fins that were described as almost limb-like. Many scientists believed it to be the missing link that Dr Gish's pamphlet was saying didn't exist. Could Dr Gish be lying to me?

Perhaps I should have raised the question of the coelacanth. Perhaps he could have explained it away. But I didn't raise the question. I wasn't here on a quest for truth and good science. I was hunting my next googlewhack and today nothing else mattered.

*

The Second Law of Thermodynamics

In a closed system, all things tend towards entropy.

You may not have been expecting that to pop up in a light-hearted travel adventure, but I feel it appropriate at this time to introduce a note of science. The Second Law of Thermodynamics, also known as 'The Entropy Law', is a fundamental law governing the way the world works. Some of you may be familiar with it in other forms. For example, Flanders and Swann, the musical comedians of the 1950s and '60s phrased it rather differently in their song 'The First and Second Laws of Thermodynamics':

Heat won't pass from a cooler to a hotter
You can try it if you like but you far better notter.
[...]
And all the heat in the universe
Is going to cool down so it can't increase
Then there'll be no work and there'll be perfect peace.
Really?
Yeah, that's entropy man.

That might not be helping, but it means pretty much the same thing and I guess the point is that I'm indebted to Messrs Flanders, Swann and Coop for the fact that it is still hanging around in my brain. (Mr Coop taught Physics at Walton High School, Stafford when I was a boy, incidentally.)

Now that I've started this alarming scientific digression I feel myself haunted by the sound of books closing. Don't worry reader, I'll be quick. We can take 'entropy' to mean 'disorder', so essentially the law says that all things tend to become more disordered and chaotic ... *in a closed system*. The 'closed system' bit is important.

To quote the law without that bit means nothing. It would be like saying 'It is illegal to buy alcohol in Britain' when the law actually states that it's illegal to buy alcohol in Britain if you're *under 18 years of age*. Unless you quote every clause of the law, you run the risk of looking stupid.

So ... what does the 'closed system' bit mean? Well, if you put an apple in a dustbin and leave it there it will eventually rot. In other words it becomes more disordered and chaotic. The apple is in a closed system, it gets eaten by bacteria and eventually the bacteria die and decay themselves, leaving the dustbin with nothing more than goo.

However, if instead you put the apple in the ground – and the conditions are right – something new will emerge. It will grow, it will thrive, it will bear fruit. It will become *more* ordered and *less* chaotic, grabbing atoms from the atmosphere and the soil to construct a complicated, ordered structure otherwise known as an apple tree. This happens because this apple isn't in a closed system because the sun shines, the rain falls and the earth nourishes.

I mention this because, even with my basic high school understanding of this fundamental physical law, I was aware that the highly qualified scientist sitting in front of me didn't seem to have a grasp of it at all.

There I was, biting my knuckle, when he suddenly threw in the following curve ball: 'Evolution [...] is an *absolute violation* of the Second Law of Thermodynamics […] if you have simplicity it cannot transform itself upwards into the system we have today.'

Whether or not you've followed my amateurish explanation of the Second Law of Thermodynamics you should know this. What Dr Gish said about it was not true. He had either chosen to ignore the 'closed system' bit or perhaps he had chosen to define the world wrongly as a 'closed system' in which case he was ignoring the presence of the vast universe that surrounds us. As it goes, the universe as a whole is obeying the Law perfectly well thank you very much in that it is expanding and cooling down. What happens on our speck of a planet is, in the grand scheme of things, irrelevant.

Either Dr Gish had spent his entire scientific career failing to understand the Second Law of Thermodynamics or he had chosen to deliberately misrepresent it to lay people like myself in an attempt to back up an argument he must have known it was flawed. I was convinced in that moment that he was deliberately telling me lies.

This was the first moment in which I was aware of thoroughly disliking any of the googlewhacks I'd met. Until that moment Gish may have seemed like a vainglorious, faintly ridiculous old man, but he had still been a cuddly, old-fashioned, well-mannered, cartoonishly physiqued old man with a passionate belief in something and I'd found him endearing for all of that.

Now I really believed he was a liar.

I found myself not liking Dr Gish but I didn't like myself for not liking him. Liking people is far easier and much more fun than not liking them. I *wanted* to like him. I *needed* him to like me. I started trying to persuade myself that I'd misheard him. Maybe I wasn't following the argument properly; after all, *he was* the qualified scientist, not me. Maybe he'd said it properly and my cynical attitude had caused me to hear a lie where there was none?

I lowered my gaze and pretended to study the pamphlet in my hands. But my eyes immediately landed on the words 'The

Second Law of Thermodynamics'. There it was being miscon-strued again, this time in his printed literature. It wasn't just me. I hadn't misheard him. It wasn't even a slip of his tongue. No, I didn't like this preposterous old man. Now everything he said seemed ridiculous.

I reached across the table and picked up a different book. A big book, big enough to hide my face behind. This was a hardback book, aimed at kids, the same size as the *Beano* annual that would be in my Christmas stocking each year as a kid (and as a grown-up).

The Amazing Story of Creation from Science and the Bible by Duane T. Gish, PhD. I opened it at a random page and immediately had to bite my tongue. There was a picture of an animal: half cow, half whale. The front half was a cow, with legs, hooves and horns while the back half was a whale with a tail and fins and so on. The caption read: *'Transitional forms would have been extremely vulnerable in either of the worlds they theoretically were bridging.'*

Well, he was quite right! Had the *whalecow* tried to live in the oceans it probably would have drowned with its cow lungs! Had it tried to live on land it probably would have been eaten by a predator with its lack of hind legs and big flapping tail! You can't use a fictitious, nonsensical 50/50 whalecow as an argument against evolution. No-one has ever suggested that such a creature ever existed.

I began to feel frightened. Frightened of laughing. If Dr Gish said another word or I turned another page I was in danger of laughing it all back into his pudgy little face. If that happened, there would be no way of persuading him to whack his Google. I had to contain myself. I had to move the conversation on to the more sensible realm of googlewhacking. Behind the big pages I took in some deep breaths.

'Well, this is all very fascinating, Dr Gish,' I said. 'You've given me a lot to think about there. But really, the reason I came was in the hope that you'd be able to find me a couple of googlewhacks…'

He stared blankly at me. I rephrased it.

'The other thing … just as a favour … you know that I'm here because I put the words dripstone and ingles into a search engine … Google … and I'm hoping to have a … kind of chain reaction where you find another two words and …'

I wasn't getting through. His eyes were clouding over again. Maybe I could show him a googlewhack and explain it that way.

'Could we possibly get on a computer together …'

His eyes brightened.

'We have a … er … an email … er … a website,' he said. There was hope in his voice. He wanted to help me and he thought this might be what I was after.

'Yes … yes, I know you have, Dr Gish,' I said, tiptoeing my way through the logic. 'One of the reasons I'm here is because someone else found a googlewhack on your website …'

'… our site… is er … my email… I can give you our computer … our … er website. The number … is … ah … www er … dot … icr … er … dot o. r. g.'

The language of the internet didn't sit well with Dr Gish's clacky teeth. It was obvious that he wasn't au fait with the big wide world of the world wide web. He was 81 years of age. His secretary had replied to my email. He didn't want to sit at a computer so I wasn't able to demonstrate what a googlewhack was.

Of course there's no reason why I should expect an 81-year -old to know his way around the internet and I'm not picking on him because of the apparent bewilderment with which he views the new technology that surrounds him. But it does go some way to illustrate how difficult a message it was for me to convey.

Trying to explain what googlewhacking was to Dr Gish was about as difficult a piece of communication as I've ever attempted. Imagine telephoning your grandmother and trying to explain to her how to set a video recorder. Now imagine that the connection is bad and the telephone is crackly. Now imagine that your grandmother doesn't have a video recorder. Now imagine that sitting beneath her telly is a cake. A cake baked into the shape of a video recorder. *That's* how difficult a message this was to convey. It was impossible. I tried. I failed.

'Thank you for your time, Dr Gish,' I said, my teeth gritted.

'You're very welcome,' he said, his clacky.

And so the man who didn't believe in evolution had stopped my chain of googlewhacks from evolving. Rarebit Nutters begat Bushranger Doublespeak begat Bibliophilic Sandwiched begat Dripstone Ingles and there the chain died.

We shook hands and I walked out of his office. I passed the offices of other scientists, I passed a wall with six paintings, each depicting one of the days of creation and I emerged into a warm and glorious Californian evening. The sun was fading but the earth had stored up a day's heat and I could feel it gently rising through the soles of my feet.

I walked away from the ICR defeated. I passed the local gun store with its sign proudly boasting 'Under New Management!' and before long I found myself a small motel for the night. Fifty or so rooms clustered around a small pool. I was the only person in all of California not driving a car so a quick survey of the parking lot showed me there were only eight other residents that night. It wasn't expensive.

It would have taken me forty minutes to put the dreary suburb of Santee behind me. Forty minutes and I could have been in the vibrant heart of San Diego. But I didn't have the stomach for it. My chain of 'whacks was over, my morale was low. A paltry four in a row! I didn't deserve San Diego. I walked to the 7-11 store and bought myself some bad food: a meal that involved boiling a kettle, and a bottle of cheap wine. I opened the wine, sat by the pool and watched the sun setting. Behind the distant mountains the night sky glowed a magnificent firey red. A glorious view but small comfort.

And yet, I supposed, there was hope. OK, that chain might have died, but another chain was still alive. Rarebit Nutters had begat Bushranger Doublespeak who begat Bibliophilic

Sandwiched who begat Dripstone Ingles who begat bugger all, but Rarebit Nutters had also begat Hippocampi Wallpaper who begat both Verandahs Plectrums and Catnips Gargoyle. Emails had been sent and I was still awaiting the replies. I had to hope that there was more googlewhack-begatting to be done.

If not… well, if not; the journey was over. I'd have to go back home. For the first time in a while I thought about Jake. They say an optimist's glass is half full while a pessimist's is half empty. I poured myself a full glass of wine.

twelve

Verandahs Plectrums

Verandahs   noun: plural of verandah; a porch or
                    balcony extending along the outside of a
                    building. Normally roofed.

Plectrums   noun: plural of plectrum; a small piece of
                    plastic, metal, bone or similar, used to
                    pluck the strings of a guitar or similar
                    instrument.

On 2 March 1987 my father cooked a roast chicken dinner to celebrate the 16th birthday of me and my twin brother, Nick. The two birthday boys had wrapped our scrawny little pinkie fingers around either branch of the wishbone and pulled. The bone broke in my favour and I kept my wish silent in the hope that it would come true.

Nearly 16 years later, in January 2003, I found myself en route to Holland to hang out with a couple of lesbians. Odd the way life works out if you give it time.

Sneek (which the Dutch sneakily pronounce 'snake') is a tiny town in the north of Holland. It's in the Friesian region which is famous for its cows. Actually, that's a guess, but relax, I'm not trying to write a guidebook, but it *is* called the Friesian region so there has to be some kind of cow connection.

I didn't plan on spending very long in Sneek. Even Nene, the woman I was set to meet, had told me there wasn't a lot to see here so I figured once I'd got a couple of 'whacks from her I'd return to Amsterdam for the night and work out my next trip from there. That way I'd be able to indulge in some less cow-based fun as well.

I'd never been to Holland before but my first impression was good. I bought a sandwich from a fast food restaurant at the train station. It wasn't a special sandwich, in fact it was pretty much what you expect to find at a train-station fast-food outlet and yet it did possess one truly remarkable quality: it looked exactly like the picture that was displayed above the counter.

Wherever else I've been in the world it seems to be standard practice in these so-called restaurants to display pictures of food that look at least three times better than the corresponding item in real life. It might entice you, but it inevitably leaves you feeling disappointed when the fresh, juicy, plump item you plumped for turns out to be a stale, dry and limp imitation. Not in Holland, where the picture accurately depicts the thoroughly average and dull sandwich on offer. It's less enticing to be sure, but I left feeling satisfied that I'd got what I paid for. My expectations weren't dashed on the rocks simply because they were never raised high enough.

That seemed to sum up Holland for me. Nothing was spectacular, but everything did what it said it would do. The trains seemed as dirty and smelly and poorly maintained as British trains and the journey from Amsterdam to Amersfort to Leeuwarden to Sneek seemed to take an inordinately long time, but that was OK because the timetable said it would.

Sneek itself was beautiful. It was early evening when I got there and the light was drawing in, but a light dusting of snow was adding a highlight to the small turrets and spires of the old and ornate architecture and a comforting crunch underfoot. A huge watertower dominated the skyline looking like *Chitty Chitty Bang Bang*'s Caractacus Potts had turned his mind to designing a redbrick space rocket. In the sixteenth century the town had been a fortress waterport and what looked like a tiny fairytale castle was still standing over the waterway to the old town.

Beyond this the roads grew progressively smaller and more crooked. As I walked along the narrow lanes there were times when it seemed the sky had disappeared and I was alone with my frosty breath but I knew I was closing in on my target.

I knew Nene's partner Corrie was an artist. She sold her paintings from a small artist's studio in the old part of Sneek and the two of them lived in an apartment above the studio.

As well as their apartment the two shared a space on the world wide web and from my look around their site I was familiar with Corrie's painting style: funny portraits of round-bellied, round-faced figures made with a clean line and bold colours in acrylic and ink. When I found a collection of these on small 10 cm square blocks of wood staring out at me from a window I knew I'd found the home of Verandahs Plectrums.

Nene welcomed me in. She had short, wispy blonde hair, a round face, a button nose and a big smile.

'Come on in,' she said. I was surprised to hear an American accent, one with a hint of a soft Southern, *Gone With The Wind* drawl. 'Be careful on the stairs, they're a bit steep.'

I clambered up behind her on the stairs that were more than 'a bit steep'. Any steeper and it would have been a ladder. I gripped the banister tightly but it felt like it was just as likely to come away in my hand as it was to offer me any stability.

We emerged in a tiny living room-cum-kitchen. Actually it was more of a kitchenette. Come to think of it, it was more of a living-roomette too. It was *tiny*. And it was full. Full of homely clutter but also occupied by three people (Nene, Corrie and me), one dog (Mo), two guinea pigs (Elvis and Muk), six zebra finches (Coco and Babette and their four offspring Lola, Trudy, Boppi and Flo) and two computers.

I'd like to say that the zebra finches were proof of evolution; some hybrid as strange as Gish's fictional whalecow, a stepping stone on the evolutionary journey from finch to zebra but, disappointingly, they're all finch and no zebra. I examined Boppi, Lola, Trudy and Flo.

'Is Boppi a boy's name?' I asked.

'Yeah,' said Corrie, a mop of curly dark hair atop another smiling round face and button nose combination, but with a Dutch accent.

'They all look the same to me,' I confessed. 'Which one is the male?'

'They're all male,' said Nene.

'Before they got their adult plumage we thought three of them were female,' added Corrie.

'It doesn't matter though. They're all gay anyway,' said Nene.

'Sometimes they're just gangbanging away!' said Corrie

'Boppi, Lola and Flo take it in turns to hump Trudy,' said Nene, 'like some spur of the moment orgy.'

'But they groom him and feed him so he gets something out of it,' said Corrie with a shrug.

'The feathered slut,' said Nene. A phrase that brought out the Scarlett O'Hara in her accent.

Any plans I'd had to return to Amsterdam were soon forgotten, I was enjoying the company too much for that. Nene and Corrie shared one mind, but what a lovely, funny, chatty mind it was.

They had a nice way of picking up each other's stories and sharing the telling. If I closed my eyes, it was only the change of accent that gave away the change in speaker; the tone of voice, manner and timing seemed to be that of a unit. They'd shared that tiny living space for five years so I suppose life had forced them to integrate every aspect of their lives completely.

The two of them had met on the internet, an idea that summons up a mental image of fat, insecure male menopausees and their resigned-to-the-fact Thai brides, but nothing could be further from the truth here.

Nene is a writer and she'd been posting her fiction online. In fact, having only just discovered the genre of fan fiction, I was amazed to discover that, while Nene now penned her own entirely original work, she had been a part of the fan-fic world too, her chosen fandom being *Xena, Warrior Princess*. (I wonder how Dr Gish would feel if he knew he was the meat in a gay and lesbian fan fiction sandwich?)

Corrie had discovered Nene's writing and written to say that she liked her work and they'd struck up a correspondence. They quickly discovered that they had a lot in common, a shared love of Mel Brooks's movies and big band music for instance, and before long their emails contained love poetry.

The two fell in love long before they met, but then the one thing they didn't share was geography. Corrie is from Sneek, Nene from the US. They started planning to meet one Valentine's Day but it was May when Corrie finally ventured to the States.

'I went with knees knocking and sweating bullets; I was very nervous,' said Corrie, perhaps the less worldly of the pair.

Nene comes from a military family and had spent her life moving from place to place, but Corrie had spent her entire life in Sneek, and I don't suppose you can find a much more sheltered environment than a fortress waterport.

As first dates go it was quite a commitment but it went well and that July Nene had travelled to Holland. That was over five years ago and she's been there ever since.

'We're together 24 hours a day,' said Corrie.

'As you can see, we have very little space,' shrugged Nene, 'but we never argue.'

'We've been rich and poor; we know it works,' said Corrie.

Corrie sat at the computer and I sat on the sofa stroking Mo while Nene prepared supper. The conversation continued to flow, interrupted only by the occasional random word thrown from Nene to Corrie as part of a potential googlewhack.

'We haven't been visited by the old man,' said Nene, chopping an onion, '...felicitation?'

'Perhaps that's because you're here, Dave,' said Corrie, typing.

'Who's the old man?' I asked.

'He's the ghost,' said Nene, '…oligarchy.'

'He smells and moves around the room,' said Corrie, '… no, Felicitation Oligarchy gets 26 hits.'

'He smells and moves around the room? Are you sure that's not the dog?' I asked, deceitfully stroking Mo.

'It's not the dog,' said Nene, she turned to Corrie, '…pernicious?' and then to me again. 'Occasionally you hear him shuffling around the room.'

I looked at Mo. She was a little smelly (inasmuch as she was a dog), she was certainly able to move around the room (inasmuch as she was a dog) and I'm sure you could describe her movement at times as a 'shuffle' (inasmuch as she was a cairn terrier).

'Are you sure it's not the dog?' I asked.

'No, it's not her,' said Nene. 'juniper?'

'I beg your pardon?' I asked, unsure for a moment which thread of conversation was where.

'Pernicious Juniper.'

'No. 603 hits!' said Corrie. 'The dog can't get upstairs. The old man can.'

And so the conversation went on. Part googlewhacking, part ghost story. I'm not really one to believe in ghosts but then Nene said the same was true of her before telling me three stories about them. Once, when she was living in the States – gargantuan – she swore – crevice – that she – *950!* – could hear the sound of ten pin – hunchback – bowling. The next day – quoits – she asked around and – *19* – discovered that the apartment block was – caramelised – built – diphthong – on the site of an old – *2! Oof!* – bowling alley.

It was like talking to someone who has a polite and verbose version of Tourettes syndrome.

*

I was woken in the morning by the sound of church bells. They were playing a Beatles medley.

'That's the bell man,' said Nene.

'He plays all sorts of odd things,' said Corrie, 'last week it was *The Sound of Music.*'

'Come on, you have a long journey ahead of you. We'll walk you to the station,' said Nene.

'We can show you the fortress,' said Corrie.

*

When the Leeuwarden train pulled in I gave Corrie and Nene a squeeze and a hug. Ready for my long, slow-as-advertised journey back to Amsterdam and beyond. The train started to chug and we heaved out of the station. I stood between the carriages waving frantically.

'Thank you so much,' I said

'Good luck with Psychosomatic Rambunctiousness,' said Nene with a smile.

thirteen

Psychosomatic Rambunctiousness

Psychosomatic   adjective: relating to an illness or disorder with physical symptoms originating from mental or emotional causes.

Rambunctiousness   noun: the quality of being rambunctious. Boisterous and disorderly.

'I *am* Psychosomatic Rambunctiousness,' said Wendy between forkfuls of salad. The California sun was beating down, I had to squint to make out her silhouette. 'I *am* those words. Those two words *define me*. I *am* Psychosomatic Rambunctiousness.'

We were sitting outside a restaurant, Le Petit Greek, part of a pretty parade of shops in Larchmont Village, which seemed to be a nice part of LA.

It feels a bit weird typing those last few words. I've been to Los Angeles on several occasions over the years and it's only in recent times that I've come to accept it has any nice parts at all.

I used to hate the place. While other cities have a personality, some kind of defining character that flows from the heart of the city, LA has none. It's a sprawling vacuous mass, occupying a thousand square miles, but it doesn't have one area you would call the centre and without a physical heart, it seems to lack a metaphorical one too.

Because it's so spread out it's impossible to get around without a car. There's barely any public transport and taxis (if you can get one) cost a small fortune. It's a terrible place to be poor, but many people are, rubbing up uncomfortably against the wealthy neighbourhoods with their swimming pools and (two car) garages. The dependency on cars is probably the reason it's also a depressingly sober place.

What made me appreciate Los Angeles was finding a friend there. Her name was Julie. Rob, my agent, had introduced me to Julie a couple of years earlier when all three of us found ourselves in Aspen, Colorado. I suppose you could say we bonded over a shared appreciation of Steve Martin's singing testicles. Julie lives in LA with her English husband, Dan, a former Wiltshire farm boy who's now an LA-based TV producer.

Julie bought me a two-foot tall wooden bear for my 30th birthday because she thought it would be fun for me to carry it through customs on my way home. It was.

On subsequent trips to LA, I'd stayed in Julie and Dan's spare room, a very welcome change from the usually soulless hotels on offer. The first LA location that I had identified as a 'nice place' was their house, high in the mountains above Studio City.

Not so long ago, while I was staying with them for a couple of days, Julie and I had a fantastic night out at the Four Seasons Hotel bar drinking overpriced cocktails. We'd ended up sharing a bottle of champagne with the surprisingly down-to-earth pop star and mono-name, Seal. Part way through the evening, Seal dashed off to have a chat with former prime minister John Major who'd just entered the bar. According to Seal, John Major is 'really sound'. Those kinds of things happen when I'm with Julie. Julie thinks those kinds of things happen when she's with me.

Knowing Julie and Dan has made LA a different place entirely. The shallow weirdness (and indeed the weird shallowness) that pervades is no longer the be all and end all. Instead it's become something to marvel at, something to sample, safe in the knowledge that there's a safe haven somewhere in the smog-bound city, a place that feels almost like home.

Having tapped into this LA positivity I have been able to recognise it in others too. If you ask any incomer in LA how long they've lived there they always say the same thing: 'Too long.' To some of them it means, *I wish I'd never come, every minute I've spent in this Godforsaken place has been a minute too long*, and from others it means, *I've been here so long I'll never be happy anywhere else, for all its faults I love this place.* I think I was now able to tell them apart.

One of the things that sets these people apart is their ability to live in LA while remaining themselves. Julie and Dan were the first people I'd seen hold a conversation in LA without looking over the other person's shoulder to see if someone more important had entered the room. You have to love them for that.

And Wendy Mogel displayed this quality too. She seemed very happy with her life in LA but she didn't seem *very* LA. Los Angeles is gaudy, Wendy is elegant, it's frivolous, she's earnest, it's all surface, she's all substance. With her short silver hair and intelligent demeanour her natural habitat would be a New York coffee house but she still seemed at ease with herself and her surroundings.

Wendy writes about parenting; the words psychosomatic and rambunctiousness had been found on a bookselling website in an extract from her book, *The Blessings of a Skinned Knee: Using Jewish Teachings to Raise Self Reliant Children.* I guess you could live anywhere in the world and write about parenting so it seemed odd to me that Wendy should choose to live in this shallow suntrap.

'How long have you been in LA?' I asked.

'Too long,' came the inevitable reply with a smile and a shrug.

'So how come you're here?'

'My husband writes screenplays…'

'Anything I'd know?' I asked, expecting not to.

'He wrote *The Player*,' came the casual response.

I love that film.

'I love that film!' I said, forgetting to pick my jaw up when I'd finished.

Wendy smiled.

The Player is a fantastic film. A scabrous satire on the movie industry it's brilliantly directed by Robert Altman, stars Tim Robbins as a Hollywood executive and it was written by … who was it written by?

'So you're married to …?'

'Michael Tolkin.'

'Yes!' I said, kindly confirming to Wendy that she'd got the name of her own husband right. 'Michael Tolkin. I really love that film.'

The Player epitomises the ability to live in LA without becoming an LA kind of person. Only someone who had lived there and remained themselves could have written that screenplay. Or someone who wanted to leave Los Angeles altogether.

'He wrote it to try and *get out* of LA,' said Wendy with a wry smile.

'But the plan backfired because the film was a success!' I said enjoying the irony.

'Yeah.'

'I'm glad it backfired,' I said.

'So's he,' said Wendy dryly. 'So am I.'

'I love that film,' I said as much to myself as to Wendy.

I was beginning to annoy myself with the repetition so I'm sure I was annoying Wendy too.

'So, tell me more about this googlewhacking thing?' she asked

'OK,' I started, 'so how familiar are you with the internet?'

'Oh, I'm *addicted*!' said Wendy. 'I *love* the internet. The thing is I love it too much.'

'How d'you mean?'

'Well today, when I got to my office my cable modem was down. I couldn't get online. It was fantastic. I got *so much* done. When the internet is there I do much less writing.'

'Really?' I asked, but of course, I knew better than most how distracting the internet could be.

'Absolutely!' said Wendy.

'So if I ask you to find me two more googlewhacks am I threatening the future of your next book?' I asked.

'I wouldn't go that far,' said Wendy.

'No,' I said under my breath, 'I think that's just me.'

'I beg your pardon?'

'Oh … nothing,' I said, 'I was just thinking about something else.'

'Have you heard of a movie called *Adaptation*?' asked Wendy from nowhere.

'I don't think so,' I shrugged, 'did your husband write it?'

'No,' Wendy looked a little embarrassed. She leaned in towards me in a conspiratorial manner and lowered her voice a fraction, 'I'm in it.'

'Really?'

'Yeah,' said Wendy. 'Are you sure you haven't heard of it, it's a Spike Jonze movie? Written by Charlie Kaufman?'

'They did *Being John Malkovich*!' I said, my jaw once more hitting the table. 'I *love* that film.'

'Yeah. Well they've made another movie. *Adaptation*. It might not be out in the UK yet, it's relatively recent over here.'

I was intrigued.

'So who do you play?'

Wendy shrugged.

'Myself.'

'So you play "Wendy Mogel"?'

'Well, not as such,' she sniggered. 'But I play an obnoxious New York intellectual.'

I laughed.

'So what's it about?'

'It's kind of a movie about a man's failure to make a movie,' chuckled the New York intellectual without even a whiff of obnoxiousness about her.

An idea flashed through my mind: a book about a man's failure to write a novel! I dismissed it.

'I'm only in one scene,' continued Wendy. 'I have dinner with Meryl Streep!'

'It sounds great!' I said vacuously. It might well turn out to be a great movie but knowing that your current dining companion appears as one of Meryl Streep's dinner guests doesn't actually inform you either way on the film's potential for greatness. 'I bet I *love* that film.'

'My husband sort of knows Spike Jonze. He wanted some people to play obnoxious New York intellectuals. The casting director rings up and says, "Spike *needs* you." I said, "No." She rings again, "Do you like shoes?" I say, "I love shoes. Why?" She says, "Because for doing this one day's work, you'll be able to buy yourself some very, *very* nice shoes." So I did it.'

I laughed. Wendy had the brain and the career of the New York intellectual but maybe her feet were well and truly in LA.

*

That night I stayed with Julie and Dan. It was the first time since the start of the year that I'd met someone who wasn't a stranger. I felt like I'd made some new friends, but it was a joy to relax in the company of some old friends for a while. It was fantastic to see them.

'So what are you doing in town?' asked Julie.

'I had a meeting this afternoon,' I said, which while being the truth was clearly nothing of the sort.

'That's great,' said Dan. 'Things must be going well. What kind of meeting?'

'Oh, with a writer,' I said, pouring myself another glass of wine so as to avoid their gaze.

When the wine was poured there were still two pairs of raised eyebrows waiting to hear more.

'Well, she's not just a writer, she's an actress too,' I said. 'She's been in a movie or two. Her husband wrote *The Player*...

but the meeting was about a secret project. I can't tell you any more.'

Julie and Dan exchanged glances. They were impressed. They didn't know what with, but they were impressed. Of course they didn't know that I was in town to meet Psychosomatic Rambunctiousness, did they?

'Actually, I'm waiting on some news,' I said, still sticking to the misleading truth. 'Can I use your computer …?'

fourteen

Pomegranate Filibusters

Pomegranate   noun: an Asian shrub or small tree
cultivated in semitropical regions for its
fruit. Or the fruit of this tree; it has a tough
reddish rind, juicy red pulp and many
seeds.

Filibusters   1. noun: plural of filibuster being:
(a) the process of obstructing legislation by
means of long speeches or other delaying
tactics.
(b) those who engage in such tactics.
2. verb: to filibuster. The action of delaying
legislation by these means.

In the breakfast room of the hotel, over a stodgy banana
muffin and a cup of lukewarm coffee I watched out for the
arrival of my next googlewhack. At precisely ten o'clock a
silver sports car pulled up. I knew this was my man; no one
with a car that nice would be staying at a lowly hotel like this.
I dashed out to meet him.

'You must be Byron,' I said.

'I sure am,' said Byron. 'So … do you wanna drive to
Mexico?'

That must be the best opening gambit I've ever heard,
knocking Suzi Appleby's 'Do you want to see my knickers?'

into second place. (I should add that Suzi and I were both four at the time.)

'Mexico?' I pretended to give it a moment's thought. I had no idea how far away from Austin, Texas it was, but I didn't really care. 'Absolutely!'

Byron chuckled. The chuckle passed through his right leg and the engine chuckled too.

'I'll need to run upstairs and get my passport though,' I said, adding a dash of responsibility to an otherwise reckless conversation.

'OK,' said Byron, coolly.

I'd taken a few steps back towards the hotel when he called out.

'Hey, I figure some time today you're gonna start tryin' to persuade me to find some of these googlewhacks, right?'

'Right.'

'Well, I already found 'em. You might as well have them now. That way we can talk about real things while we're driving.'

Every second I was with Byron I found myself liking him even more. He was the googlewhacking Fonz. These were happy days.

'I got Dubitable Quaalude and Propolis Dhow,' he said.

Byron was like the new kid at school who was supercool. The one with the good bike that you immediately wanted to be your best friend. I bet he'd be really good at conkers.

'There are at least three words there I can't spell,' I said, only confident that I could spell dubitable, indubitably.

'I wrote 'em down for you,' said Byron, producing a neat piece of paper. Googlewhacking didn't come much better than this.

'Would you mind if I spent a few minutes looking these up,' I said, a bit uneasy. The new boy was offering to take me to Mexico but I wanted to do my homework first. 'I'll need to look around the websites and find the email addresses, you see. The sooner I email them the better.'

'Take a look at the other side of the paper,' said Byron, not missing a beat.

I did. There, in his neat handwriting, were two email addresses. I looked them both over. One was an anonymous office address, the other went to someone by the name of Julia Roberts.

'So, d'you think, Dubitable Quaalude leads to—'

'No, Dave. I shouldn't think it's *that* Julia Roberts,' said Byron, matter-of-factly. 'I think a Hollywood actress of her stature is highly unlikely to spend her spare time running a website about quilting.'

'No. You're probably right.'

'Take ten minutes,' he said, turning the engine off, 'email them, get your passport, then we'll go. There's no rush.'

'Cool,' I said while rushing very uncoolly.

*

'So how far is Mexico?' I asked as we hurtled down the freeway.

'I'm not sure. Maybe 300 miles or so,' shrugged Byron.

Byron looked like an aristocratic Englishman: tall, pale and with a floppy fringe, that wouldn't have seemed out of place accompanying a stuttering Hugh Grant accent but his manner was Texan through and through. He wore a brown leather flying jacket and a pair of shades and he spoke with a slow, cool drawl.

'Do I sound Texan to you?' he drawled.

'Yeah.'

'Good.'

If there's one thing Texans love in the world, it's Texas. I hadn't been there long but even in my short journey from the airport to the hotel I'd worked that much out for myself. Wherever you look you're constantly reminded that you're in the Lone Star State. Why have just a plain bit of iron railing when you could have it worked into the shape of the Lone

Star? Why have plain flagstones outside your parking lot when you could have them with a Lone Star on? How many Lone Stars do you have to put on the side of a building before the word 'lone' stops making sense? It's clear that Texans either love Texas, or they have very bad memories and worry that they might forget what state they're in on the journey to work each morning.

'So what do you know about Texas, Dave?' asked Byron.

'Not a lot really,' I confessed. 'It's big.'

'Did you know it was once an independent country?'

'Really?'

'Oh yeah,' nodded Byron. 'From 1836 to 1845 Texas was an independent nation.'

Byron launched into a Texan history lesson. He vividly explained the Battle of the Alamo, brought to life the characters of Crockett and Bowie and explained how Austin came to be the capital city.

If history had been taught like that at school I might have been more interested. Then again, most subjects would be improved if the classroom was a high-performance sports car travelling at 70 mph with a cool but enthusiastic teacher at the wheel but I don't suppose that's possible in this day and age. You know, what with large class sizes and all that.

'Have you had a chance to see the Capitol Building since you've been in Austin?' asked Byron.

'Yeah,' I replied. 'I walked past it on the way to the hotel.'

'What did you think?'

'It looked like the National Capitol in Washington DC,' I said. 'Only bigger and grander.'

'You understand Texas pretty well,' said Byron with a sly chuckle.

In order to pay for such a splendid building the state had sold off three million acres of land. That's an area bigger than Yorkshire and Lancashire combined. Of course, Texas can afford to throw away that kind of land because it's so huge. It's roughly three times bigger than Britain and with only a third of the population.

'So, what were you expecting me to be like?' asked Byron.

'I've stopped expecting anything of anyone,' I said. 'I don't think googlewhacks are like other people.'

'How d'you mean?'

'Well, nobody's really been what I expected,' I said. 'I thought Bibliophilic Sandwiched was going to be a gay man but she turned out to be a happily married woman.'

'What made you think she'd be a he?'

'She writes stories in which the characters from the *Highlander* TV series have lots of gay sex.'

'That figures,' said Byron. 'So you didn't have any pre-conceptions about me as a Texan?'

'Not really,' I shrugged. 'I mean there's the accent and stuff and maybe I would have expected a cowboy hat and ... I don't know, Texans have guns, don't they?'

'Yup,' Byron nodded.

I looked across, not sure how much information was contained in that 'yup'. There was no sign of a cowboy hat. I paused.

'So ... do you have a ... a gun?' I asked.

'Yup,' said Byron.

I was now pretty clear on how much information was contained in *that* 'yup'.

'Right,' I said because I preferred it to the silence.

'So, what do you think about guns?' asked my cool and *armed* host.

'They scare me,' I said honestly.

'Not having one would scare me,' came the equally honest reply. 'Now, I have a special licence that means I can carry a concealed weapon.'

'Really?'

'Uh huh. Not everyone can do that. It involves a background check, a training course, lecture and firearms proficiency demonstration. It's worth it. I figure it's better to know what you're doing, right?'

'I guess so,' I said, my pitch rising nervously.

'I think it's a good law. It's a good deterrent to the criminal because he knows that somebody well trained might be carrying a weapon,' said Byron. 'There are restrictions. For instance, I'm not allowed to take it into a bar or anywhere that makes over 51% of its income from the sale of alcohol.'

'That's good,' I said, my voice climbing a little higher still. I made a conscious effort to start lower down because I was planning a longer sentence next and wasn't sure I could make it to the end if I kept on going up.

'The thing is,' I said, but my voice came out too low, I sounded like I was doing a bad Barry White impression. I started again. 'The thing is,' that's better, 'it's not *you* owning a gun that scares me. It's the fact that everyone else can get one.'

'Well, *that's why* I want to have one,' said Byron matter-of-factly.

'But if no one could have one, you wouldn't need one,' I said, trying to rationalise it for myself.

'But the bad guys are gonna get one whether they're allowed one or not,' said Byron. 'I have a wife and family and I want to be able to protect them.'

'Yeah but—'

'Would you like to hold my gun?' asked Byron.

'Um …'

'You would, wouldn't you?' he prompted and however much the idea frightened me, he was right.

'Yeah … kind of,' I said nervously admitting it to myself.

Byron opened up a little compartment that sat between our two seats and produced a small pistol. He made a small and careful adjustment and passed the gun my way.

'The safety's on,' he said.

I'd never held a gun before. I'd played with toy guns when I was a boy, copying cop shows and war films from the telly, but holding a toy gun and holding a real gun are very different things. I knew *how* to hold a gun but I didn't want to feel a trigger under my finger, I didn't want to look across my hand and down the barrel, I didn't want to acknowledge that I had a *real* gun in my hand and so I picked it up between my thumb and finger and held it away from myself, like an unwilling father taking a newly filled nappy to the bin.

Byron threw me a glance. It contained the faintest hint of a snigger. Stung, I shifted the gun into my hand properly. It was heavy. The metal was cold in my palm. The sweat was cold in my palm too. The safety catch might have been on but still, I knew that in my hand I held a machine designed to kill and it felt very, very, wrong. 99% of me was scared of what I held in my hand, the other 1% was excited by it and surely *that's* the scariest part of the equation. I tried to hold it below the level of the window for fear that a passing motorist might mis-understand, but of course, they wouldn't have batted an eyelid. My fingers felt like they didn't belong on my hand which felt like it didn't belong on my arm which felt like it didn't belong on my body which felt like it didn't belong in Texas.

'How does it feel?' asked Byron.

'Cold ... heavy ...'

'Uh huh.'

'... and frightening,' I said. 'Can I give you this back now? I'm really not comfortable.'

'Of course,' said Byron calmly offering his hand.

I wasn't sure on the manners involved in passing a gun to someone. Is it like a pair of scissors? Do you pass them the handle or the barrel first? Does the barrel point at you or them? I tried to do neither, holding it out on my flat palm, allowing Byron to pick it up as he saw fit. He did and soon the gun was safely stowed away.

'Fascinating,' said Byron to himself as we rounded a big wide bend in the road.

We travelled a few miles in silence.

'So, have you been to Mexico before, Dave?' asked Byron.

'No,' I said.

'From your email I figured you were the kind of guy who'd appreciate the experience,' he said. 'I thought I'd try and make your trip to Texas memorable.'

'Well, it already is that,' I said.

'I bet most of the people you've met doing this didn't lay on a trip to Mexico, did they?' he asked.

'No they didn't,' I said. 'Most of the people I've met so far just … kind of … met me.'

'And besides, I want to buy some coke,' said Byron.

My mouth moved but no sound came out.

Slowly I took in the facts. I was in a car with a complete stranger. We were driving to Mexico. He had a gun. He wanted to buy some coke.

My mouth had another go but still nothing emerged.

I wasn't very happy. There was something unsettling about that list of facts. I couldn't quite put my finger on what it was, but I *think* it was probably the whole stranger-Mexico-gun-drugs thing. Aaaaagggggghhhhh! Yes, *that* was it!

What the hell was I doing? That doesn't happen in real life! People don't really carry guns and drive to Mexico to buy coke, do they? That only happens in movies, doesn't it? The kind of movies where people get shot? I don't want to get shot. Thoughts started swimming through my head. Too many thoughts. I suddenly realised my dad's birthday had passed two weeks earlier and I hadn't sent a card. Damn. Hang on, what about the gun and the coke and the … Aaagggggghhhhh.

My mouth was still moving and still there was no noise.

'Are you OK?' asked Byron.

'No. No, I'm not *actually*,' I said, my voice squeaking out at last. I tried to invest the words with some kind of moral indignation. I breathed deeply and filled my lungs, trying to pull my shoulders back and give myself some extra height but the car had bucket seats and whatever I did only caused my arse to slip further down, cancelling my efforts out. It's hard to take the high ground in a sports car.

'What's wrong?' asked Byron, seemingly unable to fathom anything untoward about the situation.

'What's wrong?' I spat. 'What's wrong? Well maybe I don't *want* to go to Mexico to buy coke. Huh? Maybe that's what's wrong.'

'We can get some Pepsi as well if you like?'

'Wha …?'

'I wanna buy some Coca-Cola,' explained Byron. 'They changed the recipe and started making it with corn syrup over here.'

'Wha …?'

'But in Mexico they still make it with sugar. I prefer it with sugar.'

'So we're going to Mexico to buy Coca-Cola?' I asked, unwinding, calming down, giggling childishly and immediately forgetting my father's birthday once more.

'Yes,' said Byron.

'I'm sorry I thought you meant we were going to buy drugs,' I said, my eyebrows throwing in a *'tsk – get me'* gesture for good measure.

'Oh yeah,' said Byron. 'I forgot to say we're going to get some drugs as well.'

'Wha …?' I said, my head spinning immediately back into confusion.

Nightmarish images of Mexican jail cells flashed through my mind. Somewhere in the back of my brain a cruel and corrupt police officer with a Zapata moustache and stubble you could light a match on cackled insanely at the sadistic pleasure ahead.

'Look,' I said. 'I don't know what was in my email or what makes you think I'm up for this kind of thing, but I'm really not very happy about this whole buying drugs thing …'

'Well, it's perfectly legal,' said Byron with a shrug, 'and prescription drugs are much cheaper over the border.'

'*Prescription* drugs?'

'Yup.'

'So we're going to Mexico to buy Coca-Cola and prescription drugs and that's it?'

'Uh huh.'

'So we're not going to buy anything illegal?'

'No,' said Byron. 'I might buy a Cuban cigar, but I'll smoke it while we're in Mexico so that's OK.'

'And that's it?'

'Uh huh.'

'So there's nothing illegal about this? You're not a drug dealer?'

'No.'

'You own this car?'

'Yes.'

'Good.'

'Fascinating,' said Byron with a rueful shake of the head.

As my heart returned to a more regular beat I started to chuckle. I looked across at Byron. He wasn't going to let on, but he was quite pleased with himself. The corner of his mouth twitched a little. He was funny, Byron.

A few more miles passed in silence.

'So, you must have travelled a lot recently?' said the law-abiding citizen at the wheel. 'D'you get on well with folk?'

'Yeah,' I said, 'I generally do. I think most people are good people.'

'That's a nice way to be,' said Byron, 'and I think you might be right, but do you really *like* everyone?'

'I've liked every googlewhack I've met,' I said, a bit too quickly.

'Really?' asked Byron, clearly unconvinced by my happy answer.

'Really,' I said unconvincingly.

'Really?'

'No.'

I always crumble under interrogation.

'So, who didn't you like?'

'Well, Dripstone Ingles was weird. He was an 81-year-old creationist,' I said. 'I mean *obviously we* didn't get on! They're all loonies, aren't they? Creationists? It's incredible in this day and age that people hold on to that kind of view of the world and—'

I stopped. Byron wasn't nodding along. There was no 'uh huh' of encouragement.

'Just so you know, Dave,' he said. 'I'm a creationist.'

'Ha ha … right,' I said. 'Yeah … the coke is Coca-Cola and the drugs are prescription drugs and … and … you're not joking, are you?'

'No.'

'Really?'

'Really.'

Damn. I didn't know where to look or what to say. There was a horribly awkward pause. I was grateful when Byron finally took up the slack.

'Don't worry, Dave, you haven't offended me,' he said. 'I have a very thick skin.'

'I'm sorry,' I said, 'but … but …'

I was floundering, trying to find a way out of this conversation without causing offence but then I suddenly realised it didn't matter. I didn't have to stand on ceremony here; I already had my googlewhacks. The emails had already been sent. It wasn't important for Byron and I to get on, there was no need for me to watch my words. What was the worst that could happen?

I mean, OK, he could abandon me in Mexico, but apart from that, what's the worst that could happen?

Well, yes, he has a gun so, yeah, I guess the worst case scenario is pretty bad, but really … apart from *that* what's the worst that could happen?

'I'm sorry,' I said, 'I just can't see how creationism can be true. Besides, what really got me with Dripstone Ingles was the lies …'

'What did he tell you?'

'He said that evolution contradicts the Second Law of Thermodynamics,' I said, and prepared myself to explain as best I could why that wasn't so.

'Well, that's just plain wrong,' said Byron who didn't need an explanation. 'He shouldn't have told you that. It's not true and it doesn't help the argument any.'

'Right,' I said, surprised by our ready agreement on that part of the issue.

'But of course neither of us knows how old the world is because neither of us were there,' said Byron, 'and *I* believe the story of creation.'

'But—'

'Well, you weren't there, were you?'

'Well no, but—'

'Well then, we're both choosing to believe what someone else is telling us ... and I look around the world and I see how beautiful it is and I think it must have been *designed*.'

For the rest of the day the subject of creation versus evolution was never far from our conversation. We disagreed about it all the way, but we both did it with a smile on our faces and I know that I for one I enjoyed the conversation.

It made me feel a little guilty about my meeting with Dr Gish. I wished that I'd engaged in the same kind of robust debate with him. Instead I'd tried to nod and agree and appease my way through it, allowing my feelings to fester inside and become something more malign. Don't get me wrong, I still disagreed with him and I still loathed his (mis)representation of the facts, but I wished I'd said so at the time. I'm sure I'd have liked him more if I'd done so and I know I'd have liked me more too.

*

Laredo was a dusty, downtrodden and downbeat kind of town. It's known as the *city under seven flags* because, obviously enough, it's been governed by seven nations. Most of Texas has, in its turbulent history, been governed by Spain, France, Mexico, the short-lived independent Texas, the Confederacy and of course the United States, but Laredo was also part of the even-shorter-lived Republic of the Rio Grande. In fact Laredo was the capital city of the country, which existed for less than a year in 1839/40.

I don't know the ins and outs of setting up a country – although for tax reasons I might look into it – but less than a year does seem like a particularly poor showing. I doubt you could get much country-style stuff done in that time. It's not just flags that need designing; there are uniforms, stamps, currency, passports and national anthems to think of. I bet someone ended up with a warehouse full of sheet music they couldn't sell. But I digress.

The border between Mexico and Texas has been the subject of much dispute over the years but eventually they decided that nature had provided the obvious boundary in the form of the Rio Grande and so, Laredo being on the north bank of the river, it ended up being part of Texas. The Laredo Mexicans who wanted to be in Mexico immediately moved to the south bank and set up a new town, cunningly named Nuevo Laredo, and these days the bridge that joins the two is the busiest crossing on the whole frontier.

It was across this bridge that Byron and I walked, paying a mere 25 cents each to stroll unimpeded into a foreign country. No one examined our passports; we just paid the money and walked through the turnstile.

We spent a couple of hours walking round Nuevo Laredo but I didn't feel like I was getting an authentic Mexican experience. Both Laredos, old and Nuevo, are shaped by their relationship with each other. The two economies are vastly different which means most things can be bought cheaper on the Mexican side. Seeing as getting there involves only a three-minute stroll and a 25-cent door-charge it must be pretty difficult setting up a competitive business on the American side. Of course the other side of that coin means that on the other side of the river, Nuevo Laredo is a hustling bustling marketplace, a cacophony of noise with hundreds of small shops competing to sell you knock-off goods and tacky souvenirs for the best price they can. Cheap plastic goods compete for window space with home made Mexican piñatas representing icons of American (and now world) culture: Homer Simpson, Bugs Bunny, Spiderman.

Laredo seemed to exist purely as the gateway to Nuevo

Laredo and Nuevo Laredo seemed to exist purely to take money from tourists. I guess I *had* visited Mexico but only in the same way that someone who does a booze-cruise to a Calais wine superstore has visited France. I'd crossed the border but seen nothing of the country.

We walked back over the bridge. Byron had a crate full of sugary Coca-Cola, a carrier bag full of cheap pharmaceutical goods and lungs full of Cuban cigar smoke. I had an 'I've Been To Mexico' fridge magnet to add to my collection.

Walking through the turnstile cost us a full 50 cents each this way and, unsurprisingly, our passports were scrutinised this time.

The crate of coke was heavy and quite awkward for one man to carry so we walked through the streets of Laredo with it suspended between us. As we approached the car park we found our path blocked by an incredibly large woman who in turn found her progress blocked by two men and a crate of Coke. I guess the two units were about as wide as each other and a little wider than the sidewalk. We shuffled one way and then the other a couple of times before one of us realised that Byron and I had the advantage of being able to split up and let her pass through the middle.

'Did you see her T-shirt?' I asked, taking half of the crate back.

'No,' said Byron.

'It said, "God made the Big Bang!"' I said. 'Maybe that's the answer to our creation/evolution argument?'

'But maybe it isn't,' said Byron, committing us to another 300-mile long debate on the topic.

*

In fairness, while the subject of creationism was never far away we did talk about other things. Byron must be one of the most fascinating men I've ever met. He's full of entre-preneurial spirit, he's an authentic dotcom millionaire (on paper at least) and he seems to have achieved this in a wholly admirable fashion.

His company, pagewise.com, has, among other things posted the entire 1911 edition of the *Encyclopaedia Britannica* online. There are two reasons for choosing this particular edition.

The first reason is that it's widely considered to be the best encyclopaedia ever written. It's known as the 'scholar's edition' because of its ridiculously star-studded list of contributors. Among the 1500 authors there were 47 Members of Parliament while various world-renowned experts wrote about their specialist subjects. It's hard to argue with an encyclopaedia that has Henry Ford writing the entry on Mass Production while the subject of Anarchism is ably defined by Prince Peter Kropotkin, a famous Russian anarchist of the day.

The second reason is that it's out of copyright.

Even so, putting 44,000,000 words on the internet isn't easy or cheap and yet it's there, online as a free service to anyone who cares to visit.

Essentially the company makes money by creating websites that contain genuinely interesting information that you can't find elsewhere online, which means they'll get a lot of visitors, which in turn means they can sell advertising space. But there are clearly far more tawdry ways to attract people to your website and the evangelical zeal that appeared in Byron's eyes when he talked about the 1911 *Encyclopaedia Britannica* showed me that he was genuinely passionate about the educational content of the project.

Byron was a wonderfully entertaining raconteur with a host of absorbing anecdotes and I found it impossible to second guess him on almost any subject, such were the apparent contradictions.

He gleefully described a day spent as an extra on the movie *Miss Congeniality* …

('I spent the whole day sitting next to Candice Bergen and William Shatner.'

'Did he? I expect she was furious.'

'What?'

'If William sha … oh never mind.')

… but he also proudly declared, 'I don't own a television machine.'

He once ran for office and yet he doesn't vote.

He's met every US president that's served in his lifetime, which is quite a thing in itself, but the manner in which it's been achieved only makes it even more impressive. He hasn't used his business contacts and influence; instead the stories mostly seemed to involve him having a brass neck and pretending to be a waiter. (Byron that is, not the president concerned.)

Spending time with Byron wasn't exactly relaxing. The conversation was never throwaway; instead he constantly challenged me to think about my beliefs and consider my words and he expected the same kind of challenge from me. At the end of the day I felt as though my brain had been to the gym. But I enjoyed the workout.

In fact, I don't think I've ever enjoyed disagreeing with someone quite that much. His religious convictions (and my lack of them) mean that he's convinced I'm going to Hell and yet I really liked him. And I think he liked me too.

Byron dropped me off at the hotel, I waved him off and walked back up to my room exhausted and exhilarated at the same time. I boiled the kettle even though I had no intention of standing up again once I'd sat down on the bed.

I lay back and looked at the ceiling, taking in patterns that weren't really there. I suddenly realised that that was about the longest I'd gone without thinking about googlewhacks all year.

The instant that thought hit me, I was thinking about them again. Byron had delivered me two beauties that morning, the emails had been sent, all I had to do was wait for the replies. Well surely, I figured, a 600-mile round trip to Mexico was wait enough. My exhaustion disappeared. I sprang into action.

Like most of the American hotels I'd stayed in there was an

in-room internet service using an infrared keyboard and the TV set. It was a bit slow and clunky and the keyboard was a bit unreliable, but it only cost $10 for 24 hours and my morning's use meant it had already been added on to my bill for the day. It was time to check my mail.

I opened up the TV cabinet, propped myself up on the edge of the bed and got online. The hotel was probably full of scenes like this: lone men crouching over unfamiliar keyboards, awkwardly negotiating their way around the net. Businessmen checking their stocks and shares, travelling sales reps emailing home, bored tourists killing time. But I wasn't one of those people. I was a hunter. I'd set my traps this morning and now I was returning to see if Propolis Dhow or Dubitable Quaalude had taken the bait.

I knew that everything rested on this. I needed at least one of these two to deliver or it was all over. But I was confident; failure didn't even cross my mind. Why would it? These 'whacks had come from Byron, the googlewhacking Fonz; how could they fail to come good?

With supreme confidence I clicked into mail2web.com and scrolled through the list of names in my inbox. My buoyant mood didn't last long. I felt like I'd taken a punch to the gut. My email to Propolis Dhow had bounced. Suddenly the frailty of the project was all too apparent. Every chain of 'whacks was no more than a fragile house of cards, threatening to collapse at any time. What about Dubitable Quaalude? Where was it? Feverishly my eyes roamed up and down the screen desperately seeking a missive from what was now my last hope.

'Yes!' I yelled and punched the air in delight. It *was* there after all. There, sitting in my inbox, almost lost, swamped by a morass of junk email adverts, the name 'Julia Roberts', the subject, 'Googlewhacking'. 'Yes!'

Surely this could mean only one of two things:

1. The star of *Pretty Woman* was getting in touch because she'd heard of my adventures. Maybe she wanted to buy

the film rights and, being a wily media type, was planning to bed me as a way of negotiating a favourable price. (Look, I'd been travelling alone for a long time, all right?). Or:

2. Dubitable Quaalude had hit 'reply' and I would soon be meeting an expert quilter.

Whichever way I looked at it, it was going to be a result.

I clicked on the link and the email opened up before me and, this being the real world, it was from Julia Roberts: quilter.

My blood ran cold. My body turned numb. My eyes lost focus. My hearing turned muddy. There was a third option I hadn't considered:

From: Julia Roberts
To: Dave Gorman

Subject: Googlewhacking.

When will you creeps leave me alone? I'm putting a block on this address so your emails won't reach me anymore. I'm taking my website down. It's not worth it. Eat shit you moron. I hope you die.

And that was it. The room started spinning. Propolis Dhow had delivered a body blow, but now Dubitable Quaalude had followed through with a perfect uppercut. I was floored, flat on my back, out for the count. Dead. Who did she think I was? What did she think I'd done? What kind of hellish behaviour went on in the world of quilting to inspire such anger? What had I done? What could I do? It was over. My googlewhack adventure was over. For good.

There was nowhere else to go. Rarebit Nutters had found me two googlewhacks, setting me off on two chains. One chain took me to Bushranger Doublespeak, Bibliophilic Sandwiched, Dripstone Ingles and then nothing. The other chain had taken me to Pomegranate Filibusters via Hippocampi Wallpaper,

Verandahs Plectrums and Psychosomatic Rambunctiousness but now, again, nothing. And that was it.

I caught a glimpse of myself in the mirror. I was pale. I'm normally pale; I have skin the colour of an aspirin but now I looked transparent. Nothing made sense any more. What was I doing? Why was I here? 4000 miles from home and for what? What had I done with January?

Nothing made sense any more. Had it ever made sense? What was the point? What *was* the point? I'd spent a month running. Running *after* googlewhacks or running *away* from life? I was angry. I was upset. I was embarrassed. I was confused. I couldn't feel my fingers or my toes. I felt like all of my mass had pulled itself into my gut, concentrated itself into the size of a fist, deep in my belly. Every ounce of flesh and blood and phlegm and bile and shame and rage and fire, knotting itself up into a ball then swelling, welling up inside of me and I tried to scream but no sound emerged, just tears, tears, I couldn't stop the tears. I fell back on to the bed and gave into the tears, let them come, let them fall. Clutching a cheap pillow to my chest I sobbed, each sob making me feel more pathetic but what else did I deserve? I was a pathetic, wretched waste of time and space.

I turned myself inside out. Then I sobbed some more ...

*

... until eventually there was no more sobbing to be done.

I needed to pull myself together. I went to the bathroom and splashed cold water in my face. I stared at myself, at my red puffy eyes and I hated what I saw. I hated who I was. I hated myself. I was a liar.

My beard made me so.

I'd grown that beard to tell the world I was putting my life of youthful folly behind me. But it wasn't behind me, was it? Here I was in a hotel in Austin, Texas having spent weeks trying to meet ten googlewhacks in a row. Not only was I still *doing* stupid things, I was *failing* at them. Not only was I still living a life of youthful folly, but I'd got worse at it!

I'd grown that beard to tell the world I was going to write a novel. But there was no novel, was there? I hadn't written one pissy word. I hadn't just failed to write a novel, I'd failed to realise that there was no novel in me. It was time for me to face the facts. I had to face my demons.

So, this is who I really am, I thought. Novelist? Pah! That's nothing more than an act of vanity on my part; a preposterous idea above my station. I'm no more a novelist than I am an astronaut. Face up to yourself, Gorman, be who you really are. You've run away from it for long enough but now there's nowhere else to run, it's time to turn and face the music. It's time to give up and give in. The beard represents the lies, shave it off and be true to yourself; be the person you're clearly meant to be: a young idiot. Stop being a bearded liar and become a bare-faced teller of truths.

I strode out of the hotel into the cool, early evening air, across the road and into a pharmacy. I bought myself a pack of disposable razors and some shaving gel and returned full of determination.

In the bathroom I lathered up my lying chinny chin chin and prepared to make an honest face of it. I'd shave myself honest and then I'd ring Jake and confess. I'd tell him there wasn't a novel, that I'm not a novelist and I'd find a way of giving him back the money.

I lifted the razor to my cheek. I held it there steady, the blade reaching for the first contact. My hand began to shake. Something was stopping me. The flimsy plastic felt heavy, like lead in my hand. Why so heavy? I knew I was holding the razor at my cheek but in the mirror I could see myself holding Byron's pistol, the barrel resting at my temple, my finger caressing the trigger. I was scared and excited and scared of my excitement and … I shut my eyes, relaxed my fingers and let go.

The razor clattered into the basin and I dropped my head into my hands. I just couldn't do it. I knew it had to go, but I wasn't ready to let it go.

It's a game, Dave. That's what I told myself.

It has to go. But of course you can't just *shave it off*. Human nature means you have to try leaving different patterns and shapes first. This is your opportunity to try out different looks. If you've ever been curious about how the Hitler toothbrush-tache would sit on your top lip, or how a big gay-biker-handlebar-mo would suit, now is your chance to find out. It's a game. That's all.

But it needs careful thought. You can't try out everything you might like because some combinations cancel others out. For instance, you can go from gay-biker to Hitler but in doing so, you forsake the chance to try the Abe Lincoln chinstrap underbeard.

Back in the bedroom I picked up the notepad and pencil from beside the phone. This project required a little planning. In the bathroom I started sketching faces, mapping out journeys from full beard to clean-shaven, a facial topiary flow-chart calculating the most scenic route from A to B.

I don't know how long I spent doing this. What I do know is that I eventually found myself staring at maybe 30 differently bearded, badly drawn, cartoon faces staring back at me. What was I doing? I was manic and I needed to get a grip. Some-where deep inside of me I summoned the strength I needed. I breathed deeply. I needed to think. I needed to analyse. I needed to be calm.

I sat on the bed and took some more deep breaths. Again. And again. Think. I tried to separate my emotions – breathe – tried to work out how I really felt.

There were two sides to this. I was upset because I'd failed, because it was all over. I'd lost myself in the adventure of it all. I'd allowed this … this *thing* to consume me, to take over my life. But in failing I was being forced to confront the bigger situation. My failure on a grander scale: my failure to grow up. I'd let so many people down. I'd let myself down. And now it was time to deal with it.

But slowly. I needed to look after myself. There were two

strands to my disappointment and I would deal with them one at a time.

First, I would accept that the journey was over. The adventure had come to an end and I needed to recognise that fact. I would mourn its loss. I'd go out tonight and see it off with a drink, commiserate, drown my sorrows, whatever it took to get it out of my system.

The bigger picture could wait until tomorrow. Tomorrow I could shave my beard, call Jake and make my confessions. Tonight I would face myself. Tomorrow I would face the world.

I emptied my pockets of everything but my wallet – no need for a Mexican fridge magnet – now and headed for the door. I needed a drink.

On the advice of the hotel receptionist I headed for 6th Street. This was supposed to be the centre of Austin's nightlife, the best place for a drink. She wasn't wrong.

I turned the corner and was stunned to find a row of old Victorian brick buildings, a stark contrast to the high-rise blocks that dominated the rest of this modern city. Small signs explained the history of each building, which of Austin's forefathers had built it and what business he pursued there, but now they were all bars and each one seemed to be hosting some form of live music. Walking down the street past the open doorways was like spinning the dial on a radio, hearing split second snatches of different styles of music before the next doorway and the next tune grasped for a foothold in your consciousness.

Neon lights hung in the windows, hordes of young revellers filled the street walking boozily from bar to bar. It was perfect. No one would notice me quietly drowning my sorrows amongst all of this.

I strode nonchalantly towards the first doorway without a queue.

'ID?' asked the doorman.

'What?' I asked.

'Where's your ID?' he said in patient tones.

Not *this* again. I looked up at the doorman with desperation in my eyes. He was a big man, with long dark hair pulled back into a ponytail that fell back over his muscular shoulders. He had forgiving eyes.

'Look, I don't have any ID on me,' I said, attempting to reason with him. 'I'm English. We don't really *need* ID at home. Look at my face. Look at my beard. I'm 31. I couldn't grow a beard like this when I was 21. I appeal to you to use your common sense. I've got a lot of thinking to do. All I want is a quiet drink to go with it.'

What could be more reasonable than that?

'You need picture ID,' he said, patient still.

'Look, earlier on today I walked into *Mexico* without any ID. That's a country!'

'Well, this is a bar, and you need picture ID.'

'Does your little brother work at Little Brothers in Columbus?' I asked.

'What?'

'Never mind,' I said, my hackles rising. 'You're not going to let me in, are you?'

'Not without ID, no.'

'Fine.' I turned on my heel. 'I'll take my custom elsewhere then, shall I? I'll spend my dollars somewhere I *am* wanted, thank you very much.'

I turned and strode purposefully across the road to the bar opposite. Confidence was the key.

'ID?'

I was turned away from at least five bars before I finally conceded the point. Pride didn't come into it, I *needed* to get drunk and so I *needed* to get my passport. It was sitting on the bedside table back at the hotel in a small bag with a fridge magnet. I left the pedestrianised 6th Street, hailed a cab and with fire in my eyes headed back to the hotel where I ordered the cab to wait.

Ten minutes later I was getting drunk on 6th Street. But I wasn't quietly drowning my sorrows. Now I was drowning them angrily. Now I was on a mission. I wanted to obliterate the day. How could a day start so right but turn so wrong?

'Bourbon? Sure. Make it a large one. Aaah. Another, please. Cheers.'

ID? The arrogant bastards! I'd show them I was man enough to drink in their bars.

There was a band on stage knocking out solid cover versions of classic soul songs. A poster behind the bar told me they were called Joe Valentine and The Imperials featuring Lynn, which was quite a lot of names considering they were only a three-piece band. Joe Valentine was running the show, Lynn was sharing vocal duties so presumably the guy on drums was The Imperials.

Lynn was belting out a gutsy rendition of the Aretha Franklin classic, 'Respect'. I was singing along. My pores were opening up to let some of the alcohol out and in the process some of the lyrics got in under my skin. Except the song was too fast and only the word 'respect' seeped in. Respect. That's all it needed. ID? The arrogant bastards! I'd show them I was man enough to drink in their bars.

The band took a break. As they left the stage I gave The Imperials a big thumbs up and he returned the gesture. I wanted more music. I wanted more bourbon. I wanted more. I wanted Joe Valentine and The Imperials featuring oblivion. I wanted oblivion. It was time to move on.

'Hey, dude,' called out Al, the barman.

I didn't know his name but he looked like an Al.

'Yeah?'

'You left this …'

'What's that?'

He was holding out my passport.

'Thanks, man,' I said. 'You don't know how much trouble I'd be in without that.'

I didn't know how much trouble I was heading for with it.

I moved on. Bar one. Bar two. Bar three. More? I can't remember. All? Bar none.

I'm swaggering. I'm staggering. I'm sniffing out another

experience. I'm alive. I pause in every doorway. Have I already been here? How does it look, sound, smell? This place is new to me. I haven't been here yet. It's bright for a bar. Fluorescent lights. Hang on. Of course. It's not a bar. It's a tattoo parlour, no wonder I haven't been here, no wonder ... I wonder ...

'Are you interested?' asks a voice. He's leaning on the counter. I can't focus on anything but his ears. He has piercings in his ears you could pass two fingers through.

'It makes my skin crawl,' I shudder.

'So you're not interested?'

Earlier that day I'd wanted to hold the gun.

'Well ... I'm interested.'

'Come upstairs,' he says and I follow him up.

The walls are white, the light is bright and the air smells clean. One wall is covered in pictures, each one a potential tattoo. There are hearts and Harleys and dragons and flames and anchors (they actually have anchors!) and Vikings and Chinese letters and Celtic bands and what am I doing here? I don't belong.

'So, are you interested?'

'Yeah,' I say, meaning no. 'I'm interested.'

'ID?'

Idea.

'ID,' I say, nodding.

'No. You need ID,' says holey ears.

'I know,' I say. 'And I want ID.'

'You need ID.'

'I've got ID,' I say, my passport hitting the counter. 'I want ID. Do you have a driver's licence?'

'Hey!' he calls out through a secret doorway. 'You got a driver's licence?'

'Yeah,' comes a disembodied response.

'I want one. A tattoo,' I say, 'of a driver's licence. His driver's licence,' I point through the door, 'these details,' I point at my passport, 'and this face,' I point at my face.

'This sounds cool,' says the voice emerging from the back room. He's big, he has a goatee beard, a beanie hat and a lot of tattoos. 'It's more expensive than getting something off the wall,' he says, indicating the wall of available tattoos, 'but it's more off the wall too. It's cool.'

'You can do it?'

'Yeah.'

ID? The arrogant bastards! I'll show them I'm man enough to drink in their bars.

'Let's do it,' I say.

'Cool,' they say together.

I'm sitting in a chair. A dentist's chair. I hate the dentist. The sound of the drill makes me feel feint.

Buzzuzzuzzuzzuzzuzz.

So does the sound of the needle.

Why am I doing this? I don't know. I feel a prick. I look away and grit my teeth and feel a thousand pricks, buzzing, buzz-uzzuzzuzzing away, scratching, stabbing, penetrating, piercing, permanently painting under my skin, my ID under my skin, I've got me, under my skin, I'm doing it, with a skin full of drink and a skin full of ink, I'm doing it.

ID? The arrogant bastards! I'm showing them I'm man enough to drink in their bars.

PART FOUR

WHAT HAPPENED BECAUSE I WOKE UP IN A

HOTEL ROOM IN AUSTIN, TEXAS WITH A

DRIVER'S LICENCE TATTOOED ON MY LEFT ARM

fifteen

Googlewhackless Gorman*

Googlewhackless   adjective: being without any
                        googlewhacks.

Gorman   noun: me.

I screwed my eyes up tight. Maybe I was imagining it. Maybe when I opened them again my tattoo would be gone. I opened my eyes but no, it was still there.

It was real. For the rest of my life my left arm would carry these marks, a permanent reminder of that night in Austin. The madness of the night before made me shudder. Was this how Dr David Banner felt the morning after a night of Incredible Hulking? Did Dr Jekyll ever lose control and wake up the next day to discover a tattoo? Did Hyde ever ink his hide?

And of all the tattoos to get, I end up with a State of Texas Driver's License. A legal document. With small print. Yes, my tattoo had small print. Looking down across my own shoulder the tattoo was upside down. I tried to look at it in the mirror but it's back to front. Seeing myself, bare-chested in the mirror triggered a painful memory from last night:

* This is not, itself, a googlewhack.

I'm standing in the street. My shirt clutched in my sweaty palms and I'm screaming. Screaming at bouncers, screaming at anyone who'll listen.

'I've got my ID now! You won't turn me away next time! I've got my driver's licence now! Davey's got some picture ID!'

People stop and stare. Gangs of college students point and laugh. There are wisecracks at my expense. I can only hear the laughter. But I'm defiant.

'What are you staring at? Huh? Mr Cap-on-backwards? Where's your ID, huh? I've got mine.'

More laughter.

A policeman. Two. Politely, calmly taking me to one side. Some of the crowd follow but they get shooed away. This is between the cops and me. They make it very clear to me. I don't want a night in the cells, so I put my shirt back on and start walking back to the hotel.

Ow. The memory hurt. Alone in my hotel room I found myself blushing.

Contorting my neck and twisting my arm I manage to take in the details. The tattoo was about the size of a credit card. In the top left corner sat a Texan flag. In bright red lettering (red with ink and blood) the word 'TEXAS' and then in the top right, a Lone Star. Of course. Why have a plain old ordinary left arm when you *could* have the Lone Star on it? Below that, in blue ink, the words, 'DRIVER LICENSE'. Below that: 'DOB: 03-02-71'.

Hang on. That's not even my birthday! That's my birthday *if you're American*. I'm not and in spite of the fact that it has a Texas driver's licence, neither is my left arm. *I* can't read that without thinking it says 3 February. I was born on 2 March. It will never look right to my English eyes.

Below that: 'SEX: M.' At least they got *that* right. Below that: 'GORMAN, DAVID' and an address; somewhere on 6th Street, Austin, maybe it was a bar, maybe it was the tattoo parlour, I didn't remember.

To the right of all this; the 'photo'. Oh my God. A passport-photo-sized image of a face. It looked nothing like me. Except it had a beard. A bright red beard.

I suddenly realised I was trapped in my beard for the rest of my life. If I shaved my beard off I might as well have a stranger's face tattooed on my arm. The birthday was wrong, the face was wrong; only the name was mine. (But then, I'd met plenty of other Dave Gormans, it could be any of theirs too.) If I was clean-shaven it would look like I had someone else's face tattooed on my arm and that would be even harder to explain away. It *was* me. But it was only me *if* I had a red beard.

I walked through to the bathroom and there sitting in the basin where I'd dropped it the night before, was the razor. Another painful memory came flooding into my head.

The tattoo parlour. I'm sitting in the chair. The tattooist is shaving my arm. He's an artist cleaning his canvas, preparing to go to work. He wipes my arm down with some sterilising solution. It feels cool on my skin. He's wearing rubber gloves. He places the specially created transfer on to my hairless skin, presses it down and peels it off like the fake tattoos we used to get in bubblegum wrappers when I was a kid. A feint purple line marks out the shape: a template for him to follow. If only that was it. If only it was that simple.

He produces the needle. For all the world it looks like a tiny pneumatic drill, preparing to shatter my tarmac skin. I look away.

'Ow.' I wince.

Only when he laughs do I realise the needle hasn't touched me yet.

I'd already reasoned my way through this yesterday:

Dave Gorman the bearded novelist didn't exist. I didn't deserve to be taken seriously. *Be the person you're clearly meant to be,* I'd told myself, *shave off the beard, admit who you are, be honest with the world and be that idiot.*

I'd had a two-part plan:

- Part One: Drown my sorrows with a quiet drink.
- Part Two: Shave off my beard, ring Jake and own up.

Well, Part One had gone a bit awry. Part One had gone so wrong that I'd completely scuppered Part Two. I couldn't shave off the beard now. I was trapped in it forever.

Unless ... unless ... what if I amputated my left arm?

Stop it, Gorman, you're going mad. Going? Pah. Gone.

What was I going to do next? How could I tell people about this? I didn't know the answers. Without knowing what to do next I decided to carry on as normal and work out my next move over breakfast. I got dressed, concealing my tattoo – it felt like sunburn – and then headed downstairs.

Four or five doors down the landing the tiny cleaning lady was pushing her cart full of shampoo refills down the corridor. It was bigger than she was.

'You can clean my room now if you like,' I said with my best singsong voice and smile.

The look in her eyes was one of abject terror. A short while ago she'd walked into my room to find me a desperate, manic, trouserless loon. Now I appeared to be calm and collected. The only clue that I was the same man was the carpet burn on my forehead. Maybe she was wary of entering my room, frightened that she'd be the one to find the body.

Downstairs I opened the door to find ten or twelve people politely working round each other at the self-service breakfast counter. There were four urns dispensing different brands of coffee, a selection of muffins, three toasters and my favourite item: a waffle iron. I'd never seen one of these contraptions before but it was fascinating to watch. You poured a pre-prepared batter mix into what looked like a giant sandwich toaster and closed the lid. Two minutes later the machine beeped and you had a perfectly fried piece of egg, fat and sugar latticework. Breakfast: the most important meal of the day.

The waffle iron was the most popular part of the breakfast production line and so inevitably the queue bottlenecked around it, forcing people who didn't really want to acknowledge each other into conversations. Platitudes floated around among the 'please's, 'thank you's and 'excuse me's, but when I tried to join in I met silence.

'Morning,' I said to the cheap suit in front of me.

He turned his back. The scene was watched by a young Mom with two toddlers in her skirts. I met her gaze and raised my eyebrows in a 'did-you-see-that?' way, expecting her to return the look but instead she turned away too, pulling her charges protectively towards her as she did so. Her daughter, maybe six or seven years of age, turned to look at me, but a maternal hand scooped round the back of her head and turned it away from me in an instant.

What was it about me, about my aura, that offended these people so? What was it about my appearance that made me so unacceptable? They couldn't possibly know about last night. They didn't know of my shame. Maybe it was just the look in my eyes. Whatever it was, I felt like I'd stepped into some 1950s movie, set in small-town America and I was cast as the young rebel. The one who rides into town on his motorbike, corrupting the locals with – shock horror – rock 'n' roll.

I knew there and then that I had to leave Austin. I put down my plate, picked up a blueberry muffin, turned on my heels and left. I returned to my room – it was still unserviced – threw what belongings I had with me into my backpack and pre-pared to check out. But where was I going to go? I knew I couldn't stay in Austin, but could I really go home?

Suddenly it came to me. I'd made some new friends on my recent travels but they were all part of my googlewhacking, they were part of the problem. There was only one old friend I'd seen all year. Los Angeles was a couple of hours behind but it was late enough now, Julie would understand. I picked up the phone.

'Hello?'

'Julie, it's Dave—' I stopped because I didn't know what else to say.

'Hey Dave,' said Julie brightly, 'you got any news from your top-secret meeting yet?'

'Erm … no.'

There was an awkward pause. I wanted to tell her every-thing but I didn't know how to start.

'Dave, are you OK?' asked Julie, concern entering her voice.

'Yeah,' I bluffed.

'You don't sound good, Dave,' it was clearly a bad bluff. 'Is everything OK?'

'No.' My voice cracked.

'What's wrong? What's happened?'

'I don't know, Julie. *Everything's* gone wrong. Life's just turned to shit.'

'What are you talking about?'

'I've been googlewhacking,' I gabbled. 'I've been trying to get ten in a row. I've failed. It's shit. I'm shit. I went out last night and … I've got to wear this beard for the rest of my life, Julie. I've done some *really* stupid things. I'm in trouble. I've spent Jake's money. I haven't written anything … it's all gone wrong.'

I was speaking too fast to be understood, especially for poor Julie who knew nothing about (a) googlewhacking, (b) Jake or (c) my publishing contract.

'Dave—' she tried to cut in.

'I've gone *too far* this time, Julie,' I blurted. 'Don't you see? It's out of control, Julie. *I'm* out of control. I don't know what I'm doing. I don't know what to do next.'

'Dave, listen,' she snapped, her voice the telephonic equiv-alent of a slap across the cheek. 'Tell me where you are?'

'Austin.'

'Austin? As in Austin, Texas?'

'Yes.'

'Right. Do you want me to come to Austin or do you want to come to LA?'

'What?'

'OK. Go to the airport. Fly to LA. Let me know what time you land. I'll come and pick you up.'

'But—'

'No buts. Nothing. Do it.'

*

The cab to the airport cost me $25. I reached into my pocket and pulled out my wallet. It always takes me a couple of extra seconds to select the right notes in America as they're all the same colour and size, but in this confused state of mind I was slower than normal. Adding to my confusion were other scraps of unfamiliar paper that were getting in the way. They fell out on to the back seat of the cab and with too much going on in my head I didn't think to pick them up.

'Hey, take your trash with you, mister,' said the driver.

'Sorry,' I said, reaching back in and picking up the scraps.

I was about to drop them in a bin when curiosity got the better of me. I'm glad it did because the first piece of paper had on it neatly typed instructions on caring for my tattoo. I made a mental note to look out for an ointment called 'A + D'.

The other scrap of paper was also related to my tattoo; it was a receipt. Take that fact in for a moment, why don't you? You're reading a book written by the kind of man who asks a tattoo parlour for a receipt! What was I thinking? That I might want to take it back?

The receipt's existence was damning enough to my sense of self-respect but it contained two pieces of information that really put the final nails in the coffin. The first was the price, the second was the name of the tattooist. Not only had I paid $190 to have this abomination on my arm (ow) but I'd given this money to a man named *Boo Boo*!

Boo Boo for crying out loud! Not even Yogi! Would anyone in their right mind entrust their skin to a man called Boo Boo?

No, but someone who was out of it might.

I didn't buy a fridge magnet from Austin. I already had a souvenir from this city. One that would be with me forever.

*

As I stepped off the plane into the blazing heat of Los Angeles I felt hollow. It's difficult to explain the almost complete lack of sensation I was experiencing because it was precisely that: a *lack* of sensation. I felt like I'd experienced an internal power cut. My emergency generator had kicked in, but it only had enough power to keep the bare essentials going, it couldn't cope with any of the body's more complex systems. I had to concentrate so hard just to walk and talk and even breathe that there was no chance of me exhibiting anything as draining as thought or emotion. I was numb.

Julie was in the arrival's lounge and came racing over to greet me with a big hug, inadvertently squeezing the tender tattoo and making me wince slightly. I didn't tell her about the tattoo. I couldn't. I felt such an idiot.

'Are you OK?' she asked.

'I'm fine,' I said, but it was just noise, my words meant nothing.

'You are *so* not fine,' said Julie resting her palm on my cheek. 'You're not well. Come on, let's go.'

The journey passed in a haze. As did the hours that followed. As did the rest of the day and beyond. I don't know how long I was in this zombie-like state because I wasn't really aware of the passage of time. I can remember fragments and nothing more.

I can remember sitting on the sofa and being confused because I didn't recognise the clothes I was wearing.

'Dan's away filming,' said Julie. 'I lent you some of his stuff because I'm washing all yours. Don't you remember?'

I can remember soup. And a bath. And sleep. Lots of sleep. And every now and then Julie asking me what was wrong.

'Do you want me to ring anyone?' asked Julie. 'Does anyone back home know where you are?'

'No.'

'What's happened, Dave?' she asked. 'I want to help.'

'I don't know,' I said. 'I'm OK.'

I can remember sitting on the sofa, watching a video and eating pizza, but I couldn't taste the pizza and the film was a nothingness, just pretty colours moving around in front of my eyes.

'What did you think?' asked Julie.

'What?'

'Of the film?'

'Film?'

And then one morning I ate a strawberry and it was amazing to me because it tasted like a strawberry and suddenly I remembered what it was like to taste things and smell things and hear things and see things and touch things and all of a sudden I wanted to explain and I wanted to talk about it and it all came flooding out of me right there and then in the kitchen.

Julie sat in stunned silence as I recounted my travels. I told her how it began and how it got to this point. I tore off some pieces of kitchen paper and scrawled a diagram explaining the connections between the various googlewhacks and how all the chains had broken down and then ... and then obviously I had done the same.

'I've been trying to get ten in a row,' I explained. 'I don't really understand how it became important, it just did. But I

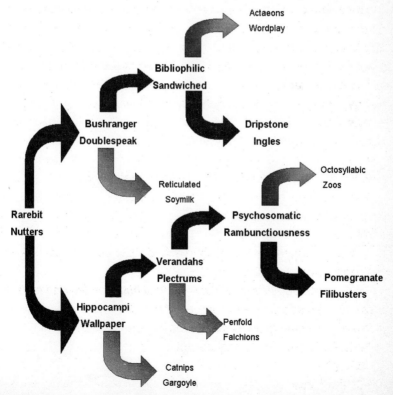

couldn't get more than five in a row. There are too many dead-ends. Look at that ...' I slid the paper towards Julie '... four-in-a-row, five-in-a-row, it's useless.'

'There's a lot to take in here, Dave,' she said, a look of utter disbelief playing across her face. 'So when you came to Los Angeles and told me you were meeting a writer and an actress you were actually meeting a googlewhack?'

'No. Not really,' I struggled for the words, 'I mean ... yes. I was meeting Psychosomatic Rambunctiousness,' I said, 'but she *is* a writer and she *has* just appeared in a movie. I wasn't lying to you, Julie. I just wasn't telling you the whole truth.'

'So instead of writing a novel you've travelled the world ... *googlewhacking*... and all you've got to show for it is a chain of four and another of five?' said Julie, her voice growing less concerned and more appalled with every syllable. '*That's* what you're telling me?'

'And another chain of five,' I said defensively.

Even though I knew I'd let the whole googlewhacking thing get out of hand, hearing the scorn creeping into Julie's voice made me feel protective towards it. Yes, it had been madness, but it was *my* madness. I tore off another piece of paper and quickly scrawled another diagram explaining my first foolish

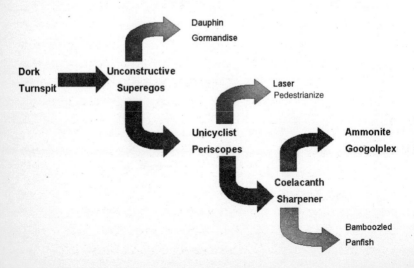

five-in-a-row foray into the googlewhacking world.

'You see,' I said, 'I just can't get more than five.'

'So, let me get this straight,' said Julie, 'the world's largest publisher has given you a contract to write a novel and you haven't written anything and *this* is the reason?'

'Well yeah, but the thing is…'

'Because you were trying to get ten googlewhacks in a row?'

'Yeah, but…'

'Dave, this *doesn't make sense*… googlewhacking is supposed to be a distraction, a half hour's worth of wordplay to while away a slow day in the office, not … not…' Julie picked up the pieces of kitchen paper with disdain, 'not *this*.'

'I know, but…' I protested.

'No,' said Julie, determined to say her piece, '*this* isn't a real game. There are no rules, Dave, you've *invented* these rules…'

'It wasn't me, Julie,' I pleaded, 'it was David Gorman.'

'*Listen* to yourself,' said Julie with fire in her eyes. '*You* are David Gorman. *You* invented these rules…'

'No,' I said. 'It was *David* Gorman. Not me. He challenged me. Meet ten googlewhacks in a row. Find no more myself. Everyone I meet can find me two more…'

'In which case,' yelled Julie, 'why has *this one* only found you one?'

There was silence. Had I heard Julie correctly? Which one? If I had… if there was… then there was still hope for the adventure. Our eyes were locked across the kitchen counter but I broke free of Julie's gaze. My eyes darted to the counter where Julie's hand rested still pointing at my badly rendered diagram. She whisked her hand away as if that would somehow make the facts disappear too but it was too late. It was there. It was obvious.

It was Dork Turnspit.

Marcus – *had* only found me one googlewhack. Of course! He'd found Unconstructive Superegos! He'd led me to David Gorman and it was only then that the rules were established. Of course I hadn't asked Marcus for a second 'whack – the two 'whack rule hadn't existed at the time.

I looked back up at Julie. She looked at me. We both knew what this meant.

'No!' she shouted at me.

'Yes!' I shouted back. 'The game is still alive. Marcus owes me one more googlewhack. Don't you see, Julie, this is my chance—'

'Your chance for what?'

'Dignity!' I cried. 'Right now there's no dignity in this situation. I've screwed up the novel, I've lost the game, I've … I've …'

'What?'

I still hadn't told Julie about my tattoo. No one knew about that and I was determined to keep it that way. That was between me and Boo Boo.

'I've gone too far, Julie,' I said. 'But what's the point in turning back now? If I go home and tell people what I've done now, I'll have nothing to show for it but a story of failure. Meeting another googlewhack isn't going to make what I've done any more stupid; it's too late for that. But if I can *do* this … if I can get ten in a row, I'll be a winner. I'll have done something. I've still got time; there's a month left. What choice do I have?'

Before Julie could offer me any choices I raced out of the kitchen and into the study. I went to work and within a few minutes I was back at WomenAndDogsUK.co.uk and looking once again at Marcus's email address.

From: Dave Gorman
To: Marcus
Subject: Whack my google one more time.

Marcus,

I need a really big favour from you. I need you to find me another googlewhack and I need it as soon as possible. Please Marcus, it's really important.

I needed him to do this for me. What could I offer by way of encouragement? Ah ha!

> I'm away from home right now but I have found a really great photo of a woman and a dog. When I get back to the UK I'll stick it in the post.
>
> Please remember the googlewhack, asap,
>
> Dave

'Julie?'
  'Yeah?'
  'Do any of your neighbours have dogs?'
  'Uh. Yeah.'
  'Great. I'll just get my camera.'

*

The next morning I checked my emails:

> From: Marcus
> To: Dave
> Subject: Hydroids Souvlaki.
>
> Hi Dave,
>
> Howzat?
>
> Marcus

'Zat' was absolutely perfect. I googled the pair and whack, there it was all present and correct. Two words, one hit and every googlewhacking rule obeyed.
  'Wicked!' I whispered. I'd never known my accent wander that far before.

I tentatively clicked on the link and watched as the page – written by a Dr M. Dale Stokes – opened up before me. It contained good news and bad news, which is how *my* doctor likes to package things too.

The good news was that an email address was very easily found. The bad news – the very bad news – was that the website was entitled: *The Antarctic Journal of Dr. M. Dale Stokes*.

Was it possible for a regular Joe like me to visit the Antarctic? I suppose I was about to find out.

sixteen

Hydroids Souvlaki

Hydroids   noun: plural of hydroid; any of several
              types of invertebrate sea creatures with a
              saclike body and a single opening or
              mouth, such as the hydra, Portuguese-
              man-of-war etc.

Souvlaki   noun: a Greek dish involving meat (usually
              lamb) cooked on a skewer.

'Come in, sit down,' said Dr M. Dale Stokes, 'would you like a
cold drink?'

This is possibly a good moment to mention that we were
not in the Antarctic.

Dale's *Antarctic Journal* had been written several years ago
and he had since returned to his more permanent residence in
San Diego. He was a research scientist working at the Scripps
Institution of Oceanography and it was there that he'd agreed
to meet me.

The desperation I'd felt at the prospect of a trip to the
Antarctic had been replaced by joy when I discovered I didn't
even have to leave the State of California to get my man.
There'd been a spring in my step as I left Julie's bound, not for
the airport, but the train station.

A magnificent, double-decker train chugged its way down
the coast covering the 100 miles in a little over two hours and

depositing me at the Santa Fe railroad. San Diego had, under the auspices of Dr Gish, been a part of my earlier downfall, but now I hoped the presence of another Dr would make it the scene of my resurrection.

From the centre of town I'd jumped into a cab and asked for La Jolla. Five minutes later, when I'd worked out that it was pronounced 'La Hoya', my 25-minute cab ride through stunning scenery had begun.

La Jolla itself was beautiful. Huge, individually designed houses delicately stacked up on a low mountainside over-looking a clear blue ocean. Palm trees cast dramatic shadows in the early afternoon sun. As I got out of the cab I saw a rich woman with too much jewellery walking a tiny dog with too much jewellery as three suntanned surfers parked their artfully beaten-up VW campervan on the side of the road.

There was a cluster of modern buildings made from dark timber with huge industrial girders and high tension steel wire pulling things together that looked like large Ikea bookshelves – only without the wobble factor – and it was on the terrace outside these buildings that Dale met me. We sat at a picnic table and opened a can of pop apiece while we chatted. Dale was possessed of a rugged Indiana Jonesy quality. He was an academic but he was an adventurer too and he held me in thrall as he told me about his time in both the Antarctic *and* the Arctic. How many people have you met who have literally been to the ends of the earth?

'But that's enough about me, eh,' he said modestly, 'tell me about yourself. Is this your first trip to San Diego?'

'Actually no,' I said, 'I was here about a week ago.'

'Really?' asked Dale. 'How come?'

'I was meeting another googlewhack,' I shrugged. 'But I've been to Holland, Texas, Mexico and LA since then.'

I suppose throwing Mexico into the mix was a little disingenuous – I had only been there for a couple of hours – but I was in the company of a real explorer and I didn't want him to think my travels weren't serious.

'So what was your other San Diegan googlewhack like?' he asked.

'He was a bit odd really,' I said awkwardly. I'd learnt to tiptoe my way around the subject of creationism.

'How come?'

'Well ...' I weighed up my surroundings; Dale was an academic, a marine biologist of all things. If anyone was going to be properly informed on the origins of life it would be him. '... Well, he was an 81-year-old creationist.'

'Pfft, I see what you mean; definitely a bit weird,' said Dale, his eyes rolling in their sockets. 'I expect he was one of Gish's lot.'

The mention of Gish's name caught me by surprise and I was mid-gulp at the time. I snorted in amazement, sending fizzy 7Up shooting up the back of my nose and out through the front. I jumped back from the table as if propelled by the jet of snotty pop.

'One of Gish's lot!' I yelled, my eyes watering from a carbonated nostril. 'One of *his lot*! It wasn't *one of his lot*, it *was* Dr Gish!'

'You've met Gish!' exclaimed Dale, his jaw dropping. He was lucky he didn't have a mouthful of anything fizzy at the time.

'Yes!'

'Oh my God! What was he like?'

'He wears a wig!'

'Fantastic!' Dale yelped with delight, we were like schoolboys sharing an embarrassing discovery about an unpleasant teacher. 'I can't *believe* you've actually met Gish!'

'I can't believe you know who Gish is ...' I said.

'What do you mean? He's one of the most powerful creationists in the world! You've met the top dog,' said Dale. 'Ooo, I hate Gish! I've seen him debate. He's a nasty piece of work. He'll go against a young, naïve evolutionist and he'll tear him a new asshole. He lies, uses bad science but he plays to the crowd.'

'What? Dr Gish?' I asked, amazed at what I was hearing about the old buffoon.

'Did he show you their museum?'

'No, not really, I went to the offices but ...'

'When I was a student I wanted to go round and trash that museum.' Dale's expression was loaded with contempt. I looked at his eyes and watched the pupils contract as thoughts were formed and then dilate suddenly as an idea hit him. 'Oh! Oh yes ... I've got something that might interest you ... come with me.'

Dale was off, taking purposeful strides towards one of the buildings. I skipped off after him, all the while trying to clear the unpleasant 7Up sensation at the back of my nose.

Dale held a door open and I stepped into a vast laboratory full of incredible looking equipment. I didn't know what any of it did, but it all looked frightfully interesting. An involuntary 'wow' fell from my lips.

'It is kind of cool, isn't it?' said Dale.

The word 'laboratory' summons up a stereotypical image: all Bunsen burners and test-tubes, little flashing lights, beeping beeps and bubbling green and purple liquids, but this was far more ramshackle than that. The equipment was big, scruffy and practical: balls, tubes, planks of wood, pipes and who-knows-what all thrown together, no doubt by big, scruffy, practical men.

'When you're doing work that hasn't been done before,' explained Dale, 'it involves apparatus you can't buy from a catalogue so you have to build it yourself ...'

'It's amazing,' I said.

'... apart from *this*. This thing was shop-bought,' said Dale, affectionately patting a small white box. 'It's probably my favourite bit of kit.'

I looked at it, trying to work out what was so special about it. It was about the size and shape of a microwave, but I couldn't begin to fathom what function it served.

'What does it do?' I asked.

'It's a microwave,' said Dale.

'What?'

'It cooks noodles. Come on, let's go to the office.'

We skipped up two flights of stairs, along a corridor and in to a small, neat office. The lack of personal touches made it obvious that Dale didn't spend very much of his time in the office but then this was the Scripps Institution of Oceanography so it shouldn't really have seemed odd that Dale spends more time in the ocean than he does at his desk.

He crouched down in the corner, opened up a small filing cabinet and started flicking through its contents.

'What are you looking for?' I asked.

'Well … I'm really a research scientist not a teacher, but we are part of the University of California,' said Dale, without looking up, 'so occasionally I have to give the odd lecture. I keep a few essays that I wrote when I was a student because they help me to structure a lesson, but there's one in particular that might interest you … hang on … yes, here it is.'

Dale handed me a few sheets of neatly typed A4 paper with a handwritten title page:

Analysis of a Creationist Pamphlet and Evidence for Evolution

by Dale Stokes.

I turned the page and began reading. It didn't take me long to work out that the pamphlet I was reading about, the creationist pamphlet Dale had analysed when he was a student wasn't just any old pamphlet. Oh no, it was 'Have You Been Brainwashed?', written by (and starring) Duane T. Gish!

'This is amazing!' I said.

'Well … I was only a student …' said Dale modestly.

'No, not that,' I said. 'This whole thing … you and Gish and me and googlewhacking! How weird is this? Google indexes three billion pages, any of those pages might contain a 'whack. It couldn't be more random. So what are the chances that I meet one googlewhack in San Diego, he gives me a pamphlet he's written and then a week later I find myself back in San Diego meeting another googlewhack who gives me his analysis of *that* pamphlet?'

'He gave you a copy of *that* pamphlet? He's still distributing that piece of crap!'

Dale's analysis of 'Have You Been Brainwashed?' made for a very entertaining read. Every point made by the pamphlet was summarily destroyed, every falsehood and half truth highlighted and ... oh joy ... my eyes suddenly rested on the following phrase: '*Dr. Gish's twisted definition of the Second Law of Thermodynamics disproves the process of evolution about as well as his anthropocentric views of the universe prove the existence of an omnipotent creator ...*'

'Yes!' I said, 'The Second Law of Thermodynamics thing! How twisted is his definition?'

'Oh, I know!' said Dale. 'How screwed up is that?'

I felt like I'd found a soul mate in Dale. United by a common enemy. Witnessing Dale's gleeful hatred for the man and his beliefs, I found my own distaste rekindled. Dale hated Gish for his creationist views, I hated him for his failure to googlewhack, but in that instant we were both united in our hatred for him.

'This is astounding,' I said. 'I've never met two more diametrically opposed men in all my life. You and Gish are like black and white, you're hot and cold, good and evil, Batman and The Joker, *you are the anti-Gish ...*

'I'll tell you something else about Gish,' I continued. Pausing dramatically, I leaned forward and lowered my voice, about to reveal a dark secret. 'He *could not googlewhack ...*' Dale's eyes widened. I seized my opportunity. '... Tell me, Dale... can *you*?'

If I live to be a hundred I swear I will never witness a more motivated googlewhacker in my life. Determined to show that the only thing he had in common with Gish was a San Diego zip code, Dale sat down and went to work. Not only did he deliver two prime 'whacks but he delivered them quickly. Two minutes, two 'whacks. Anthropocentricity Waistcoat? Whack!

Acehigh Lawnmowers? Whack! Scientists tend to be good at it when they put their minds to it but if you give one that kind of motivation you'll find yourself looking at a world-class 'whacker.

Oh yes, I was well and truly back in the googlewhacking saddle. A new chain was underway. From Dork Turnspit to Hydroids Souvlaki and beyond …

seventeen

Acehigh Lawnmowers

ACEHIGH   abbreviation (now obsolete): the Allied Command Europe troposcatter communication system.

Lawnmowers   noun: plural of lawnmower; a powered or hand-operated machine with rotary blades used for cutting grass.

I was shocked. It was the same kind of shock I'd experienced when I stepped into Tom and Lisa's living room in Seattle to be confronted by all that Mickey Mouse memorabilia. Only it wasn't Mickey Mouse, it was Elvis Presley and it wasn't just someone's living room, it was the entire city of Memphis.

I'd been in Memphis for less than five minutes when I saw my first giant cardboard cutout Elvis outside one of the airport shops and from then on I was bombarded with images of him wherever I went.

I suppose it didn't help that my hotel was just off Elvis Presley Boulevard but then I'd chosen it for budgetary reasons and that part of town was overflowing with cheap hotels, most of which seemed to be competing to see just how Elvisy they could be.

I'd never been much of an Elvis fan and I really just wanted to get a good night's sleep so I was hoping my hotel hadn't gone too far with the Preslification. I was most encouraged when I found the lobby to be entirely devoid of Elvis iconography but then a little let down when I got into my room, and discovered two enormous framed black and white photographs of him adorning the wall. I was happy to settle for that. It was probably less cloying than the Heartbreak Hotel, a few hundred yards down the road, directly opposite the Graceland mansion. Who knows what kind of Elvis experience they provided. I imagined lookalikes on reception, *Viva Las Vegas*-themed rooms and a complimentary pair of blue-suede slippers.

Even if I had been a fan, I couldn't imagine wanting to stay in the Heartbreak Hotel. Sure, it was named after one of *his* songs but lyrically the hotel was surely a metaphor for the desperate loneliness of the broken hearted and while we've all been there at some time, it's never through choice. I'd have just called it *hotelvis* and been done with it, but what do I know?

I settled in to my less Elvis-centric environment for an early night; I wanted to be up and alert in the morning ready to meet my next googlewhack, Acehigh Lawnmowers. From the website I had worked out that the man responsible was known as Professor Mu Kraken and that he was a member of something called Metaphysics Anonymous. His response to my initial email had been very exciting.

From: Professor Mu Kraken
To: Dave Gorman
Subject: Googlewhacking.

Dave,

I'm very happy to meet with you and will endeavour to find you two googlewhacks before you arrive.

I would like to show you round Memphis and hopefully I will be able to introduce you to Metaphysics Anonymous. It's always interesting.

It's a collection of bohemian intellectuals who have been trying to define metaphysics for some 20 years; a sort of private philosophy club. We used to meet every Saturday night but that has slacked off in the last few years. At an MA meeting you would have found physicists, astrologers, artists, writers, musicians and a plethora of Taoist troubadours. We may be able to get a couple of them together. I'm looking forward to this with great relish.

And because he was looking forward to it with great relish, so was I. I even found myself singing in the shower that night.

'Oh I've got a lotta 'whacking to do/A whole lotta 'whacking to do/Come on baby, to make a 'whack takes two/Oh yes, I've got a lotta 'whacking to do/A whole lotta 'whacking to do/And there's no one I'd rather do it with than Mu.'

No matter how ambivalent you are about Elvis, after a few hours in Memphis, he definitely gets under your skin.

*

It was lunchtime and Professor Mu Kraken was in the lobby waiting for me.

'Hi … Mu,' I said, unsure of how best to address him.

'Call me Ernie,' he grinned, his voice gentle and calm. 'Mu Kraken is my pseudonym.'

'I guessed that,' I said. 'I read the short story on your website: "The Quest for the Cosmic Jazzma, Disk IX: The Aves of Aramie".'

'That's quite a challenging read,' smiled Ernie. 'It's written in the surrealist jive vernacular … very challenging.'

Inwardly I breathed a sigh of relief. It had indeed been a very challenging read, full of playfully made-up words that reminded me of Lewis Carroll's *Jabberwocky*: *'Farswearing the sugarswain barlooms and the ladies unladdylike, leaving Aramie abed coldercranked.'*

(I suppose it wasn't surprising that, when real words did pop up, a googlewhack was born. It occurred to me that Ernie would make a fine lyricist for erstwhile space rockers Mr Quimby's Beard and I made a mental note to call Jerry.)

'So, where does the name Mu Kraken come from?' I asked. 'I'm not very familiar with that kind of literature, it sounds kind of Lord-of-the-Rings-y...'

Ernie laughed. The answer was far more prosaic than that.

'My surname is McCracken,' he said, as we started to drive.

Ernie had a look that was hard to pin down. He wore baggy combat trousers, and a knitted hooded top over a Hawaiian shirt. He had a wonderful copper-coloured goatee beard and the pointiest of pointy, owl-like eyebrows that lent him a permanently studious expression, an effect only added to by the pipe that hung jauntily from the corner of his mouth. Oh, and he wore a beret. There was a peacefulness about Ernie; it was in his voice and the way he moved and it was in his face too, a fifty-something face with barely a crease on it. Just being in his company was like having a massage.

'So, I got you a couple of googlewhacks and I figured we could go meet some friends of mine at the Overton Park Shell,' said Ernie. 'They have internet access there and they're very interesting people.'

Ernie was a hippie. It's a word that's used lazily these days, thrown casually at anyone who might have long hair, sandals or show an interest in green politics; hell, I was once called a hippie for ordering couscous but that's not what I mean at all. I mean hippie in the truest Sixties/Seventies-acid-dropping/pot-smoking sense. I suppose Ernie was the kind of man my grandparents warned my mum about.

It may be that, somehow, the essence of that warning had locked itself into the Gorman family genes. Or maybe my parents used to sneak into my room at night and play subliminal anti-drug hypnosis tapes while I slept. Or maybe I'd just read one too many *Daily Mail*s while sitting in various dentists' waiting rooms down the years. Whatever the reason, when Ernie started to tell me about his first acid trip at the age of 19 a small part of me, somewhere deep inside, wanted to yell, 'Stop the car! I want to get out!'

Please don't misinterpret that as any kind of moralistic reaction. (I think I've told you far too much about my relationship with alcohol to get away with anything like that.) The truth, as uncool as it may be, was simply that drugs scared me. My own experience with drugs had gone no further than alcohol and caffeine, with marijuana back in a very distant third place, but everything else – and especially those things with the whiff of a laboratory about them – had always scared me far more than was probably sensible. In short, I was a coward who chose to take neither the high ground nor the high life.

Of course, I didn't yell, 'Stop the car! I want to get out!' because I knew how weird and strange and irrational that would be. No, I said, 'Really? And you were only 19?' because I was fascinated.

'You see, you have to remember that Memphis was segregated in the Sixties,' said Ernie, reminding me that being a hippie wasn't just about taking acid and smoking pot. It was a rejection of the conventional values of the day and I suppose it's wise for us to remember just how screwed up some of those values were.

Nowadays we find it impossible to imagine a world in which schools, universities, factories, public transport and who knows what else are segregated because of race, but less than forty years ago that's the way things were in Memphis. Martin Luther King lost his life to an assassin's bullet in the city in 1968. When you see a grand old house in Memphis, the chances are it was built using a fortune earned out of slavery.

'I was in a car once with four people,' said Ernie. 'I was the only white guy and we ended up in a car chase trying to get away from some rednecks trying to run us off the road. We got away, but who knows what would have happened if we hadn't.'

We pulled into Overton Park, a large expanse of densely

wooded greenery not far from the centre of town, and parked up behind what I guessed was the Shell.

The Overton Park Shell was an outdoor performance space. A large concrete half dome formed the back of the stage, a structure that bounced all sound out front to the rows of tatty wooden benches. Ernie led me in through the back door. The front of the venue might have looked a bit rough around the edges but the backstage area was charmingly rough through and through. There were tins of paint stacked up, disused props and scenery stowed wherever it would fit and un-identifiable piles of stuff hidden beneath tarpaulin.

'Hey, it's only me,' hollered Ernie, announcing our arrival.

'Hey, Ernie,' came a reply.

My eyes followed the voice to find its owner, a scrawny little man in a ragged red pullover. He had a stubbly chin but a luxurious walrus-like moustache. Ernie introduced us.

'John, this is a friend of mine, Dave,' he said. 'I'm just showing him round Memphis. Can he use your computer?'

'Sure he can,' said John, approaching and shaking my hand. 'Welcome to the Shell, Dave.'

John wanted to take me on a tour of the venue first, so off we went through the rabbit warren corridors, dressing rooms and backstage area and out on to the stage itself. As we walked I learned that the place was tatty because it no longer had public funding. But volunteers like John had dedicated a lot of time and energy to renovating and maintaining the place because they felt it was an important part of Memphis life.

'I used to be a carpenter in a big opera house,' said John. 'It's a highly skilled job and well paid too. Then a few years ago I was diagnosed with cancer. They wanted to cut me up and do all kinds of shit but I wasn't having any of it. They told me I didn't have long to live. I lost my job and came here,' his voice thinned, but he swelled up his chest with defiant pride. 'I've been looking after this place ever since. I keep it alive and it keeps me alive. Last year we promoted 54 different live shows. 62,000 people came and sat in those bleachers and it's all run by volunteers.'

I felt guilty for thinking the place looked tatty now. As I looked out at the empty benches it looked different. It looked loved.

'I think we've got enough funds together to paint the benches now. Next year, it'll happen,' said John and I could hear the spirit in his voice and see the life in his eyes and I understood exactly how this place fed his soul.

'Do you know where you're standing right now?' he asked.

I looked around me for clues. I was centre stage, but I knew there had to be more to it than that.

'Er … no.'

'Right there,' said John, pointing at my feet, 'is where Elvis made his first ever professional appearance.'

'Really?' I asked, and again I could feel my impervious Elvis-proof skin cracking.

'Uh huh,' said John. He leaned in close to me, making it clear that what he had to say next was of great importance. 'Do you know what the coordinates are for that spot right there?'

I wasn't really sure what the question meant, so I was pretty sure that the answer must be 'no'.

'No.'

John leaned in closer still and spoke in a whisper steeped in awe and wonder.

'90, 35,' he said. 'The intersection of the 90th meridian and the 35th parallel.'

'Wow,' I said, although I didn't have a clue as to why those numbers were remarkable, only that right there and then it *did* feel remarkable.

'Do you know what's on the other side of the world from here?' asked John. 'Do you know what you're opposite?'

'No.'

John looked both ways in case anyone else was within range. His eyes widened and his voice lowered further still and he said, 'The Forbidden City. Beijing. China.'

'Wow,' I said again.

The air buzzed with the mystical significance of it all. I

didn't understand why it was impressive that I was standing on the spot where Elvis made his first professional appearance or that that spot was the polar opposite of China's Forbidden City but somehow the air seemed thinner, a cool breeze blew round my neck and my skin tingled.

John put his arm on my shoulder, the two of us were almost huddling now, and he prepared to speak again. I listened intently, ready for the next awe-inspiring fact to present itself.

'Do you like surfing porn?' he said.

My brain scrambled through the words, rearranging them, trying to decipher the otherworldly message that must surely have been in there but no, he really was just asking me if I liked surfing for porn.

'Er … not really,' I said pathetically.

'I'll show you to the computer,' said John, exiting stage right.

We walked back through to the backstage area and into a tiny office space where I was amazed to discover an incredible array of computing equipment. There were monitors and printers and TV screens all stacked up in ramshackle fashion. It looked like a small East European country was monitoring a space mission from a secret location. John saw the surprise on my face.

'It's all donated by well-wishers,' he said, 'a lot of people look after us. Every Thursday some of the staff from the local Pizza Hut come by with some pizza, we get people dropping off tinned food quite often and,' he indicated the computers, 'this kind of stuff too.'

'This is amazing,' I said. 'People must really care about this place.'

'Everyone except the City of Memphis, dude,' said the bitter voice of a blue-haired volunteer from round a doorway. He had a paintbrush in one hand and a joint in the other.

'We recently upgraded our connection speed,' said John, 'much better for porn.' He smiled. 'Sit down, it's online, just help yourself.'

I sat at the computer and Ernie came to stand at my shoulder saying, 'I got Neutrino Scrummages …'

I typed in the words, hit the Google search button and confirmed that it was indeed a 'whack. It led to a page on a Welsh rugby website where an email address was easily found. I opened up another window, surfed into the mail2web.com site and seconds later an email was winging its way to Wales.

'OK Ernie, Wales is nice,' I said, fond thoughts of Minis floating through my mind, 'but it's a long way from Memphis. I hope this next one is a little easier to get to.'

'Grandmaster Sticklebacks,' said Ernie

A few keystrokes later I was looking at uwpmag.com. The 'uwp' stood for *Underwater Photography* and the 'mag' stood for magazine.

'Well,' I said, 'it's not a .co.*uk* or a .com.*au* or anything more exotic than that. I guess it's most likely to be American.'

'And quite likely to be underwater,' suggested Ernie.

'I guess so,' I said, firing off my second email.

'That reminds me,' said Ernie, his eyes lighting up. 'We'll be meeting Captain Nemo later.'

'The submarine captain?' I said. 'From *20,000 Leagues under the Sea*?'

'No, the computer technician,' said Ernie. 'From Memphis.'

'Obviously.'

'You'll like him,' said Ernie. 'We're gonna get a small group of Met. Anon. guys together and head out to The Dreamer's place. It'll be fun.'

*

We sat in the small wooden hut. Candles flickered. Outside it was pitch black. The kind of darkness you can never find in a city, the kind of darkness you only find in the woods. An owl hooted. Either that or a BBC radio sound effects crew were outside thinking, 'Do you know what would be perfect right now? An owl hooting.'

We'd left the city far behind us some time ago. A little while later we'd left the tarmac roads behind too. This was The Dreamer's place. The Dreamer was a sculptor. He was also employed as a caretaker for this patch of land in the woods, which was a perfect arrangement for all concerned. He got to live in a sizable mobile home, with the fresh air he craved and more importantly the space and freedom to carve his stones. In return the landowners got ... well, they got to have a sculptor living on their land.

The Dreamer had long silver hair tied in a ponytail at the back and a big bushy beard, which is pretty much how I'd always imagined a sculptor who lived in the woods would look. He also looked like a dreamer.

Captain Nemo had a beard too, as anyone named after a famous submariner should. Whenever he spoke, he always sounded as though he was about to break into laughter. This meant, oddly, that when he did laugh it always took me by surprise.

The fourth member of Metaphysics Anonymous bucked the trend by not having a beard or a nickname. Bryan was younger than the others by about 30 years and I was grateful for his presence. I had a few years on him *and* a beard so even though I was the newcomer, Bryan managed to look like the odd one out and consequently, I felt like I belonged. It was a nice feeling; I liked them and I wanted to fit in.

'The bye-laws for Metaphysics Anonymous are very simple,' said Nemo. 'One: members have a right to hold and express their own opinions. Two: members may use and explain their own definitions. Three: an attempt will be made to communicate not merely persuade. Four: anyone who agrees with one, two and three can be a member.'

. 'Can I be a member?' I asked.

'You already are,' said Ernie.

'Cool,' I said, because I'd never been part of a private philosophy club before.

To be honest, I wasn't really expecting a serious philosophical discussion; I just thought we'd get stoned together and talk about nothing. Well, we did talk about nothing, but it was 'the concept *of* nothing' so I think you'll find that counts as philosophy.

We talked about semantic structures, whether or not a dream represented reality (because, after all, you *really* dreamed it), the philosophical proof for evolution (I feel I came into my own on this one) and much more besides. Oh, and we did get stoned while we were doing it, which may or may not be responsible for the fact that I was actually understanding the deep concepts that were up for discussion.

In the middle of the evening Ernie asked me to explain the idea of googlewhacks to the others. Obviously by this stage I'd explained the concept to many a stranger and as a result, I had my explanation down pat. I had an explanation that was concise and precise; a little script I trotted out without thinking whenever it was necessary. But for some reason, when Ernie asked me this time, I didn't hit the script. What fell from my lips was, I suppose, the most hippie-friendly explanation I could come up with. But this wasn't because I was trying to cater to the company I was keeping. It was just how the words came out. Somehow, during that evening, my brain had been rewired, reconfigured to work in a different way.

'There are three billion pages that Google looks at,' I said.

'Awesome,' whispered Bryan.

'And the word acehigh will probably appear on a few thousand of those websites, right?' I continued.

'Uh huh.'

'And each of those websites must be linked to a person. So imagine putting a dot on the globe to represent each of those people … and then you draw a continuous line around the world, joining all of those dots, just one, long, flowing, red line.'

With my left hand I traced a squiggly line through the air. Four rapt pairs of eyes followed my index finger's path.

'Then you do the same with a blue line for the word lawnmowers; a dot on the globe for every person who has the word lawnmowers on their website and then …', using my right hand this time, '… join those dots up with one, long, flowing blue line …'

'Uh huh,' they uh-huh-ed as one.

'Now, for most pairs of words, you'll find the two lines criss-cross all over the place,' I said, my arms entwining, 'but for acehigh and lawnmowers they only cross once. Where they cross; those two words, that website, that person … that's a googlewhack. And that person is Professor Mu Kraken.'

'Wow,' said The Dreamer.

'That is about as Taoist as it comes,' said Ernie. 'That *is* metaphysicality in the extreme.'

'You're catching the wind,' said Nemo.

'Catching the wind of the electromagnetic energy currents of humankind,' added Ernie.

'Catching the wind and finding connections,' said Bryan.

'So the world wide web is like a portal for you,' said Nemo. 'You're sitting in Memphis and you plug in two words and you just pop right out on the other side of the world and meet that person and then you do it again.' He started laughing, catching me by surprise.

'Yeah,' I agreed and joined the laugh.

'So where you heading to next?' asked The Dreamer with wide-eyed fascination.

'I don't know,' I said.

'Catching the wind,' said Bryan.

'It might be Wales, or it might be … I don't know where,' I said. 'I've got Neutrino Scrummages or Grandmaster Sticklebacks.'

'Wow,' said Bryan.

'I'll take you back to the hotel later on,' said Ernie, 'but we can go to my house first and use the computer, see if you've had a reply yet.'

'See if you can find out where you're gonna pop out next,' said The Dreamer.

*

'It looks like you have a reply,' said Ernie reading over my shoulder.

We were sitting at his desk at home. Apart from the glow of the screen, the only light came from a small lamp in the corner of the room. It was late and Ernie's wife ('She's not very interested in metaphysics') was asleep in the room next door so we spoke in whispers.

'It's from the *Underwater Photography* magazine guy,' I said, reading the address in my inbox. The mouse hovered over the link, ready to open up his email.

'So where is your underwater photographer?' asked Ernie. 'Florida? California?'

'Let's find out,' I said, my index finger clicking the mouse. 'Let's see …'

eighteen

Grandmaster Sticklebacks

Grandmaster   noun: a leading exponent of any of various arts. Especially chess.

Sticklebacks   noun: plural of stickleback; any small teleost fish of the family *Gasterosteidae*.

As the minicab left the A3 I looked out of the window and my eyes fell on a small sign planted in the patch of tatty grass decorating the inside of the roundabout. 'This area is maintained by Kingston Youth Offending Team.' It's good to be back in London, I thought; if only more youths offended, the place might look a little prettier.

We drove on in to Surbiton, technically a town in Surrey but close enough to the capital to scrape on to the bottom of the London *A–Z*. I got out of the cab. I knew I was in roughly the right area but the house numbers weren't immediately obvious from the pavement. When I saw a pond in one of the front gardens containing a statue of a whale's tail in mid-splash I knew I'd found the lover of sea life I was looking for. I slipped through the gate and approached the front door.

I was warmly greeted by Peter and even more so by his golden retriever, Shana. He was stocky with a barrel-like chest and grey hair that looked like it might once have been a quiff. (That's Peter by the way, not Shana who was dog-shaped and had golden hair that had almost certainly never been a quiff.)

We sat down in the cosy conservatory with a cup of tea and some biscuits while we exchanged pleasantries.

'You haven't got a London accent, Dave,' said Peter. 'Do you live down here these days?'

'Yeah, Bethnal Green,' I said, although it didn't feel like it was true; I felt like I lived in international airspace.

'That's East London, isn't it?' said Peter to himself. 'You've had to come right across town then. Quite a journey.'

'Actually, I've travelled five thousand miles to see you,' I said, expecting my host to be flattered.

'Five thousand miles? What do you mean?'

'I've been in America,' I explained.

'You can't have come five thousand miles to meet me,' he said.

I let him know that I had with a simple nod and a look of concern flashed across Peter's face; a look that weighed up how much hospitality he thought someone was owed after a five thousand mile journey and then decided that a cup of tea and some biscuits might fall a little short.

'Do you want something to eat?' he said, hurriedly trying to correct something that didn't need correcting.

'No, I'm fine,' I said, trying to make light of the situation.

'What about a sandwich?'

'No, honestly, I'm fine.'

'Are those just digestives?' he said, looking at the biscuits on offer. 'I think we've got some chocolate biscuits somewhere ...'

'Honestly, Peter, things are absolutely fine just as they are,' I said as reassuringly as I could. He didn't look convinced. 'Honestly.'

'Are you sure?' he asked.

'Absolutely. It's the people who don't meet me that are the problem, not the ones who do. Maybe it's people thinking *Oh no, he won't want to travel that far just to meet me* that have stopped me getting to ten in a row already.'

'I see what you mean,' said Peter, who clearly didn't.

'The point is,' I said, 'you are my next googlewhack; there's *nothing* more important than that!'

'Yeah but—'

'No. No "buts". I mean it. Neutrino Scrummages didn't reply,' I said, 'but you did. That means the world to me right now and if I have to *travel* the world in order to meet you, that's fine. Memphis to Surbiton? No problem. What's impor—'

'Did you say Memphis?' asked Peter, cutting in abruptly.

'Yeah.'

'Memphis, Tennessee?'

'Yeah,' I said, helpfully adding, 'y'know – in America.'

'Memphis! I've *always* wanted to go to Memphis,' he said, his eyes lighting up like a six-year-old talking about Christmas. 'What was Graceland like?'

'I didn't really see it …' I said.

'What do you mean?' asked Peter, the childlike glee falling from his face in an instant, confusion taking its place. 'You went to Memphis, but you *didn't* go to Graceland?'

Clearly the idea offended his sensibilities. Clearly Peter was a bit of an Elvis fan. I swear I could see the hair on his head straining to regain its quiffness.

'Well, that's not what I was there for,' I said.

'But …' Peter was struggling to find the words that would explain his confusion. In the end he settled on one. '… Elvis!'

'But I didn't go there to see Elvis,' I explained. 'I went to see Acehigh Lawnmowers!'

'You're telling me that the next googlewhack is more important than Elvis Presley!'

I paused. I got the impression that Peter considered Elvis to be very, very important. But it was true. As far as I was concerned, the next googlewhack *was* more important. It meant more to me than a photo of a woman and a dog could ever mean to Dork Turnspit, more than a Mini could ever mean to the Rarebit Nutters, more even than *Creation* could ever mean to Dripstone Ingles.

'Yes,' I said. 'It does mean more than Elvis. But that means *you* mean more than Elvis and so do the googlewhacks you're about to find.'

nineteen

Optically Scriveners

Optically	1. adverb: relating to, or producing, light.
	2. adverb: relating to the eye or sense of sight.
Scriveners	noun: plural of scrivener; archaic term for one who writes out deeds and letters etc.

This is a list of the things I knew about Seattle before I went there. It is the home of:

- Lisa, Tom and Jonelle Edwards (who love Disney, *Star Wars* and Beanie Babies respectively).
- The grunge music scene and its patron saint, the late Kurt Cobain.
- Anti-capitalist protests as witnessed by the World Trade Organisation Conference of 1999.
- The 1993 Tom Hanks/Meg Ryan romantic comedy, *Sleepless in Seattle.*
- The sitcom *Frasier*.
- The Space Needle. (A structure that looks like the space-age cartoon family *The Jetsons* might live there. Its silhouette features prominently in the opening titles to *Frasier*.)
- The 1963 Elvis Presley movie: *It Happened at the World's Fair.*
- The 1962 World's Fair (the reason the Space Needle was built).

- The cinnamoniest airport in all the world.
- John and Chris Metcalfe, aka Optically Scriveners.

You can't say I wasn't learning.

*

Far from being sleepless in Seattle, I was sleepful. I slept solidly for sixteen hours – twice as long as popular opinion recommends – and woke to feel groggy, confused and, confusingly, sleepier than I was before I slept.

I don't understand how too much sleep does that to you. It's not like it's possible to eat a meal that makes you feel hungrier or drink so much water your thirst is aggravated not quenched, but somehow a sleep-overdose can make you sleepy.

I contemplated going back to sleep but managed to talk myself out of it. After all, I'd established that sleep made me feel sleepier so surely getting some more sleep would only make matters worse and the mattress more attractive. Using that logic I tricked myself into getting up. Forgetting my room was on the ground floor I pulled back the curtains to see a bright but crisp afternoon in progress and a very surprised gardener looking back at a naked Englishman pulling back his curtains, if you'll pardon the expression. I immediately whipped the curtains shut again. My brain clearly wasn't up to thinking speed yet. Sleep really did seem like an attractive option but I fought the urge and decided a shot of caffeine was what I needed.

I looked around the room for the obligatory tea and coffee making facilities but they didn't appear to be there. To begin with I was convinced I must be mistaken – surely tea and coffee are a given in every hotel – but when I opened up a drawer to find a note saying, *'Guests wishing to read a Bible should please contact reception who will be happy to lend you a copy kindly donated by the Gideon organisation',* I knew I was in a hotel that was extraordinarily sparing with 'extras'.

Reluctantly I got dressed and went out in search of the caffeine my system craved. It wasn't hard to find. In fact, it's entirely possible that my hotel room was the only de-caffeinated 100 square feet in all of Seattle. Immediately next door to the hotel I found a Starbucks, so I ordered myself a double espresso and settled into a comfy armchair in the window from where I could see another branch of Starbucks directly opposite and a third branch a few hundred yards to my right, which was itself just next door to a Seattle Coffee Company outlet, who also had a second branch two hundred yards to my left.

'Why are there so many coffee places?' I asked the young guy who came by collecting empty cups and wiping down tables.

'What do you mean?' he asked, clearly completely non-plussed by my question.

'Is this like … *the coffee district* or something?' I asked. He looked back at me, even more confused than before, 'you know, like Chinatown, only … for coffee?'

'Dude, this is Seattle,' he said, tossing his long blond locks back over his shoulders; 'we drink coffee in Seattle. It's what we do.'

'Yes,' I said, as undudely as I could, 'I drink coffee too. It just seems odd to me that I'm sitting in a Starbucks and I can see two other Starbucks *and* two Seattle Coffee Companies. That's a lot of coffee for a small stretch of street.'

He put his tray of dirty cups down on the table with an angry clank and pulled his hands up to his hips. I'd obviously said something to upset him. His nostrils flared.

'It's called choice, dude,' he snapped defensively. 'It's how we do things in America. If you don't like it you can always leave.'

Whoa. There was me having what I thought was an idle chat about the extravagant number of coffee shops in one street and somehow he thought I was taking a vicious sideswipe at him, his lifestyle, his country, his flag and, who knows, his mother. The sheer absurdity of his overreaction meant an involuntary chuckle slipped past my lips but that made his nostrils flare again, so I bit my lip instead.

'I'm not having a go at anything or anyone,' I said, containing my smile. 'I've just never seen three Starbucks so close to each other before. It seems odd, that's all.'

'Like I say,' he said, '*this* is Seattle.'

'Yes. I get that now,' I said, although I still didn't really 'get' the logic at all. 'I didn't mean any offence. It just seems to me that five coffee shops offers *less* choice than, say, one coffee shop and four … other things.'

'Dude,' he said, the word sounding like fingernails on a blackboard to me now, 'choice is choice. Someone can choose to drink coffee in *this* Starbucks or in *that* Starbucks …'

'Or,' I said helpfully indicating number three, 'in *that* one.'

'Exactly,' he said. 'Choice.' And with that, he picked up his tray and went back to his duties.

Moments later he pulled the apron from around his waist and with a high five to one of his colleagues, signed off work for the day. I watched in amazement as he walked out of the shop, crossed the road, entered a different Starbucks and ordered himself a coffee. I strongly suspected there was a bit too much caffeine coursing through that young man's veins. I looked at my double espresso and, concerned about taking a similar overdose, I decided to leave what was left and be on my way.

My next googlewhacks, John and Chris, were going to pick me up at the hotel around seven o'clock which meant I still had a couple of hours to kill. I decided I'd do so by visiting the Space Needle because that seemed to be *the* iconic Seattle landmark. Not visiting it would be like not visiting Graceland in Memphis and only an idiot would let that happen.

*

In 1980, I was a nine-year-old schoolboy at Berkswich Primary

School, Walton on the Hill, Stafford. One day our teacher, Mrs Lowndes, asked the class to write about what they imagined the year 2000 would be like.

I distinctly remember drawing a spacecraft-cum-hovercar and writing a few words about not needing a key to get through the front door (of my pod) because instead it would recognise my palm print. As far as I can recall, no-one in the class was remotely accurate with their predictions. No-one came close to describing the phenomenal explosion in home computing and the internet, no-one predicted cheese in the crust of a pizza and no-one predicted the amazing fabric refreshing powers of Febreze. Instead we all predicted massively different homes and modes of transport. Of course we did; we were children. The idea that it was *only* 20 years away didn't make sense to us because when you're nine there's no such thing as 'only' 20 years away. We didn't understand that we wouldn't yet be 30 when the new millennium rolled round because when you're 9 being nearly 30 seems like being very, very old. Of course the houses we lived in then are still standing and in many cases our parents are still living in them. And cars aren't that much different either. We're certainly not whizzing around the skies in hovercars anyway.

If those exercise books could be found today they would inevitably tell us absolutely nothing about the twenty-first century but plenty about what it was like to be 9 years of age in Britain in 1980. My hovercar, for example, was decorated with logos for the band Madness because while I could imagine a radical change in personal transportation, I couldn't imagine a world without them in the hit parade. (The fact that I was wrong on this count still hurts.) But this is always the way with predictions. The 2015 depicted in *Back to the Future* could only have been created in the 1980s and the twenty-third century of Captain James T. Kirk and his crew is unmistakably a vision of the Sixties – just look at Uhura's miniskirt.

Well, the same is true of Seattle's Space Needle. It must have felt like a futuristic vision when it was built in 1962. Man was in space but not yet on the moon and so the space race was on. The Space Needle is basically a flying saucer placed on top of a 605-foot tower. At the time, people must have gasped in amazement and wondered how long it would be before flying saucers were commonplace. Nowadays, twenty-first-century visitors like myself come along and find it mildly entertaining in a kitsch, isn't-it-very-Sixties way. I suppose it's the architectural equivalent of a lava lamp.

Having looked up at the needle for a few minutes and enjoyed its retro appeal I bought a ticket and rode the elevator to the observation deck up top, where incidentally, they serve Starbucks coffee. By all accounts the Space Needle affords a spectacular view of Mount Rainier, the majestic snowy peak that overlooks Seattle, but sadly not in this account because clouds had come to take the afternoon's brightness away and the view just didn't carry that far. It was an impressive view of the city skyline, mind you, and Seattle is an insistently modern city with glass skyscrapers lining up along the bay. But something was missing. I couldn't work out what it was but somehow the experience felt incomplete. It came to me later when I was back at the hotel waiting for Optically Scriveners to come by. The problem was that while it had been an impressive view, it hadn't been very identifiable; it hadn't felt uniquely Seattle which is what the tourist in me really wanted. There was only one building that screamed Seattle and that was the Space Needle itself. By standing at the top of it, I had automatically removed from view the one part of Seattle I really wanted to look at.

*

I've never been very interested in cars. I have friends who get an almost sexual kick out of the sound of an engine revving. 'Listen to that,' they'll say, 'hear it purr, isn't it a beauty?' I've tried joining in, but my ears just aren't attuned to it. To me, engines don't purr or roar or throb or any of the other words petrol heads use to describe them; they just make a sort of engine-y sound and I can't tell a healthy, well-tuned V8 from a rusty old knacker.

But there is one sound a car can make that I like and recognise as a sign of superiority and that's the satisfying sound of a quality car door shutting. Not all car doors make a nice sound but when they do it says more to me than any engine ever can. The sound I mean is difficult to describe and certainly difficult to transcribe but my best attempt would probably be something like *'schwwmb'.* Yes, a good car has doors that *schwwmb*. (Incidentally, that's a silent 'b'.) It's a soft sound and it should be pretty much the same whether you're pulling the door gently to or slamming it with great force because a good car pays no attention to your mood.

The doors on my Vauxhall Corsa don't *schwwmb,* they *kerlonk*. But John and Chris Metcalfe had a car that *schwwmb-ed* with the best of them. I sat in the back and pulled the door to; *schwwmb*. The three of us respectfully let the silence settle before anyone spoke.

'OK,' said John. 'We've booked a table at a place called Etta's. I hope you like seafood.'

'Absolutely,' I said and off we went.

I'd arranged the meeting by swapping emails with John and while he'd mentioned that he and Chris would pick me up I hadn't known whether to expect a Chris of the male or female variety. As it was, they were a married couple in their early fifties. I'd seen lots of couples like John and Chris before, but only on American TV and, even then, only in commercials. They were the epitome of the happy, successful, affluent couple that America's corporate giants wanted the rest of us to aspire to be. Couples just like them (usually seen walking together through autumnal scenes or staring wistfully at an ocean) could be found advertising food, clothes, cars, insurance, medicines and who knows what else. But John and Chris had the edge on all that lot because they actually existed.

If their life could have made a noise it would have been *schwwmb.*

John had an almost military crop of grey hair. Chris was blonde, her hair cut short in a style that was both gamine and glamorous. They both wore tight black sweaters that people of their age shouldn't be able to get away with but which they carried off with style.

I felt distinctly scruffy sitting on the leather-upholstered back seat of their car in my shabby cords and a shirt that badly needed an iron (no chance of that in a hotel that didn't even provide a kettle), but John and Chris didn't seem remotely troubled by my unkempt appearance so I decided not to trouble myself with it either.

Unsurprisingly, Etta's turned out to be a rather splendid restaurant. I think a good guide to a restaurant's poshness is the number of words on the menu that you don't understand. If it's every other word then that's too posh for you and you're clearly out of your depth, but if there's nothing you don't get, you could definitely go a bit posher. At Etta's I found I could order things while failing to understand approximately one word in four, which put it easily within my comfort zone but ensured it was posh enough to feel like an occasion. I ordered a *'tasty tuna something salad'* followed by an *'Alaskan halibut with oojit onions and a whatsit vinaigrette'* with a side order of *'thingummy green beans and stuff.'* And very nice it was too. Whatever it was.

Over dinner I explained my adventure so far and they explained the story behind their website, deregulation-global.com. I'm not sure if they understood why I was doing what I was doing, but I am sure that I didn't understand deregulation-global.com.

As far as I could tell, they were involved in a network marketing business in which they sold utility services – gas, electricity, telecoms and so on – on to consumers, taking advantage of the increased competition fostered by the international trend for privatisation and deregulation in those industries. I think. How it works, why it works and whether or not it works for anyone who tries it, I can't tell you. What I can tell you is that it's worked for John and Chris Metcalfe, two former teachers who no longer find themselves struggling to make ends meet.

'We're like you, Dave,' said Chris. 'You obviously like meeting people and so do we.'

'And this business has given us a new lease of life,' said John, taking the reins. 'We're empty-nesters, our kids have left home, but we don't sit in and watch TV. We're out enjoying ourselves.'

'And just like your googlewhacking,' said Chris, 'the internet has led us to meet people we never would have met. People from all backgrounds.'

'We have a friend called Barbara,' said John. 'She's in the same business. She's a Military Mom out in Memphis …'

'She's one of the most beautiful people you have ever seen,' said Chris.

'These aren't just colleagues,' said John, 'these are the people we'd give kidneys too. Really.'

'Really,' agreed Chris.

There was a pause while they both thought about things and I watched as a thought landed behind Chris's eyes.

'Actually,' she said, 'one of the guys, Geoff; he did just that.'

'What's that?' I asked, confused.

'He gave up his kidney. Literally,' said Chris.

'That's the kind of person we're talking about,' said John.

Just then a waiter approached our table.

'Would you like to see the dessert menu?' he asked.

'Actually I know what I'm going to have,' said John with a big grin. 'I'll have the Bulletproofing Trifle please?'

'I'm sorry, sir,' he said, trying to appear more polite than bemused, 'we don't serve anything of that name.'

'And I'll have the Baptise Slurry,' said Chris, and the two of them could barely contain their glee.

The waiter's brow furrowed, bemusement was winning

over. 'I'm sorry, madam, sir, these are *not* desserts. If you would like to see the menu …?'

As I observed his confusion and their pleasure, I suddenly worked out what they were laughing at, what Mr and Mrs Optically Scriveners were laughing at. Bulletproofing Trifle? Baptise Slurry? Presumably the words weren't as random as they seemed.

'I'll have what they're having,' I said.

twenty

Baptise Slurry

Baptise	1. verb: to immerse someone in water or sprinkle water on a person as part of the Christian rite of baptism.
	2. verb: to give a name to.
Slurry	noun: solid particles suspended in a liquid, for example, a mixture of manure, cement or clay with water.

The mountain of unopened mail behind the front door meant that getting into my flat was a difficult task. Once inside I scooped up the pile of letters and carried them through into the living room, dumping them unceremoniously on the sofa. I'd deal with them another day. The little red light on my answering machine was blinking madly, telling me that it too had a stack of messages waiting for me. I unplugged it and tossed it, with even less ceremony, towards the sofa.

The flat felt strangely unfamiliar to me. I hadn't been there since I'd come home from my trip to Wales. I'd only been away for five or six weeks but so much had happened in that time that 'home' had ceased to mean anything. I felt like an intruder. I didn't want to hang around. I walked through to the bedroom and picked up my car keys; that was the only reason I was here – meeting my next googlewhack was going to be far easier with a car. My mobile phone was lying on the bed where

I'd left it. I shrugged, slipped it into my pocket, turned and left the flat.

Kerlonk, went the car door as I pulled it shut, *bee-beep, bee-beep, bee-beep*, went the phone alerting me to yet more messages. I turned it off once more and threw it into the glove compartment, alongside my gloves (oh yes) and started to drive.

If Bulletproofing Trifle had responded I wouldn't have needed to confront all these reminders of who I really was, where I lived, what I did, what my life was supposed to be like. I wouldn't have needed to leave the States for Bulletproofing Trifle. A trip to Boston would have sufficed. But *they* hadn't responded and Baptise Slurry had and so here I was; back on the roads of Blighty.

John's website, www.wirksworth.org.uk was, as its name might suggest, all about the parish of Wirksworth, Derbyshire, some 150 miles north of London. I was heading south on the M3 however, because while his website was devoted to Wirksworth, he actually lived 240 miles away in the small and sleepy seaside town of Poole, or rather its smaller and sleepier suburb, Broadstone.

When I first laid eyes on John I thought I was about to meet a giant but it turned out to be an optical illusion. He was certainly a big man, his height exaggerated by a curl of Mr Whippy ice cream hair that sat on top, giving him an extra couple of inches. He was a bit broad in the beam these days too, but he'd pulled off a real illusory masterstroke by marrying a tiny wife and living in a bungalow. As I parked the car at the foot of their drive, John, who was well over six feet tall and Rosie, a poppet who can't have been much over five feet, stepped outside to meet me and it really did look as though an average-sized woman had stepped out of an average-sized house with an abnormally large man. It's only when I got out of the car and approached them that I realised the truth.

The two of them had met when, as a young man, John had placed an advert in a youth hostelling magazine soliciting a cycling buddy for a trip round Ireland. Local girl Rosie had answered his ad and off they'd gone. You have to admire them both for that; it's one hell of a first date.

John was eager to show me the two 'whacks he'd found so he whisked me into their bedroom, a corner of which was given over to a busy desk crammed with computer equipment. For a moment I thought his computer was fitted with some kind of antique monitor but the screen I was looking at wasn't wired up to the computer, it was for viewing microfilm.

'Ah it's a beauty, isn't it?' said John, proud to own such a thing.

'I thought only spies looked at microfilm,' I said.

'Ah no, this is the hub of wirksworth.org.uk,' said John, and then, rather cryptically he added, 'it all started with the Mormons.'

'I'm getting very confused,' I said to the man who wasn't a giant, a spy or a Mormon.

'It all started when I decided to check my ancestors out … well, everyone does when they get to 50.'

I made a mental note to clear my diary in 19 years' time.

'So, I went to the International Genealogical Index. It's run by the Mormons.'

'I see,' I said. Not so cryptic now.

'It's all online,' said John, 'you should take a look at it. It's www—'

'Ooo! Ha ha ha!'

The laughter came from behind us. I turned to find Rosie bringing in a tray of tea and biscuits. The mere mention of those three w's had been enough to raise Rosie's laughter. It was a laugh that said, *There he goes again! Him and his www's, him and his internet!* They may have shared many a bike ride, but I got the distinct impression that the surfing was probably a solo affair. John smiled and started again.

'It's www.familysearch.org,' he said. 'So, I traced my family back and it led to the town of Wirksworth. Well, I got as far back as 1595 and I got *interested* in it.'

He took his time and lowered his voice for the word 'interested', investing it with as much passion as he could. I knew that he didn't really mean 'interested'; he meant 'obsessed.' It was a tone of voice I'd hear often that day.

'So I went to the Derbyshire Records Office and said, "Can I get the Bishops Transcripts?" These are copies of the Parish Registers made for the Bishop – you know, details of all the baptisms and the burials and the weddings and so on. I got them eventually and they're *400 years old.*'

There it was again. He said '400 years old' as if he was tasting a fine wine.

'Well, every time you rolled them out they'd get a bit more damaged. I didn't like that at all. So I said to the Records Office, "Look, I'll do you a deal." He paused for dramatic effect, lowered his voice again, but raised one finger and two eyebrows to compensate. *'This changed my life for the next seven years…'*

I was half expecting John to tell me he really was a spy. Maybe he was working for the county of Derbyshire, operating across the border in dangerous territory like Nottingham, say, or Mansfield. But he looked about the room, and then explained the life-changing deal he'd struck.

'I said, "You photocopy them and send them to me and I will transcribe them. I'll put them into a database".' And then, savouring the words, enjoying the sound, *'Oo I love a database,* they *fascinate* me.'

Six months after doing the deal, John had transcribed the Bishop's transcripts, putting 50 years of Wirksworth – all the births, deaths, marriages and shenanigans – online. And he had found the whole community much more interesting than just his own family tree. He'd become addicted.

'I got to know these people,' he explained. 'I thought, "Oh … *he's going out with her, is he?"* and so on… I did 1650 to 1700 in about a year and … well, *I was hooked.*'

Seventeenth-century Wirksworth had become John's soap opera of choice and like any fan he wanted to know what happened next. He'd wanted to know what the next series, the eighteenth century, had in store. So John had gone back to the Mormons and offered them a similar deal, which had allowed him access to further Wirksworth information. Over three years he spent 4000 hours filling up more of his beloved databases. I wouldn't have been surprised if he'd also created a database detailing the man hours he'd dedicated to his Wirksworth databases.

Once he'd got through all that information he just hadn't been able to stop and had managed to feed his habit by using the ten-yearly censuses, all of which were making their way from microfilm to website via John's keyboard. On the day we met he was working his way through the 1891 census and by the time you read this I dare say he'll be at the 1901 census or beyond. A two-finger typist, he estimated that he'd now typed over six million words. I was just lucky that baptise and slurry were among them.

The first googlewhack John showed me was Derailleurs Jetsam.

'Oh it was *lovely*,' he said. 'I tried derailleurs flotsam and got two hits. But the word 'flotsam' is only ever used in tandem with 'jetsam' and I could see that one of the sites had spelt jetsam wrong, so I knew that it had to be a 'whack and it was!'

'That really is lovely,' I said, searching around the site for an email address. It was a site that sold sporting books. It was clearly based in America but I couldn't work out where exactly.

'So what does derailleurs mean?' I asked, as I opened up an email and started to write to my latest prospect.

'It's a cycling term,' said John, 'part of the gear mechanism.'

'Do you still ride?' I asked, as I pressed send.

'No,' said John, ruefully. 'I used to cycle a lot. I've cycled across America, but I'm getting on a bit these days. I'm afraid I gave up exercise but I forgot to give up eating,' he said, patting his tummy playfully. 'Actually,' his voice fell to a whisper, 'I'm supposed to be on a diet ... but if you want to have a curry later, it would be a good excuse.'

'That sounds like a great idea,' I said. 'Besides, I should be celebrating; this is my longest chain of 'whacks so far. You're my sixth in a row. For the first time, I'm passed the halfway point.'

'A curry it is then,' said John. 'Now, here's the other googlewhack I found for you … Benn Bathysphere.'

'By the way,' I said, as the page loaded, 'I think I'm hearing things. I could swear you just said you'd cycled across America!'

'Twice,' said John.

'I only heard it once.'

'No,' said John, 'I've cycled across America twice.'

'But it's massive!' I said. 'It takes long enough to fly across it and I should know.'

'I've done Oregon to Virginia and California to Florida. I really wanted to go and Rosie couldn't come,' said John, 'so the first time I went I advertised for a buddy and I got ten replies … actually, it was fourteen, but four of them were ladies and I didn't want to get involved in *that*!'

'Of course not,' I said, 'you've got form.'

'So I went with this fellow, nice chap he was, and we had a great time. We did about four and a half thousand miles and it took us 66 days; the roads were good, the gradient was good; it was amazing.

'You see, the thing is,' he continued, 'there's this company that make these fantastic maps for cyclists with everything you might want to know – history, weather, recommended routes and so on. So before we went, I sat down and typed it all into a *database* …'

'You really do *love* a database, don't you?'

'Oh I do. I *really* do,' said John. 'Well I printed them off on strips of paper and attached them to my handlebars. Then you can do all the navigating on the move. Brilliant.'

'Amazing,' I said, 'now, let's take a look at this googlewhack … ah …'

'What's wrong?' asked John.

'I'm afraid Benn Bathysphere isn't a 'whack.' I felt like a vet breaking bad news to a child about a beloved pet. 'You see, benn isn't underlined so it's not in dictionary.com and in any case, it leads to a wordlist. 'I'm really sorry,' I said, 'I really am.'

'No, no,' said John, being very brave about the whole thing, 'that's fine.' He looked out of the window and composed himself. 'Benn Bathysphere is no good, but that's OK because I can find a new 'whack, can't I?'

'Of course you can,' I said, geeing him up, 'and it'll be just as good, if not better.'

John began 'whack hunting and while he thought of random words and tried them out, he regaled me with more tales of travels and databases. His home was littered with souvenirs of his travels, and so was his conversation.

'See that, Dave,' he'd say, pointing at something that looked like a rock and was the size of two fists. 'That's the kidney stone from a cow.'

'Have you ever seen one of these before?' he'd enquire, holding up something long, straggly and dead. 'It's dried beef. It's called "biltong"; it's like Kendal Mint Cake for meat eaters.'

'Never have an egg in Peru,' he'd advise. 'It's too high up, they can't boil it properly.'

I wasn't surprised to discover that a man who provided such eclectic conversation made for a talented googlewhacker and before long he'd discovered a replacement 'whack in the shape of Yoyo Triptychs.'

'Well done,' I said, delighted with the find. 'Now, let's take a look at Chinese-art.com …'

The site was obviously concerned with Chinese art but it was impossible to work out where it was based. It carried news about Chinese artists living all over the world and links to galleries not only in Beijing and Hong Kong and so on, but also in Paris, Switzerland, San Francisco and New York, for example. One link led to a gallery called Chinese Contemporary, which was located just off Oxford Street in central London. The man responsible for the site went by the distinctly un-Chinese name of Robert Bernell. I hoped he worked at Chinese Contemporary, but more importantly, wherever he was, I hoped he'd agree to meet me.

As I fired off the email, Rosie appeared in the doorway.

'How are you two boys doing?' she asked.

'It's going swimmingly,' said John. 'Two lovely googlewhacks.'

'Absolutely,' I added, 'and do you know what? It's been such a pleasure and this is now the longest chain I've had so I'd like to celebrate. I don't know if the two of you like a curry?'

'Oh yes,' said John, 'what a good idea.'

'You know you shouldn't,' said Rosie, 'but seeing as we've got company …'

John winked.

*

I slept in my own bed in my own flat that night. It felt cold but I liked it that way. I didn't want to get too comfortable. Any desire to stay would be unhelpful. Nothing was going to get in the way of my googlewhacking.

I woke early the next morning and went straight to the desk, my own desk, and checked my emails. Yes. The longest chain was going to get longer. Robert Bernell, Yoyo Triptychs, had come good.

I rushed out of the house. Five minutes later I was at Bethnal Green tube station; 25 minutes later I was emerging on to Oxford Street. I walked up Regent Street, past the familiar shop fronts, H&M on my left, Nike Town on my right. McDonalds, Burger King, Starbucks; I could have been walking through any city, anywhere in the world but then the road curved round and suddenly the landscape was unmistakably London. For a split second I stood and looked in awe at the splendour of All Souls Church with its gothic spire and classical rotunda and then at the glorious galleon-like BBC Broadcasting House, but I didn't have time to hang around; I had somewhere special to go.

I crossed the road and completed the bend taking me into Portland Place and a parade of tall, grand Georgian buildings and I was there. The Embassy of the People's Republic of China.

I joined the back of the queue. I had my passport, two passport photos and 45 quid. If I was going to go to Beijing, I needed to apply for a visa.

twenty-one

Yoyo Triptychs

Yoyo

1. noun: a toy consisting of a spool attached to a string.
2. noun (*US & Canadian slang*): a stupid person.
3. verb (*informal*): to change one's opinion repeatedly.

Triptychs

noun: plural of triptych; a set of three pictures or writing tablets.

The next day I returned to the Embassy to collect my passport. As I approached the counter, I crossed my fingers and hoped that my visa application had been approved.

I had cause for concern. In the past I'd worked in a few foreign countries and as a result my passport already contained several work visas. Yesterday's application had only been for a tourist visa for China, but when I'd handed over my passport the presence of three or four US work visas had seemed to arouse their suspicion. The clerk I was dealing with had taken my passport to her senior at the next-door desk and the two had engaged in quite a conversation.

Because the conversation had been in Chinese I'd had no idea if it was something to worry about or not. For all I knew, they might have been laughing at the array of bad passport photos involved, but at the same time it could have been more serious than that. If my visa application had been turned down, the journey would be over.

As luck would have it, all was well. My passport was returned to me with a smile. I flicked through the pages and sure enough there was my visa. Stapled on top of it was a small piece of paper, maybe two inches long and half an inch wide. The message on the piece of paper had been typed on a manual typewriter:

```
You are politely reminded that
this is not a journalistic  visa.
You are not permitted to report
on events in China.
```

twenty-two

Langur Dandelions

Langur
noun: any of various arboreal monkeys of South and South East Asia having long hair surrounding the face, a slender body, long tail. Genus: *Presbytis*.

Dandelions
noun: a plant, native to Europe and Asia, having yellow rayed flowers and notched basal leaves. They can be used in salads or wine. *Taraxacum officinale*.

'So how come you're back in Washington?' asked Danielle.

'Yeah … I don't get it,' said David scratching his head.

'Well,' I said, pausing to take a sip of coffee and compose my words. Kramer's Bookstore was the kind of place you could take a long pause in and no one minded. 'I'm going for it: ten googlewhacks in a row before my 32nd birthday.'

'But I thought you were supposed to be writing a novel,' said David. 'Last time we saw you, you definitely said you *weren't* accepting the challenge.'

'That's a bit rich coming from you!' I said, taking playful offence. 'You're the one who found me Coelacanth Sharpener! I didn't *ask* you to. You're the one who said I should go to Boston!'

'Yeah but—' started Danielle but I cut her short.

'And don't *you* start,' I said. I was on a roll. '*He* only found me Coelacanth Sharpener because *you* bought me that Teeny Christmas Google!'

'What?' she asked. 'So it's my fault?'

'Yeah!' said David and I in unison, making each other laugh. Danielle skewed her mouth to one side in a mock sulk that quickly gave way to laughter too.

'Right,' she said, 'but the point is you are going for it and you're back in town so I presume your next googlewhack is in Washington?'

'I think so,' I said.

'*Think* so?' asked David, the surprise catching him mid-sip and forcing him to spit some of his coffee back.

'Yeah,' I said. 'I *think* so. Number seven in a chain took me to China to meet Yoyo Triptychs and he found…'

'*China!*' said David, recycling his coffee for the second time. 'You went to China? What was that like?'

'Oh, it was absolutely ████████ I said. 'My googlewhack was an ██████████████ , he insisted that I visit the ████████ of ██████ before he gave me my next 'whack. We went out for the night and he introduced me to a ██████████████████ who licked my ███████.'

'That sounds amazing!' said Danielle.

'Yeah, it was,' I agreed. 'But most importantly he found two googlewhacks: Langurs Nasturtium and Langur Dandelions.'

'He likes a langur,' said David.

'He certainly does. But that's two 'whacks that can take me to eight in a row. Langurs Nasturtium leads to KathysCritters.com. Kathy lives in LA and she's agreed to meet me. I'm flying out later on today.'

'And Langur Dandelions?' asked Danielle.

'The website was about a TV show. A documentary about a country called Bhutan. It was written and produced by a man called Harry Marshall. I couldn't find an email address or a phone number but the production company are based in Washington. They're on Connecticut Avenue NW.'

'So you've come to Washington on the off-chance that Harry

Marshall is working at their office?' asked Danielle, a little incredulous.

'Well, the website says they're the production company and he's the producer so it's not that far-fetched,' I said defensively. 'And besides, it's on my way.'

'What?' said David and Danielle in disbelieving unison.

'I'm going from London to LA,' I said. 'Washington *is* on the way. It's going to cost me half a day at most. If Harry's there I get him and then I go to LA and meet Kathy. If it works out, I'll have two people in the number eight slot; if it doesn't, I've still got one. Two number eights means four potential number nines means eight potential number tens. It gives me a far better chance of getting to ten. I've had chains fall apart and it could easily happen again. It's only costing me half a day so I think it's a risk worth taking.'

'Makes sense to me,' said David with a shrug, before a look of concern flashed across his face. 'Oh my God. *That* made sense to me. *You're* making sense to me. This is very worrying.' He took a big gulp of coffee, and this time he managed to swallow it down. 'Come on,' he said, 'I'll give you a lift.'

*

Devillier Donegan Enterprises were based in a dark, dull, plain 1970s office building with ugly green plastic detailing that did nothing to soften its edges. It looked more like an underfunded public library in Croydon than the home of a savvy TV production company. In the lobby of the building a notice-board informed me of the various companies that were renting office space within. Most of them appeared to be in the financial sector but in among them, I saw DDE, so I took the elevator up to their floor.

'Hi ... can I help you?' asked the receptionist. From her tone of voice it was clear she suspected I'd got out of the lift on the wrong floor. I clearly wasn't dressed for a power meeting and looked like I didn't belong.

'Hi, I'm trying to find Harry Marshall,' I said confidently

'I don't think there's anyone here of that name,' she said looking down at the notes on her desk, shattering my confidence in one fell swoop.

That wasn't good news. Harry obviously wasn't a full-time employee; he obviously wasn't in the building.

'He wrote and produced a show you made for PBS,' I said.

I was hoping that would jog her memory, that she'd suddenly say, 'Oooohhhhh, *Harry*! Why didn't you say? He's just next door!' but instead she said, 'O ... kaaaay?', pausing mid-word, teasing me with the prospect that it was just a long and confused 'oh'. Oh well, at least she slowly seemed to be coming round to the idea that I had a legitimate enquiry.

'The show's called *Bhutan: Land of the Thunder Dragon*,' I said, still hoping to jog her memory.

'Well, if you wait here I'll see what I can find out,' she said, before disappearing into the office beyond. I crossed my fingers.

Maybe he was in town and I'd still be able to meet him before heading to LA and my meeting with Kathy. Then again, he worked in TV, and in America that meant it was odds on that *he lived* in LA. That would be an amazing result! I crossed my fingers.

'I have an email address for him if that's OK,' said the receptionist as she returned, a Post-it note hanging from her finger. She gave me the address and my heart sank. I immediately knew that Harry wasn't in Washington or LA because it was clear that he wasn't in America. Four letters and a couple of punctuation marks told me that: the email address I had for Langur Dandelions ended in .co.uk. He was in Britain!

twenty-three

Langurs Nasturtium

Langurs   noun: plural of langur; any of various arboreal monkeys of South and South East Asia having long hair surrounding the face, a slender body, long tail. Genus: *Presbytis*.

Nasturtium   noun: any of various plants of the genus *Tropaeolum*, having round leaves and yellow, red or orange trumpet-shaped flowers.

Ophelia was wriggling around on my face, Portia was sliding around tickling my ears, Hamlet was resting his head on my shoulders and Kathy was giggling.

This might be a good moment to mention that Ophelia, Portia and Hamlet were snakes and only Kathy was human. She was blonde and glamorous and looked to be in her thirties but a VHS poking out of the video player labelled 'Kathy's Big 50th' gave her secret away. Kathy was the proprietor of Kathy's Critters and when she'd asked me if I fancied meeting some of the critters, eager to please I'd rather unwisely said yes.

'Well, I used to work at the zoo,' said Kathy, explaining how she came to be in loco parentis to so many animals. 'And I used to take the critters out and do educational work; school visits and so on. I got asked to do some birthday parties because kids love bugs and snakes and critters …'

'Ri-ight,' I said, my voice rising as Hamlet made his way up my torso and around my neck.

'Well, obviously they weren't my animals but I asked my boss and he said, "OK, we're not using them at the weekend," so I started doing them and it built up and eventually I started Kathy's Critters.'

'So meeting Hamlet, Ophelia and Portia would be a treat for an eight-year-old?' I asked, confused because being a corn snake's adventure playground didn't seem as much fun as, say, having some cake.

'You're lucky I didn't bring the python upstairs,' said Kathy. 'Being a Brit, you'll like this. His name's "Monty".'

I chuckled a slightly lame chuckle, not because I didn't think the Monty Python reference chuckleworthy but because my attention was elsewhere. Hamlet appeared to be trying to get inside my T-shirt and Ophelia and Portia were taking an arm each.

'I used toys to help with the education,' Kathy continued, 'you can get some anatomically correct stuffed toys and things, and people started asking where they could get them so I started selling those as well. That's when I started RealCoolToys.com and pretty soon my biggest sellers were edible insect candies so I started InsectCandy.com too.'

'And they're sweets shaped like bugs and stuff?' I asked.

'No, they're real insects,' smiled Kathy. 'You know, ants covered in chocolate, mealworms, that kind of thing. Boys love 'em. I'll give you some later.'

'That'd be lovely,' I lied. 'You will get me a couple of googlewhacks too … won't you?'

twenty-four

Paeans Uppercuts

Paeans
noun: plural of paean being:
1. an ancient Greek hymn sung in praise of a deity.
2. any song of praise.
3. enthusiastic praise.

Uppercuts
1. noun: plural of uppercut; a short, swinging upward punch delivered to the chin.
2. verb: to hit with an uppercut.

For the second time in my life I found myself looking at part of the Great Wall of China. The last time I'd looked at a part of the Great Wall of China it was attached to the rest of it. This time I was in Chicago where, oddly, a piece of the Great Wall was embedded into the side of the Chicago Tribune Building.

In 1922, the *Chicago Tribune* had held an architectural competition, the intention being to 'build the most beautiful office building in the world' and this was the result. And beautiful it was; a stunning gothic tower block that wouldn't look out of place if Batman was seen swooping down from the roof. The publisher of the day must have been on something of a power trip because he'd asked his reporters to bring back chunks of world-famous landmarks and over 140 of these were now jutting out from the building's walls. Presumably he hoped his building would benefit by having some of their greatness grafted on to its DNA.

So now a gargoyle that was supposed to be warding evil spirits away from the Houses of Parliament was instead cemented into the wall of this Chicago skyscraper alongside a chunk of rock from Stonehenge and a bit of a Pyramid and so on. I started to wonder about the veracity of some of the claims. Maybe a cub reporter, eager to impress the boss, had brought back some garden rubble and claimed it was part of the Parthenon. In a way, I hoped that was the case because otherwise the Chicago Tribune Building was responsible for some appalling cultural vandalism. I was pretty sure that the part of the Taj Mahal I was looking at had looked nicer when it *was* a part of the Taj Mahal rather than playing a bit part in this gauche mish mash. From across the road the Chicago Tribune Building was one of the most impressive skyscrapers I've seen, full of character and style, a symbol of the thrusting, ambitious decade in which it was conceived. Up close it appeared to be a freakish climbing wall, built on pillage and thievery.

The *Chicago Tribune* was part of the Tribune Group, which owned 24 different TV stations, making it America's fourth largest media empire. Among its employees was a man called John F. Kuczak (pronounced Koo-schy) who, outside of work, was responsible for a little media empire all of his own, having created two or three different websites. One of them, DaveKingman.com, a fansite dedicated to a former baseball star, was home to both paeans and uppercuts. John was going to be the twenty-first googlewhack I'd met so far but, crucially, he was the ninth in a chain. Hopefully he would serve up number ten and victory would be mine.

When John emerged from the Chicago Tribune Building lobby, he had a jolly round face, a crewcut and a very welcome willingness to 'whack.

'Hiya, how're you doing,' he said, offering his hand.

'I'm very well,' I said, 'very well indeed.'

'Good,' said John, 'so why don't we head back to mine and get some of these googlewhacks?'

The moment John said those words I knew that victory was almost assured. If he was ready and willing to 'whack, then I had no doubt that he would be able. And if he could find me two more, I was confident that I could meet one of them. After all, it seemed to me that the easiest googlewhack to meet must be number ten in the chain. For numbers one through nine I needed the approval of the 'whack. If they weren't prepared to meet me then they clearly wouldn't be prepared to google-whack either and so the chain would end one way or another. But with number ten it was different. I didn't need them to do anything *other than* meet me. Even if they expressly said that they didn't want to meet me it would still be possible. If I knew where they lived or worked there would be nothing to stop me turning up on their doorstep unannounced, ringing the bell and shaking their hand. And that was all I needed. Had Dr Gish been tenth in a chain his failure to googlewhack wouldn't have mattered a jot because I'd met him all the same.

We drove through the wide streets of Chicago. To an uneducated eye like mine it looked like New York only without the pressure cooker attitude, perhaps because, unlike the island of Manhattan, Chicago can expand; spreading out into the flat prairie land to the West. Out in the low-rise suburbs, we parked up outside a modern apartment block.

'It's a little untidy,' said John apologetically, leading me in through a laundry room.

We emerged into a living room that was so full of stuff I'm not sure it could ever be tidy. It positively screamed bachelor pad. There were framed posters on the wall of various cartoon superheroes, there were toy cars and characters from *The Simpsons* dotted about the place and in the far corner, surrounding the TV, was a vast collection of neatly arranged and labelled videos, science fiction and comedy clearly defining John's tastes. I was struck by how much of a British influence there was in the room, alongside the complete series of *Babylon 5* were several British shows like *The Prisoner* and *The Hitchhiker's Guide to the Galaxy*. On top of the TV was a stuffed Monty Python exploding penguin and on the shelf to my right was a model of К9, *Doctor Who*'s robot dog. Most alarming of all, on a filing cabinet beneath that shelf there was a Sam Fox fridge magnet, though quite how a thirtysomething from Chicago comes to have a 1980s British Page Three girl fridge magnet was beyond me.

I would have asked, but before I could articulate anything, John spoke.

'This is my computer game collection,' he said, proudly.

I turned expecting to find a shelf of PlayStation games to rival the mammoth collection of videos but I found myself looking at something far more impressive than that. Against the wall, behind the door, were three, full-size, free-standing, coin-operated arcade games.

'Oh my God!' I said, struck with awe. 'You have a Miss Pacman!'

'Yeah, it's kinda cool, isn't it?' said John, beaming with pride.

'Can I have go?' I asked, lighting up with childlike excitement.

'Of course you can,' said John, reaching on to the top and flicking some mysterious switch. 'There you go,' he said as the machine flickered into life, 'it won't need any coins now.'

'Wow,' I said, loosening my shoulders in preparation for the joystick action to come.

'Now, while you do that, I'll get to work on these googlewhacks.'

When I left John's I had Doppelganger Hippopotami, Candyfloss Draughtsmen and the Miss Pacman high score. The high score gave me a taste for victory and I liked it that way; I didn't want it to leave. All I needed to do now was to meet one of these two 'whacks and it would all be over. I would be the winner.

Doppelganger Hippopotami

This googlewhack led me to yet more fan-fiction. It was a short story written by someone called T. F. Revor (I suppose he has to use his middle initial to prevent being mistaken for a Trevor) and it was based on a TV series called *Gargoyles*. I'd never heard of the show before but I didn't think it had aired in Britain. I assumed that Mr Revor (the T, I discovered, stood for Thomas) was based in the States.

Right at the top of the page there was an email address inviting comments on the story. But there was also the ominous phrase *'completed September 25, 1996'*.

The page was seven years old and I knew that an untended website could easily turn to seed. I knew there was every chance that the links would no longer work and that the email address was quite likely to be defunct. I wasn't at all surprised when it bounced straight back to me but nor was I prepared to give in.

I'd met two fan-fiction writers in the shape of Bibliophilic Sandwiched and Verandahs Plectrums. Both were committed writers who'd maintained a longstanding web presence. I didn't think that fan-fic was something T. F. Revor could easily have given up. If he was writing fan-fiction in 1996 I was convinced he'd still be doing it now. I went straight to Google and looked for information on T.F. Revor. Yes! You can use it as a search engine too! I searched for his name in every combination I could; T. F. Revor, tfrevor, Thomas F Revor, Thomas Revor, Tom Revor all cross-referenced with fan-fiction or *Gargoyles* and I found quite a few matches. I ended up with 25 different email addresses. Maybe they were all him, maybe they weren't; there was only one way to find out and before long I'd sent 25 emails floating off into the ether.

Twenty-three of those emails bounced. Two received no reply. There were no clues as to where T. F. Revor could be found. It was a dead end.

How dare he be so elusive? Surely I had every right to find

this stranger's personal details! Didn't he realise that he was number ten in my chain? Secretly I vowed that, if in a few years time I did encounter T. F. Revor, I would wreak my revenge for this frustration; I would call him Trevor.

Candyfloss Draughtsmen

I was looking at the home page for someone called Jason Tan (and his dog, Sleepy). He was a student at something called the Royal Melbourne Institute of Technology (Jason, not Sleepy) and the page seemed to contain his research on the representation of Asian cinema, particularly films from Hong Kong.

RMIT? Would I have to go to Australia to meet number ten? There was still time left for a trip like that if it had to be done. I was approaching the end of February and that meant that I was approaching the deadline; my 32nd birthday on 2 March.

I clicked my way around the site looking for contact details and it didn't take me long to find them. But it didn't inspire me with confidence. Just below his email address, it said the following:

'Copyright © 1998 Jason Tan. This Home Page was created by WebEdit, Monday, October 26, 1998. Most recent revision Monday, October 26, 1998.'

It had been both created and abandoned on that fateful day back in 1998. Would his email address still work five years later? He was almost certainly no longer a student at RMIT; he could be living in Melbourne still but he could have moved on too.

I wrote him an email and hit the send button, all of which is quite difficult with your fingers crossed.

Having sent the email my next stop was Google once more and pretty soon I was looking at http://www.eta.immi.gov.au –

the kind of address that scares technophobes away from the internet with its impenetrable system of meaningless letters and dots. It should really be called HowToGetAnAustralianVisa.com because that's what it does. Australia, being the lovely, progressive country that it is, allows you to apply for something called an ETA, or Electronic Travel Authority, online. You visit the website, pay 20 Australian dollars (about £7.50) and give your passport details and, hey presto, the ETA is yours. You're free to visit Oz for up to three months. No queueing at the Embassy, no officialdom to contend with, nothing stapled into your passport forbidding you from reporting on events in the country; in short, no worries. What could be simpler?

Or in my case, what could be more complicated? A message popped up on the screen in front of me saying:

There has been a problem with your application. You will need to visit your local embassy. Your credit card has been charged $20.

The cheeky bastards!

Not that it mattered, because moments later my plea to Jason Tan bounced back to me. Not wanting to admit defeat I Googled his name and discovered 2570 pages of information. I sifted through it and came away with a list of 300 potential email addresses for people with that name. It was hopeless. Some were obviously not him: elderly academics who couldn't possibly be the fresh-faced youth in the photo; one wrote on his site that he'd 'never had a pet' and so on, but even so, there were hundreds of addresses that could have been my man. I emailed them all. It led nowhere. I'd reached another dead end.

I'd taken this chain to nine and there it had died. I was down but not out. On the subs bench was an eighth place googlewhack: the writer and producer of *Bhutan: Land of the Thunderdragon,* the unwitting creator of Langur Dandelions.

twenty-five

Langur Dandelions 2

Langur	noun: any of various arboreal monkeys of South and South East Asia having long hair surrounding the face, a slender body, long tail. Genus: *Presbytis*.
Dandelions	noun: a plant, native to Europe and Asia having yellow rayed flowers and notched basal leaves. They can be used in salads or wine. *Taraxacum officinale*.
2	noun: the cardinal number that is the sum of one and one. Often used to denote a sequel.

'The company is called Icon Films,' said Harry over sushi. 'We make a lot of documentaries. We're working on things at the moment about the Barbary pirates, what killed Charles Darwin and the Natural History of the Cow; that kind of thing.'

'I see,' I said, as if those three subjects were actually *a kind of thing*. 'And one of the shows was about Bhutan, right?'

'Yeah,' said Harry, 'it was our production but we work with American distributors.'

'Hence my trip to Washington …'

'Exactly,' said Harry. He sipped thoughtfully at his green tea. 'You didn't *really* go all the way to Washington on the off chance did you? When we were here in Bristol all along?'

'Well,' I said, 'it was on my way.'

'On your way *where*?' asked Harry, incredulous.

'LA.'

I think I noticed Harry moving his chair a little further away from the table. Harry was charming in a slightly foppish way. He had a neatly trimmed goatee beard, a floppy public-school fringe and a remarkably relaxed manner for one so busy. ('I have a conference call at three but I can squeeze you in,' he'd said. 'That's the thing with the Americans, they love a conference call.')

His company had been going for a while now and he exuded the calm confidence that only really comes with long-term success. He knew what Icon Films were good at and he knew that other people knew it too.

'Do you know Donald Sutherland?' he asked.

'Of course,' I said, 'he's an amazing actor.'

'He narrated the Bhutan film,' said Harry, looking justifiably pleased with himself. 'I'll give you a tape before you leave if you're interested.'

'You know, this whole thing is just getting a bit weird,' I said.

'What is?'

'This whole googlewhacking thing, it's like … it's like a coincidence magnet,' I said. 'There are connections all over the place. Like I've met two googlewhacks in San Diego. One of them gave me a pamphlet he'd written about creationism. The other one gave me an essay he'd written destroying *that* pamphlet.'

'That's pretty amazing,' said Harry, 'but what's it got to do with Donald Sutherland?'

'Well,' I said, still shaping the words in my head, 'I met Psychosomatic Rambunctiousness whose husband wrote *The Player* which was directed by Robert Altman who also directed *M*A*S*H* which starred Donald Sutherland!'

Harry looked a little nonplussed by my revelation.

'One of my googlewhacks,' I explained again, 'is married to a man who wrote a film that was directed by a man who also

directed a film that starred a man who narrated a documentary that was made by one of my other googlewhacks …
you!'

I think Harry's chair moved a little further from the table
and a little closer to the door once more.

'Actually,' I said blushing slightly, 'now that I've heard myself
saying it out loud, it doesn't seem quite as remarkable as I first
thought.'

'No,' said Harry, cautiously trying to steer the conversation
back on track. 'It was amazing working with him though.'

'I bet it was,' I said. '*You've* written a script … for Donald
Sutherland! Wow.'

'He was a real perfectionist in the sound booth,' smirked
Harry. 'He was convinced that there was some background
noise spoiling the takes. He ended up getting undressed in
case it was his clothes rustling.'

'When you say "perfectionist", do you mean "madman"?' I
chuckled, but Harry just smirked some more at the memory
and changed the subject.

'Now,' he said, 'you want me to give you some googlewhacks, don't you?'

'Yeah. Two if that's possible.'

'And then you plan to go and meet them, right?'

'Uh huh.'

'So do you want me to give you two that lead to nice places,
or do you want two that are close to home?'

'I want the first two you find,' I said. 'Besides, I would have
thought it was almost impossible to deliberately find googlewhacks in specific locations.'

'No, but I've found a few already,' said Harry. 'I could give
you googlewhacks that lead to Chicago and New York or
Switzerland or Leeds or Glasgow. It's up to you.'

It was a tempting offer. I wrapped my hands around the
small china cup, let the warmth seep through to my fingers
and thought about it long and hard. Harry was offering me the
chance to make life easier for myself. I could be back at nine

in a row in next to no time but it would involve cheating and where would the satisfaction be in that? I'd been through too much to start cutting corners now. No, this had to be done properly or it wasn't worth doing at all.

'I'm afraid it has to be the first two,' I said with a deep sigh. 'There are rules. Each googlewhack can only find me two. If you find more and let me pick and choose that's cheating.'

'OK,' said Harry. 'If we go back to the office, the pages I've visited will still be stored in the computer and we'll work out which were the first two.'

'Thanks,' I said, 'I'm very grateful.'

'That's OK,' said Harry. 'I understand ... You're a perfectionist.'

twenty-six

Spendthrift Glaswegians

Spendthrift   1. noun: someone who spends money in
an extravagant way.
2. adjective: of or like a spendthrift.

Glaswegians   1. noun: plural of Glaswegian, an
inhabitant or native of Glasgow.

Shortly before Carlisle and with Scotland rapidly approaching, I pulled into a motorway service station. I refuelled the car and myself and then I opened up the glove compartment and took out my phone. Eric, my latest 'whack, had asked me to give him a call when I got into town so I thought it best to check that my phone was working.

I turned it on. *Bee-beep, bee-beep, bee-beep* it sang, announcing that a new pile of messages had built up. I wasn't in the mood for any distractions. I didn't want to speak to anyone but Eric. It was time for a new phone number.

I bought a pay-as-you-go sim card, levered the battery from the back of my phone and slid it into place. There, I had a number that no one in the world knew. My phone sat silently on the passenger seat, unable to distract me, unable to remind me of the life I was shutting out.

I'd got lucky with Harry's 'whacks. I was climbing back up to ninth place with a trip to Scotland. It wasn't Glasgow as he'd first thought. Eric Laurier worked at Glasgow University but he lived in Edinburgh and it was there that I would be meeting him.

Once in the city I called Eric and he guided me, like air traffic control, into the car park of a grand hotel. I strolled through to the bar and arrived at our table moments after the arrival of tea and scones for two. Organised. I liked that.

Eric was a sociologist, which struck me as a difficult job. It's his business to understand the way society functions but that involves being aware of his own foibles too.

'I have two cats,' he said in his gentle Scottish accent. 'I mean, obviously in a way they're a child replacement. I mean, they're not, but in a way they are.'

'I'd hate to be so aware of why I do things,' I said.

'Yes,' said Eric, spreading jam on his scone. 'I do sometimes find myself becoming an observer when I should be a participant.'

I never know if it's meant to be jam and then cream or cream and then jam so I studied Eric's scone technique and copied him. We both took a bite out of our scones and although this time the synchronicity was coincidental it made me feel self-conscious. What if Eric thought I was copying him? He delicately dabbed a napkin to his mouth and I was instantly convinced that a bit of clotted cream was hanging around in the bristles of my beard. I desperately wanted to wipe it away but I couldn't, not yet. I leaned forward to pick up my tea and Eric did the same. Ah ha! He was copying me this time. I stopped mid-lean, and wiped my mouth instead, breaking the cycle. I let him return his cup to its saucer and then, nonchalantly, I went for my own cup, an independent gesture from an independent man.

'I think what you're doing is fascinating,' said Eric, 'but then I am a sociologist.'

Oh my God. He was on to me. He could read my mind. Were my socially awkward thoughts that transparent?

'Well, I never know if it's jam and then cream or cream and then jam,' I blustered.

'No,' said Eric, looking a little scared. 'I mean the google-whacking thing. Fascinating. Connections.'

'Oh, I see,' I said, blushing. 'Yes. Thanks. I think. Well, remember that I don't want you to be just an observer, you're a participant.'

'Of course, so what do you want me to do?' asked Eric.

I explained it all: the chain, the deadline, everything.

'So you need one more and you need to meet him by your birthday which is March the 2nd?' said Eric, making sure he had all the relevant facts straight.

'No,' I said. I knew I had to be as clear as possible. 'Before that. The challenge is to meet ten in a row *before* my 32nd birthday. March the 1st is the day that counts.'

'But it's February the 25th,' said Eric.

'I know.'

'So what are we doing wasting time with tea and scones?' he asked. 'You go and get in your car and start driving to London.'

'What?'

'I'm going to a computer to googlewhack,' said Eric. 'You need to be in the best hub for international transport when I get them. Get going. You were the last person to call me, so your number is stored in my phone. I'll ring you as soon as I've got the 'whacks. Let's go.'

As we rose to our feet I felt empowered. I was being marshalled by an expert general, a man with a plan of action and the desire to see it through. I breathed deeply, filled my lungs and headed straight to the car.

Only later did it occur to me that neither of us had paid for the tea and scones.

*

Only one person had my phone number so when the phone rang I knew it was Eric. I slowed the car down and pulled on to the hard shoulder. I know it's meant to be for emergencies only, but this *was* an emergency.

'Hi Dave,' he said. 'Have you got a pen?'

'Yes,' I said, scrabbling around in the car for a biro. 'Yes, I have. Fire away.'

'Spatulas Denouement,' said Eric and I scribbled it down, 'and Trimarans Crimps.'

twenty-seven

Trimarans Crimps

Trimarans   noun: plural of trimaran; a three-hulled
vessel, with two hulls flanking the main
hull.

Crimps   1. verb, to crimp. To fold, bend or press
into ridges.
2. noun: plural of crimp. A tight wave or
curl in the hair.

Spatulas Denouement would have been the perfect denouement to my adventure if it hadn't led to a completely useless website.

I say completely useless; it consisted of a list of peculiar phrases translated into Japanese so if you ever find yourself stuck in Japan and needing to write down the phrase *blocky wood patio furniture* (がっしりとした木製の屋外用の家具) or *plump handled spatulas* (丸みをおびた取っ手のついたへら) then this is the website for you. But if you wanted to know who'd written the page, why they'd written it, how to get in touch with them or, more importantly, where the hell they were, the site was useless.

Trimarans Crimps, however, was surely as good a piece of fortune as has ever landed in my lap. It led to the website of the Marinestore Chandlery, a shop dealing in sailing equipment that was based in Maldon, Essex.

Essex! After two months of extreme travel and with the

deadline almost upon me it was about to end in Essex. In the first two months of 2003 I had travelled over 71,000 miles. I had spent over 183 hours in aeroplanes. That means that in the first eight weeks of the year I had spent more than one week with bad leg room. In January and February, my average speed was over 50 miles per hour! And after putting myself through all that, all I had to do now to claim victory, was drive 41 miles.

I didn't ring the Marinestore Chandlery. I didn't email them either. It didn't matter. I didn't care if they wanted to meet me or not. I knew where they were, I knew their opening hours and so I knew it was possible for me to meet them. All I needed to do was to walk through their door and shake the hand of someone working there and I would have met ten googlewhacks in a row while complying with all of the rules laid down by David Gorman.

It didn't take me much longer than an hour to get to Maldon, a pretty little town at the head of the Blackwater Estuary. I breathed in the salty sea air and it tasted of victory.

I stood outside the Marinestore Chandlery, a humble, modern, red brick little building and knew I was about to win. I was excited and I was nervous. Nervous because when I'd won, it would be over and when it was over I would have to come back down to earth. I'd shut Jake out but he hadn't disappeared forever. The novel hadn't magically written itself in my absence. Real life was still out there and pretty soon I would have to find my place in it once more.

But the overwhelming sensation was one of excitement. I was about to complete something huge. There were times during my googlewhack adventure when nothing in life had made much sense to me. There were times when I'd felt I was losing control but, if I could win, then it wouldn't all have been in vain. Victory would give purpose to the last two months of my life.

I approached the shop, my heart beating faster and faster. I tried to compensate, breathing deeper and deeper. I paused at the door. My hand rested on the handle. This was it. This was the moment everything else had been building up to. Images of the recent past flashed through my mind; all the places I'd been to, all the people I'd met, and my heart glowed with pride and with love.

I took my hand away from the handle and fished my mobile phone out of my coat pocket instead. I wanted to share my excitement. I wanted to share the nerves and the pride and the love that was making my skin tingle.

My phone only knew one number. The last person to call me: Spendthrift Glaswegians: Eric.

'Eric, it's Dave,' I said.

'Hey, Dave,' he said sounding nervous. 'How're you doing?'

'I'm doing just great,' I said, nineteen to the dozen, my words tripping over themselves in their eagerness to be heard. 'I just wanted to say a proper thank you. I'm about to meet number ten and it's all down to you. I owe you a huge favour. Any time you want anything, just call. I'll be there in a heartbeat. I can't believe it's about ...'

'This is brilliant,' said Eric interrupting my gushing. 'Which one of them is it? Which one is number ten?'

'It's trimarans and crimps,' I said.

'What?'

I felt a pain across my chest. His 'what' was full of concern. He sounded worried. The excitement stopped turning and knotted itself up inside me, an unbearable tightness while I waited for him to expand and explain. It didn't happen. There was silence.

'What do you mean "what"?' I croaked, my lungs struggling for enough air.

'That isn't the googlewhack I found,' said Eric.

'What do you mean?' I yelled, the tension releasing itself in a scream, unleashing a torrent of words, twenty to the dozen, now. 'What do you mean, it's not what you said? I looked it up; it is a googlewhack! You don't trip over them in the street, you can't accidentally mishear one, it doesn't make any sense, what do you mean?'

'I'm being honest with you, Dave,' said Eric. 'I didn't say trimarans crimps,' he paused, 'I said … Trimaran Scrimps.'

The air fell out of my lungs completely. I didn't know what to do. I fell to my knees and let out a howl, a primal scream of fury as everything, everything I'd achieved in the last two months suddenly turned to dust. I heaved for breath. The salty sea air tasted of salt. I looked down at my right hand, the phone still connected to Eric. I raised it to my ear and heard:

'I'm sorry Dave. Dave? I'm sorry … Dave?'

twenty-eight

Trimaran Scrimps

Trimaran   noun: a three-hulled vessel, with two hulls flanking the main hull.

Scrimps   verb, to scrimp. To be very sparing or economical.

Trimaran Scrimps was indeed a googlewhack. A googlewhack that led to the following website: au.geocities.com/ I_wish_I_was_a_Minogue.

Well, you don't need many guesses to work out where that site was based, do you? There's a pretty big clue at either end of it, the 'au' and the 'Minogue' both pointing to Australia. So, I thought, what's this site all about?

I started to read:

So, what is this site all about? Well, it's my chance to really work out who I am. Do I want to be:
    A) A straight man with a steady girlfriend.
    B) A shy voyeur on the fringes of the gay club scene.
Or   C) A Minogue?

Crikey. This website belonged to one very confused man. It explained that he worked in the financial district of Sydney. At the end of his working day he would go home to his girlfriend. They shared a flat and were very much in love. What his girlfriend didn't know was that once every couple of months he'd go out cruising on Sydney's vibrant gay club scene. She was also unaware that he wanted to be a Minogue.

It seemed his gay friends knew nothing of his straight life and his straight friends certainly knew nothing of his gay life. The only place in which he was honest about the two was in his website, although for obvious reasons he remained anonymous.

He seemed tormented by his double life and claimed that he wanted to choose Option A *or* B, adding, *'I can't lose C as I will always want to be a Minogue!'* The prime concern of his website was inviting visitors to let him know what they thought of his life. He asked for advice, guidance, criticism and even abuse in the perhaps forlorn belief that if he read enough opinions it would help him come to some sort of conclusion about how to live his life.

I suppose his website was his own personal *Jerry Springer Show*, a chance to workshop his complicated personal life in public.

From my point of view it provided a glimmer of hope. There, at the bottom of the page, were the words, *'Happy 2003'.* Not, *'Completed September 25, 1996'*, not *'This Home Page was created by WebEdit, Monday, October 26, 1998. Most recent revision Monday, October 26, 1998'*, the phrases that had spelled doom for me the last time I'd been at nine in a row. No. *'Happy 2003.'*

I knew where in the world he lived. I knew there was a link to an email address that would work, and I knew it was a current website, a living, breathing website. And I knew that he was 10,000 miles away and that time was running out.

*

'Hi,' I said, as I reached the front of the queue. 'I applied for an Electronic Travel Authority but the website said I had to visit my local embassy. There was some kind of problem.'

'OK,' said the cute girl behind the Australian Embassy counter, her inflection rising sharply at the end of the word. 'Can I take your pass*port*?'

'Of course you *can*,' I said, my accent wandering towards hers, my inflection rising sharply at the end of the sentence too.

'I'll just be a couple of min*utes*,' she said, sliding down from her stool and disappearing round a corner.

I still hadn't had a reply from *I_wish_I_was_a_Minogue* but obviously I had to be able to get into the country to meet him and there was no point waiting to find out. I imagine she was running through some checklist to see if I was a desirable visitor or not. I bet imitating the Australian accent at the counter had blotted my copybook.

'There you *go*,' she said with a smile as she handed the passport back.

I flicked through the pages, looking for the new documentation.

'There's nothing here,' I said. 'Have I been turned down?'

Maybe I could pay for *I_wish_I_was_a* to come to England?

'It's electronic,' she said, 'there is no paper*work*. It's all *fine*.'

'Thanks,' I said, feeling a little foolish. 'Do you mind me asking what the problem was, why I had to come in, in person?'

'Oh, it's nothing really,' she said. 'Someone with the same name as you and a very similar birthday is on our *list*, so the computer flagged it *up*.'

A few years ago that would have been music to my ears, proof that another Dave Gorman existed, a sniff of a lead that might eventually take me to another namesake encounter. But that was a few years ago. This namesake had caused a problem with the ETA. He'd delayed me, held me back when time was of the essence. It seemed a cruel twist of fate that now, the success of *this* quest had been jeopardised by another Dave Gorman.

*

I headed home and checked my emails once more, praying that I would see *I_wish_I_was_a_Minogue*'s name in my inbox. It wasn't there. I sent him another email. It was probably my fifth or sixth so far.

I checked the details for flights to Sydney. It was still possible to meet *Trimaran Scrimps* on 1 March if I flew now. If I left it any longer I would be too late. I wouldn't be able to get there *before* my birthday. I had no choice. I could wait for him to reply but that would guarantee failure or I could go now, fly blind, and give myself a chance of success. If I waited a day and found a reply from him agreeing to meet me it would be impossible to get there on time. I could meet him, but I would be 32 years of age. That would make me a failure.

I headed to Heathrow Airport. I got online at an internet kiosk and booked myself into a cheap hotel in Sydney. That was it; I was committed. I surfed in to my bank account and checked the balance. I knew how much money Jake had given me, I knew how much money I'd spent. I knew I hadn't written one solitary word of the novel and I knew what that meant. Legally, contractually, morally, completely correctly, I owed Jake all of that money back.

I looked at the small amount of money propping my account up and knew what I had to do. Sod Jake, sod reality, sod everything, there was a fire in my belly. I knew this was my last throw of the dice; win or lose, this was the last trip I would be making, this was Custer's last stand, Gorman's last 'whack and I, David James Gorman was going to fly business class.

I put my credit card down and bought the ticket before visiting a bureau de change. I emptied my pockets and my wallet of all the money I had, a few pounds and quite a few more US dollars, and I changed it all into Australian. I'm pleased to report that the Australian economy wasn't faring very well and I got a lot of Australian currency for my money. I felt quite rich with a business class ticket in my pocket and a deceptively large wad of Australian cash in my hand.

There were a couple of hours to kill before the flight so, as usual, I headed to a bookshop for a browse. Even with the relative luxury of business class to look forward to, the rule *never, ever, ever set foot on a plane without a book to read* still stood. Especially when I was facing a journey time of more than 24 hours. I picked up *Black Box* by Nick Walker because I'd never heard of it and *The Water Method Man* by John Irving because I had. John Irving, I noted, shared my birthday, so it seemed appropriate that I might share my birthday with him. I'm a twin and I still think of birthdays as something to be shared.

It was only as I approached the till and pulled out my wallet that I remembered that I had no British money on me. A few coins maybe, but not enough to cover the cost of my reading matter. I opened my wallet, hoping I was mistaken and a mysterious fifteen pounds would float out from some hidden flap or pocket. And it almost did. As I rustled through wedges of receipts vainly hoping to discover some errantly stowed fiver a flash of silver foil caught my eye. I stopped. My thumb and forefinger retraced their steps back a little: there it was. The foil was embossed on to one of two book tokens. Fifteen pounds' worth to be precise, my winnings from the *Observer* cryptic crossword, stuffed into my wallet and long forgotten.

'Yes!' I said under my breath as I punched the air. A few people stared awkwardly. Punching the air isn't very bookshop behaviour.

*

I climbed out of the taxi and walked into the lobby of the hotel. It was nearly 11 pm on 28 February. I had 25 hours in which to meet my man.

My hotel was one of many offering cheap accommodation in and around Pitt Street, a lively, well … studenty … well, all right, downright grotty part of an otherwise stunningly attractive city. It was full of late-night bars and tatty shops and,

I was delighted to discover a parade of three, adjacent 24-hour internet cafés.

Before going to bed that night I checked my email one more time. Not one of the names in my inbox expressed any desire to be a Minogue. I wrote yet another email.

From: Dave Gorman
To: I_wish_I_was_a_Minogue
Subject: Please!

Hi I_wish_I_was_a_Minogue,

Me again. I'm just writing to let you know that I'm in Sydney. You know that I want to meet you. Well now you know how much I want to meet you. Enough to travel this far.

By the time you read this it will probably be March 1st. That's the day I need to meet you. The day after is my birthday and that means my time is up.

I know you've had a few emails from me already, but I wanted you to know how much this means to me. I only need one minute of your life and I will obviously travel to wherever you happen to be.

This means the world to me. I've come this far, please call me at my hotel on (02) **** **** or email me at this address. I'll try to check them both as often as I can.

Please look kindly on this request IWIWAM, I need this to happen.

Dave

I pressed send, waited for ten minutes and checked for a reply.

Finding none I returned to my hotel. It was clean, basic and cheap with white plastic furniture and no frills.

Exhausted, I fell into bed and closed my eyes but, like a ten-year-old on Christmas Eve, I didn't sleep for hours. *My* big day was tomorrow, I wanted it now and I was afraid that if I let sleep take me I would miss it. Of course, time kept on ticking by at one second per second and eventually sleep won out.

*

At 9.30 the next morning I was back in the internet café, checking my emails again. Was there a Minogue in my inbox? I should be so lucky. I wrote another email begging him to meet me and returned to the hotel, hoping for the phone to ring.

At 10.20 I was back online. At 10.40 I was back in the hotel. I yoyoed between the two all day. Each time I checked there was nothing and each time I wrote him another email imploring him to meet me. Time was running out but I wasn't giving up; reader, I harried him.

I was in one of the world's most beautiful cities, a city that was young, vibrant, brash, bold and exciting but I wasn't able to enjoy anything that Sydney had to offer apart from the sensory deprivation chamber of my room, and a downbeat internet café full of teenage backpackers playing network computer games against one another as if that was what a gap year was for.

It was a day of heartbreak. Every time I visited the café, I allowed my hopes to rise only to have them dashed on the rocks moments later and then, at around half past six, for the first time, I saw I_wish_I_was_a_Minogue's name in my inbox.

My heart stopped. Then accelerated. This was truly it. I held the mouse over the link and tried to click but my finger wouldn't obey. My index finger seemed frightened that it would be held responsible for what it was about to uncover. I focused all my energy on that button, on that finger, I reassured my digit that it would be OK and finally it moved.

Click.

In two, three, four agonising seconds his message filled my screen and ...

From: I_wish_I_was_a_Minogue
To: Dave Gorman
Subject: Re: Go on, please meet me?

No. Sorry.

That was it. Two words. Appropriate I suppose, that a journey inspired by pairs of words should be ended by another. If you Google *'No Sorry'* it'll give you 11,300,000 hits and right then I felt like I'd been hit that many times, each one a punch to my gut. It was all over. I wasn't king of the googlewhacks, I was the world's biggest chump.

*

It was a Saturday night; there was a festive atmosphere abroad on the streets of Sydney as gangs of youngsters gathered to kick off their big night out. And I hated them for being so happy, so cheerful, so carefree. How dare they party while my life was collapsing?

As I neared the hotel it became obvious that some big event was happening that night. Huge crowds were gathering on the fringes of Sydney's Hyde Park. (Is nothing original?) Scores of people were flooding the streets, many of them in fancy dress. The place was awash with colour and a cacophony of noise filled the air. People were honking horns, blowing whistles and hooters and there was the throaty roar of motorcycles revving engines but underpinning all that was the hubbub, the excited chatter and laughter of crowds preparing to enjoy themselves.

Hundreds of thousands of people seemed to be gathering for the world's largest party and it felt like they were there to celebrate my failure. *Have you heard? Dave Gorman failed to get ten googlewhacks in a row! Let's paaaarrrr-ttttty!*

I took the lift up to my room and closed the door behind me. I wanted to pretend they weren't there, that the revelry wasn't happening. I wanted everyone to be as unhappy as I was but the noise from the streets easily penetrated the hotel, trespassing on my life some more. I wanted to crawl under a stone and die. Instead I undressed, crawled under the duvet and pulled a pillow across my head to shut out the noise. Everything was silent … apart from the low, dull thud of my heartbeat and then … then the low, pathetic, hollow sobs. It sounded like someone else, but I knew that it was me. I felt detached from the world, my body numb, I felt nothing. But there I was, sobbing myself to sleep, listening only to my own tears.

*

I woke around 8 am. I was alone. I was on the wrong side of the world. I was a failure. I'd thrown away the opportunity to write a novel. I'd vandalised my body, I'd squandered so much money; why the *hell* had I flown business class?

Happy birthday, Dave, I thought, *happy birthday*.

It was a pretty bleak situation to wake up in. I wished I hadn't woken up. I didn't want to face the world. Out there, beyond the windows, people were getting on with life. I didn't want to know about that. I just lay there, almost comatose, unable and unwilling to get the bed off my back. And then the phone rang and so I had to.

'What is it?' I asked grumpily, annoyed that I was being forced into confronting a little bit of reality.

'It's recep*tion*,' said a female voice, 'there's someone downstairs who wants to see *you.*'

'No there isn't,' I snapped. 'I don't know anyone in Sydney, you've rung the wrong number.'

'No, he's definitely here to see you, Mr Gor*man*,' she said.

'His name's Danny and he says "Happy Birth*day*".'

Thoughts started racing through my brain, crashing into each other chaotically. He knows it's my birthday? Oh my God. Danny? It couldn't be …? Could it really be … how? And why? And …

'Mr Gorman?' said the voice in my ear.

'Yes. Sorry,' I said. 'I'm still here. Um … you'd better send him upstairs.'

Hurriedly I got dressed, threw cold water at my face and patted myself dry.

Suddenly, sooner than I expected, there was a rat-a-tat-tat at the door. Gingerly I opened the door to see a man, a complete stranger, staring at me. He stretched out his arms like a magician's assistant in ta-da!-mode and in a sing-song voice he yelled, 'Happy Birthday!'

I looked him up and down. He wore a smart white shirt and dark green chinos and he had short blond hair. It felt like someone had ordered me a singing Man-At-Marks-&-Spencers-agram.

I took a few paces back away from the door, into my room.

'Err... Thank you,' I said.

We stared awkwardly at each other for a few moments. It felt like minutes.

'I don't suppose you wish you were a Minogue do you?' I ventured.

'Yes,' came the simple reply. I think he blushed slightly.

'Danny isn't your real name is it?' I asked.

'No,' he confessed. 'But Kylie rather gives it away.'

'I suppose you'd better come in,' I said. 'Would you like a cup of tea?'

'That'd be lovely,' he said.

He walked through and sat on one of the two upright chairs. We froze awkwardly for a moment, not knowing what to say to each other. I picked up the kettle and carried it through to the bathroom. I turned the cold tap on and while the kettle filled I looked at myself in the mirror. My eyes were bloodshot and teary. And it was *his* fault. I walked back into the bedroom, plugged the kettle back in and flicked the switch.

It was as though a switch had been flicked in my head also. Suddenly I couldn't contain my rage.

'Why didn't you come and meet me yesterday?' I wailed. 'Why not? You knew how much it meant to me. You read my emails. You knew about it yesterday, you read them yesterday, you replied yesterday so you could have bloody met me yesterday! But you didn't, did you? I needed one minute of your life. That's all. One minute! Why? Tell me why?'

'I couldn't!' he yelled, his anger matching my own, throwing him forwards out of his seat and shocking me into silence. Tears were welling up in his eyes. 'I couldn't do it. Yesterday was the hardest day of my life. Every year it happens and every year it's the hardest day of my life. I couldn't do it.' He started to blub, tears rolling down his cheeks. 'I couldn't do it and I'm sorry.'

'What do you mean?' I asked, my anger dissipated, replaced by confusion and concern.

'Yesterday was Mardi Gras,' he said through gritted teeth, trying to fight back his tears but giving in to them.

'What?'

'Mardi Gras,' he said, angry that I wasn't taking in all the information he thought his words contained, angry that I was forcing him to talk some more. 'It's a gay and lesbian parade. It's huge. 400,000 people come out to watch it go by, not just the gay and lesbian community; grandma and granddad and mom and pop and kids in pushchairs go out to watch the parade.'

'I heard it' I said. 'Last night, I heard it.'

'My girlfriend loves Mardi Gras,' he said, his eyes wide and wild, 'and she expects me to go with her, and I do. And every year I stand there thinking, *this is the moment my two lives collide. This is the moment it all goes wrong.* I see gay friends of mine in the parade, I see gay friends of mine in the crowd. I see straight friends of mine in the crowd and I don't know who I am.' The tears came again. 'I. Don't. Know. Who. I. Fucking. Am!' he screamed. 'How do I wear my hair? Is my collar up or down? How do I stand? How do I speak? Which me am I that day? I live all day with my heart in my mouth knowing that it could all implode, that someone might say something to bring it all crashing in on me. I have too many secrets and I'm in too deep and I can't turn round and I don't know what I'm fucking doing but I do know that Mardi Gras is always the most difficult day of my life and I couldn't cope with you as well. You know about my website. My girlfriend doesn't. It couldn't happen. I couldn't meet you, and I'm sorry, but we all have our shit to deal with!'

Silence.

'No,' I said. 'I'm sorry. It never occurred to me when I wrote any of my emails that I was ever making anyone else's life more difficult. I apologise. I'm sorry.'

As I said that the kettle reached its peak, bubbling away, shaking slightly and as it did so, my anger resurfaced, boiling, bubbling its way to the surface too.

'But why have you come to tell me this now!' I yelled. 'It's hard enough being me this morning without knowing that I made somebody else's life harder. I'm struggling enough with my own situation, thank you very much.'

'Really?' he asked, indignant that I dared to be anything but contrite. 'Well, I came by to say thank you. My website says "Tell me what you think of me", but you ignored that, didn't you? All you were bothered about was your stupid little selfish game. All you ever did was ask if you could meet me, you never bothered to tell me what you thought of me, did you? And then last night you did. Last night you finally bothered to give me your opinion and I thought *well done him*. Well done. Thank you for being so honest. Thank you for telling me what you think of me.'

Because I had.

When I'd read *'No. Sorry.'* I'd hit reply. I'd sent him one more email.

From: Dave Gorman
To: I_wish_I_was_a_Minogue
Subject: Re: Re: Go on, please meet me?

Right. Well, while I'm here let me just say that I think
you're being a complete and utter shit to your
girlfriend. She is an adult. A grown-up human being.
She is entitled to make grown-up, adult choices about
her life based on real information as given to her by
the people who claim to love her, you absolute fucking
cunt.

I'm not proud of my language and I apologise for presenting
you with *that* word but that is the truth of what I wrote at that
time. I suppose I wasn't really expressing myself as well as I'd
like to think I'm able, but the red mist had descended and my
vocabulary had shrunk accordingly.

'So you've come to thank me for what I wrote, have you?' I
asked.

'Yes,' he said. 'I'm not going to take your advice but I
appreciate the honesty with which it was given. Thank you.'

'Right,' I said quietly, filling my lungs in preparation. 'So
what we are now is a pair of dickweeds in a hotel room in
Sydney. My life is royally fucked up right now and from where
I'm sitting, your life is even bloody worse.'

'Yeah,' he said. 'Maybe you're right. Maybe it is. Maybe you
can't help me, maybe no one can. But I might be able to help
you.'

'Oh yeah?' I sneered.

'Yeah.'

'Oh yeah?'

'Yeah,' his eyes locked on to mine, challenging me to trust
him. I met his gaze. 'What time do you make it?'

I looked at my watch. 'About 9.30.'

'So what time does that make it in England?'

Slowly it dawned on me. The time difference: eleven hours.

It was still *yesterday* in England. It was 10.30 pm! Oh. Oh my. That meant it was 11.30 yesterday back in France! I leapt across the room and hugged Trimaran Scrimps with all my heart.

'Thank you,' I said and he returned my hug.

I was frantic now. I ran to my bag and scrabbled around looking for the phone number I needed, then bounded across the room and picked up the phone. I dialled while my Minogue-wannabe stared in shock at the frenzy of activity.

'Bonjour,' said a sleepy Canadian accent.

'Hello, David Gorman, it's David Gorman here,' I said.

'What?' he asked. I'd obviously roused him from his bed. 'What are you doing? What time is it?'

'I was about to ask you that,' I said. 'Go on David, what time is it?'

'It's about … 11.30,' he said.

'And what day is it, Dave?' I asked.

'It's … it's … Saturday,' he said.

'No, David, what's the date?'

'What? It's … it's March the 1st.'

'Exactly!' I yelled. 'And I'm just ringing to tell you that *this* is the day before my 32nd birthday and I have met TEN GOOGLEWHACKS IN A ROW! I. AM. THE WINNER!'

*

'I'd like to apologise for earlier on,' I said to the girl on reception. She was cute with her pageboy haircut and jewelled nose stud. 'You called my room earlier and I snapped at you. I was in a bad mood. I'm sorry.'

'That's OK,' she said. 'Shit happens. You don't look like you're in a bad mood any more.'

'No. No, I'm not,' I grinned. I was on top of the world that day. I could do anything, even ask out a cute receptionist if I wanted. 'But … look, I don't want to be forward, but I'm on my own and it's my birthday … I don't suppose you're finishing your shift any time soon, are you?'

*

We sat by Sydney Harbour and drank champagne together, Lisa and I, while I told her the story I've just told you. With the Sydney Opera House to our right and the Harbour Bridge dead ahead it was as spectacular and magical a view as I've ever seen. I was having a truly amazing birthday.

'You should take a boat trip round the harbour,' she said. 'To celebrate.'

'OK,' I said. 'Let's go.'

We walked towards the ferries along Writers' Walk, so named because large brass medallions are sunk into the sidewalk each quoting a famous writer's words about Australia.

'So it started with an email from Australia and it ended with a trip to Australia,' said Lisa.

'Yeah,' I said. 'I suppose it is quite an Australian story, all told.'

'Come here,' she said, beckoning me over, pointing at the medallion at her feet.

'Who is it?' I asked.

'Mark Twain.'

'Did you know he wrote most of his books in a cabin at his sister's farm in upstate New York?' I asked.

'No,' she said. 'But look at what he said about Australian history.'

I stood over the large brass disc.

'Australian history is almost always picturesque ... It is full of surprises, and adventures, and incongruities, and incredibilities, but they are all true, they all happened.'

'You're right,' said Lisa, 'it's a very Australian story.'

'Come on, let's get this boat,' I said.

'No,' she said, 'I can't. I have to go. But you should.'

'But I thought—'

'No. I don't really like beards.'

Epilogue

Conversation 1

'I'm sorry about last night, Dave,' I said, lying down on the hotel bed, the phone pressed against my left ear, held in place by my cocked head and shoulder.

'It's OK,' said my namesake. 'I understand. I think. You were excited.'

'Yeah,' I paused. 'Oh, by the way, have you ever had trouble getting into Australia?'

'I have actually,' said David, surprised. 'How did you know?'

'I applied for an Electronic Travel Authority,' I explained. 'Because of another David Gorman I wasn't allowed to get it online, I had to go to the embassy. I guess the same thing would have happened to you too!'

'Oh, it was years ago when I had trouble,' explained David. 'I was living in London at the time and I flew to Australia. I'm Canadian, I'm living in the UK, I figure that Australia's part of the Commonwealth too so I didn't think I needed a visa. So I just flew in and got turned away. I was on the first flight back to London, then I got my visa sorted out and then I flew back the next day.'

We both laughed lightly at the ridiculousness of it all. And then a thought hit me. What had the girl at the embassy said? *Someone with the same name as you and a very similar birthday is on our list.*

'David,' I said, 'you might be the reason I had the trouble. You turning up without a visa might be the reason *our name* is on the list! When's your birthday?'

'February the 3rd,' said David, 'why?'

I raised my left arm and cocked my head some more. I saw my tattoo. With the date of birth given as 03-02, not 02-03.

'Do you have a ginger facial hair?' I asked.

'Yeah.'

'I forbid you to grow a beard.'

'Whatever you say, Dave,' said David. 'Say, what are you going to do about the novel.'

'I've got an idea,' I said. 'I've got an idea.'

Conversation 2

'Look, Dave,' said Jake. 'It's very simple. You owe us the money back. That's all there is to it.'

'But I've got an idea,' I said.

'What?'

'How about I write a book about my googlewhack adventure?'

'But that wouldn't be a novel,' said Jake. 'I commissioned a novel, a work of fiction.'

'Well, what if I changed the name of the central character. Called him Gavin? Then it'd be a novel.'

'Don't be stupid, Dave. You've let us down. You owe us the money.'

Conversation 3

'Hello Rob.'

'Dave.'

'I'm sorry about all that … *stuff*,' I said.

'That's OK,' he said. 'It's your own stupid fault for thinking you could write a novel. Ridiculous, Dave. You were very busy. I had a lot of work lined up for you, things were on a roll.'

'And now that's all gone?' I asked.

'Well, I've got a few ideas,' he said. 'Have you got your diary?'

Conversation 4

'Thanks for the money, Dave,' said Jake. 'I think we should draw a line under that and leave it there. It's in the past.'

'I doubt you'll ever want to speak to me again after all this,' I said. 'I am sorry.'

'Actually I have got a few things I'd like to talk about,' said Jake. 'I've been speaking to a few people in different departments and I've had an idea I think you might like.'

'Go on.'

'Non-fiction are interested,' he said. 'How about you write a book about your Googlewhack Adventure?'

'That's brilliant, Jake,' I said. 'I wish I'd thought of it!'